Robespierre and the Festival of the Supreme Being

Manchester University Press

Studies in
Modern French History

Edited by
David Hopkin and Máire Cross

This series is published in collaboration with the UK Society for the Study of French History. It aims to showcase innovative short monographs relating to the history of the French, in France and in the world since c.1750. Each volume speaks to a theme in the history of France with broader resonances to other discourses about the past. Authors demonstrate how the sources and interpretations of modern French history are being opened to historical investigation in new and interesting ways, and how unfamiliar subjects have the capacity to tell us more about the role of France within the European continent. The series is particularly open to interdisciplinary studies that break down the traditional boundaries and conventional disciplinary divisions.

Titles already published in this series

Emile and Isaac Pereire: Bankers, Socialists and Sephardic Jews in nineteenth-century France
Helen Davies

From empire to exile: History and memory within the pied-noir and harki communities, 1962–2012
Claire Eldridge

Catholicism and children's literature in France: The comtesse de Ségur (1799–1874)
Sophie Heywood

Aristocratic families in republican France, 1870–1940
Elizabeth C. Macknight

The republican line: Caricature and French republican identity, 1830–52
Laura O'Brien

The routes to exile: France and the Spanish Civil War refugees, 1939–2009
Scott Soo

The Society for the
Study of French History

Robespierre and the Festival of the Supreme Being

The search for a republican morality

JONATHAN SMYTH

Copyright © Jonathan Smyth 2016

The right of Jonathan Smyth to be identified as the author of this work has been asserted by him in accordance with the Copyright, Designs and Patents Act 1988.

Published by Manchester University Press
Altrincham Street, Manchester M1 7JA
www.manchesteruniversitypress.co.uk

British Library Cataloguing-in-Publication Data
A catalogue record for this book is available from the British Library

Library of Congress Cataloging-in-Publication Data applied for

ISBN 978 1 5261 0378 9 *hardback*

First published 2016

ISBN 978 1 5261 0379 6 *paperback*

First published 2018

The publisher has no responsibility for the persistence or accuracy of URLs for any external or third-party internet websites referred to in this book, and does not guarantee that any content on such websites is, or will remain, accurate or appropriate.

Typeset by Out of House Publishing
Printed by Lightning Source

Contents

	List of illustrations	*page* vi
	Acknowledgements	ix
	Abbreviations	xi
	The Revolutionary Calendar – An II	xii
	Introduction	1
1	Towards a new republican morality	10
2	The national response to Robespierre's proclamation	31
3	The celebrations in the capital	49
4	The celebrations outside Paris	78
5	Financing a national festival	103
6	Contemporary comments on the Festival	127
7	After the Festival	146
	Conclusion	154
	Bibliography	160
	Index	175

Illustrations

Figures

1. The route of the procession in Paris — page 54
2. The *sections* assemble in the Jardin National for the procession
   Fête à l'Être Suprême dans le jardin des Tuileries, le 8 juin 1794 ou 20 Prairial An 2ème de la République. Engraving, Pierre-Gabriel Berthault and Jean Duplessis, 1794. Paris, musée Carnavalet ref: 36634-1. Copyright © Musée Carnavalet/Roger-Viollet — 57
3. The Festival of the Supreme Being on the Champs de la Réunion
   La Fête de l'Etre Suprême au Champ-de-Mars, le 8 juin 1794 ou 20 Prairial An 2ème de la République. Oil on canvas, Pierre-Antoine Demachy, 1794. Paris, musée Carnavalet ref: 23991-15. Copyright © Musée Carnavalet/Roger-Viollet — 60
4a. The medal struck in Lyons in celebration of the Festival of the Supreme Being
    Lyon, June 1794. Coloured plaster, Jean-Marie Chavanne, 1794. Paris, musée Carnavalet ref: 57421-10. Copyright © Carole Rabourdin/Musée Carnavalet/Roger-Viollet — 86
4b. The medal struck in Lyons in celebration of the Festival of Reason
    Lyon, November 1793. Coloured plaster, Jean-Marie Chavanne, 1793. Paris, musée Carnavalet ref: 57423-1. Copyright © Carole Rabourdin/Musée Carnavalet/Roger-Viollet — 86

Tables

1. Submissions made to the *Comité d'Instruction publique* regarding the Festival of the Supreme Being between 23 Floréal and 7 Thermidor Year II — *page* 45
2. Analysis of the different names for the Supreme Being used by Robespierre in his speech of 18 Floréal to the Convention and in his speeches at the *Fête* on 20 Prairial — 63
3. The costs of the *Fête de la Réunion* held in August 1793 — 107
4. Summary of payments made by Fructidor Year II (September 1794) — 109
5. Stage payments made by Hubert to the major contractors on 16 Prairial (4 June 1794) — 113
6. Expenditures for the Jardin National and the Champ de la Réunion — 114
7. Shortfall in real against estimated income for the city of Angers, 1793–94 — 116
8. Official commodity prices established by the Law of Maximum 4 Ventôse Year II (22 February 1794) — 122
9. Comparative rates of pay between specialist tradesmen (journeymen) in Paris and London — 123

Acknowledgements

Ever since I first became interested in the enigma which was Robespierre, his launching of the Festival of the Supreme Being has always struck me, as it has most commentators, as a peculiarity, a one-off event, apparently unconnected with the rest of the period of the Terror, and a most unlikely aspect of his personal vision of the Revolution. I hope that this book will perhaps lead other scholars to re-examine their estimate of its importance to his vision of republican morality as I have had to.

A very large number of people have been of immense help to me throughout the long journey towards the publication of this book. I must express my deep gratitude to Professor Pamela Pilbeam, who took on the Herculean task of trying to turn a total non-academic into a passable historian for her support and enthusiasm. I also owe a great debt to my fellow historians of the Revolution, all of whom have been kind to the stranger in their midst. I would like to thank especially Dr Rodney Dean, Professor William Doyle, Professor Joël Félix, Dr Marisa Linton and Professor Julian Swann. Their help in reading some of the chapters and in commenting on my ideas has been enormous. Any errors in this book are entirely my own.

I am very grateful to my French family and friends who put me up and put up with me during my research and to the Archivists and Librarians of the Municipal and Departmental Archives in Angers, Amiens, Bordeaux, Lyon and Strasbourg, and of the Archives Nationales, the Bibliothèque nationale de France and the Bibliothèque Historique de la Ville de Paris, all of whom were unfailingly welcoming and helpful.

Very special thanks go to my brother, Roger, who found time, in between writing his own books, to read and improve successive versions of the text. He also prepared the index.

I would also like to mention two people, unfortunately no longer with us, who were responsible for opening my mind to the joys of History at different times in my life; Arthur Sopwith, who taught History many years ago at Latymer Upper School, and more recently Alan Clinton who was my Tutor at the Open University. They are both owed more than they ever knew.

Finally, I dedicate this book with love and gratitude to my wife, Monique, who has supported me and looked after all my needs, and, with devotion beyond price, read and commented positively, firmly and helpfully on all my work. Without her this book could not have been written.

This book is produced with the generous assistance of a grant from Isobel Thornley's Bequest to the University of London.

Abbreviations

A.D. + name	Archives Départementales (e.g. A.D. Maine-et-Loire)
A.M. + name	Archives Municipales (e.g. A.M. Amiens)
A.N.	Archives Nationales, Paris
A.P.	*Archives Parlementaires de 1787 à 1860. Recueil complet des Débats législatifs et politiques des Chambres Françaises*, fondé par MM. Madival et Laurent, continué par l'Institut d'Histoire de la Révolution française, Université de Paris I (Paris: Éditions du Centre National de la Recherche Scientifique, 1972)
C.I.P.	*Procès-verbaux du Comité d'Instruction Publique de la Convention Nationale*, M.J. Guillaume, ed. (Paris: Imprimerie Nationale, 1889)
Moniteur	*Réimpression de l'ancien Moniteur: seule histoire authentique et inaltérée de la révolution française depuis la réunion des États-généraux jusqu'au Consulat (mai 1789–novembre 1799)* (Paris: Plon, 1858)
Robespierre Œuvres	*Œuvres complètes de Maximilien Robespierre*, Marc Bouloiseau *et al.*, eds (Paris: Phénix, 2000)

The Revolutionary Calendar – An II

	Day	1793		Day	1793		Day	1793		Day	1794		Day	1794	
	1	S	22	1		22	1		21	1		21	1		19
	2	E	23	2	N	23	2	D	22	2	J	22	2	F	20
	3	P	24	3	O	24	3	E	23	3	A	23	3	E	21
	4	T	25	4	V	25	4	C	24	4	N	24	4	B	22
V	5	E	26	5	E	26	5	E	25	5	V	25	5	R	23
	6	M	27	6	M	27	6	M	26	6	I	26	6	U	24
E	7	B	28	7	B	28	7	B	27	7	E	27	7	A	25
	8	R	29	8	R	29	8	R	28	8	R	28	8	R	26
N	9	E	30	9	E	30	9	E	29	9		29	9	Y	27
	10		1	10		1	10		30	10		30	10		28
D	11	O	2	11		2	11		31	11		31	11		1
	12	C	3	12	D	3	12	1794	1	12	F	1	12	M	2
E	13	T	4	13	E	4	13	J	2	13	E	2	13	A	3
	14	O	5	14		5	14	A	3	14	V	3	14	R	4
M	15	B	6	15		6	15	N	4	15		4	15		5

A	16		7		16		6		16		6		16
	17	T	8		17	V	7		17		7		17
I	18	O	9		18	E	8		18		8		18
	19	B	10	I	19		9	C	19	S	9		19
R	20		11	R	20	M	10	E	20	E	10		20
	21	E	12	E	21		11	M	21		11		21
E	22		13		22	B	12	B	22		12		22
	23	R	14		23		13		23		13		23
	24		15		24	E	14	E	24		14		24
	25		16		25		15		25		15		25
	26		17		26	R	16	R	26		16		26
	27		18		27		17		27		17		27
	28		19		28		18		28		18		28
	29		20		29		19		29		19		29
	30		21		30		20		30		20		30

The Revolutionary Calendar – An II

			1794			1794			1794			1794			1794	
	1		21		1	21		1	20		1	19		1	18	
	2		22		2	22	M	2	21		2	20	J	2	19	
	3	M	23		3	23		3	22		3	21		3	20	A
	4	A	24	A	4	24	A	4	23	u	4	22	u	4	21	U
	5	R	25	P	5	25		5	24		5	23		5	22	G
	6	C	26	R	6	26	Y	6	25	N	6	24	L	6	23	U
G	7	H	27	I	7	27	M	7	26	T	7	25		7	24	S
	8		28	L	8	28	E	8	27	E	8	26	Y	8	25	T
E	9	F	29		9	29		9	28		9	27		9	26	
	10	L	30		10	30	S	10	29	E	10	28	U	10	27	
R	11		1	A	11	31		11	30		11	29	C	11	28	
	12	O	2		12	1		12	31	R	12	30		12	29	

M	13		3		13		2		13	S	13		1		13	I	13	S	30
	14	A	4	R	14		3	I	14		14	M	2		14		14		31
I	15		5		15		4	R	15	I	15		3		15	T	15	E	1
	16	P	6	M	16	J	5		16		16	I	4	A	16		16		2
N	17		7		17		6		17	D	17		5		17		17	P	3
	18	R	8	A	18	U	7		18		18	D	6	U	18	I	18		4
A	19		9		19		8	A	19	O	19		7		19		19	T	5
	20	I	10	Y	20	N	9		20		20	O	8	G	20	D	20		6
L	21		11		21		10	L	21	R	21		9		21		21	E	7
	22	L	12		22	E	11		22		22	R	10	U	22	O	22		8
	23		13		23		12	Y	23		23		11		23		23	M	9
	24		14		24		13		24		24		12	S	24	R	24		10
	25		15		25		14		25		25		13		25		25	B	11
	26		16		26		15		26		26		14	T	26		26		12
	27		17		27		16		27		27		15		27		27	E	13
	28		18		28		17		28		28		16		28		28		14
	29		19		29		18		29		29		17		29		29	R	15
	30		20		30		19		30		30		18		30		30		16

Jours Complémentaires Sans-culottides

1	2	3	4	5
17	18	19	20	21

SEPTEMBER

Introduction

> There is one type of institution which must be considered an integral part of public education, by which I mean the national festivals. Bring men together and you make them better ... give a great moral or political meaning to their meeting and love of the truth will fill their hearts.[1]
> Maximilien Robespierre, *Rapport sur les idées religieuse et morales* (1794)

On the 20th Prairial Year II of the Republic (8 June 1794), the whole of France was united in the celebration of the Festival of the Supreme Being. Two days later, Vaud, the secretary responsible for incoming correspondence, reported to the Convention on the exceptionally large number of letters which had been received relating to the great festival. He described them as demonstrating the joy which the nation had expressed at the idea of 'a family of twenty-five million brothers and sisters rising before daybreak to lift their hearts and voices toward the Father of all'.[2] His was not the only voice to express these feelings. Three days later, the official report on the Festival in Paris stated that 'Of all the festivals celebrated since the beginning of the Revolution, none had demonstrated more harmony, brotherly love or solidarity'.[3] It concluded the report on the day's events with the following words:

> The beauty of the day, the purity of the decorations, the open happiness of the people, the solidarity of feelings expressed by every attitude, every movement, every utterance by the citizens, finally the friendliness and good order which marked every aspect of the ceremonies created the most beautiful of festivals, one whose memory will last for ever in the records of the Revolution.[4]

Even allowing for the tendency of the scribes of the Revolution to use the over-flowery and oratorical prose of the period, it would seem the festival of June 1794 was indeed something special in the sequence of great national

Revolutionary Festivals. Not only was the event received with warm words, the contemporary commentators noted that the ladies had brought out their pre-revolutionary finery for the occasion.[5] It is therefore all the more surprising that, with this type and level of reaction, this particular festival has been almost universally regarded as a dull uninteresting event, most often seen as an unsuccessful attempt by Robespierre to impose his dictatorial rule on republican and Revolutionary France. The manner in which historians have looked at this seminal event has changed from the political histories of the nineteenth century, and the socio-economic perspective of the early twentieth century, both of which concentrated on the political importance of the Festival. More recently there has been an increasing acceptance of the idea that the Festival was an equally important key cultural event within the overall context of the Revolution.

With the lone exception of Ernest Hamel who boasted of being 'Robespierre's apologist',[6] the early French and English historians of the Revolution all vilified Robespierre – as they did Saint-Just – as the source of all that was bad in the early years of the Revolution, and as the bloody tyrant of the Terror.[7] It was only after the insistence by Aulard and Mathiez that historians should only work from verifiable sources, rather than from what was often highly selective, if not downright dubious, anecdotal data, that historians began to examine the evidence more deeply. Even so, Aulard dismissed the importance of Robespierre and his moral concept. To begin with he refused to see in Robespierre the personification of the Revolution, 'I refuse to personify the French Revolution in the person of this pious liar and mystical assassin.'[8] He further denigrated the importance of Robespierre's concept of a Supreme Being against Chaumette's Cult of Reason since, in his view, 'The Cult of Reason or the Cult of the Supreme Being were, as far as public opinion, especially in the provinces, was concerned, the same thing ... So while worshipping Reason before 18 Floréal one could claim to be worshipping God, in the same way, after 18 Floréal, while worshipping God one could claim to be worshipping Reason.'[9]

Contemporary accounts, such as those by Sylvain Maréchal a noted atheist and member of the Convention, the jurist Vilate and the publicist Fiévée, all of whom claim to have been present at the Festival, are at one in agreeing that the Festival was a great popular success. They also indicate that the reason behind the Festival was purely political, a carefully constructed bid for total personal power by Robespierre. They were however all writing in the period immediately following Robespierre's fall, and were largely concerned to minimise, if not deny totally, any part they may have had in the Jacobin administration. Modern scholarship, based on closer examination of the available evidence, especially Robespierre's own written and spoken words, does show a steady progression in his personal thinking on public morality. This can be seen to reach its peak in late 1793 and early 1794 when he appears to be moving towards the acceptance of the necessity for the establishment of some form of acceptably revolutionary yet still fundamentally Deistic, moral code. Logically – and Robespierre was nothing if not logical – this led to his attempt to meld his own predilection for the stern and unbending moral code of the 'man of virtue' with a semi-Rousseauvian form of Deism. The result, as he suggested in his speech of 18 Floréal, was the vision of a virtuous Nation advancing in unison towards the ideal Republic, under the benign protection of a Supreme Being.

Early historians of the Revolution, such as Mignet or Buchez and Roux, using the evidence from the letters received from the provinces, saw the Festival of the Supreme Being not only as a great event, but as one particularly notable for the depth of national participation. Regrettably, from then onwards, the great classical historians and their successors from Michelet and Quinet through to Aulard and successive holders of the Chair of Revolutionary Studies in Paris, maintained the view that the Festival should be regarded as an oddity, an aberration, an uninteresting one-off. Any suggestion that it might have been a genuine attempt by Robespierre to try to move the revolution towards a new and acceptable republican morality was totally dismissed. This view of the Festival continued through into the mid-twentieth century until, shortly before the Bicentenary, some historians began to look for an explanation as to why not only this particular Festival, but also other major Revolutionary Festivals, were considered so important within their own time.

It was during the Colloquium on the Revolutionary Festivals held in Clermont-Ferrand in June 1974 that the lines began to be drawn publicly between the two completely different readings of the importance and meaning of the Revolutionary Festivals in general, and that of the Supreme Being in particular. In separate sessions, Mona Ozouf and Michel Vovelle laid down not merely their own readings of the importance of the Festival but effectively the battle lines of what became a bitter controversy through the celebrations of the bicentenary of the revolution in 1989.[10] Ozouf invited historians to look more closely at 'everything we can see and hear, everything that was moved and carried, everything that was sung, sculpted, mimed, declaimed, inscribed in the festivals'.[11] Vovelle replied by dismissing this in unequivocal terms, 'there is a different reading, a different encoding between the approach of historians and those of many of our literary colleagues ... I believe these two readings are incompatible. No compromise is possible. The one must disappear should the other prevail.'[12] Ozouf set out the area of debate clearly in her major work, *La Fête Révolutionnaire 1789–1799*:

> Is the Festival of the Supreme Being (as Daniel Guérin holds) an ingenious conceit, a clever stratagem designed to strengthen the position of those in power, or is it, as Mathiez maintains, a serious attempt to reconcile patriotic Catholicism with the Revolution? Is it, as Aulard claimed, the result of a religious vision, the product of a naturally mystical thinker? In short, when Robespierre instigated this festival was it as a clever politician or as a real believer? Plotter or priest?[13]

Despite considerable work by local historians on the Festival in their own areas,[14] the majority of commentators have tended to concentrate on the Festival's centralist and political aspects, most often limiting themselves to the Parisian celebrations, thereby not only seriously undervaluing the Festival's impact in the rest of France, but strengthening the tendency to see the picture through the distorting mirror of Paris.[15] Aulard's dictum that no-one outside Paris cared a jot for either the Cult of Reason or the Cult of the Supreme Being remained the accepted wisdom. This, in turn, led to a general disregard for the potential importance of the evidence available in provincial archives, evidence rather cavalierly dismissed by Ozouf as being nothing more than 'minutes of meetings, often inelegant, invariably dull'.[16]

The first hurdle to be overcome for any historian attempting to evaluate the genuine popular experience of a particular phase or aspect of the Revolution is the availability of reliable evidence, particularly when the area of inquiry is outside the capital and away from the narrow confines of the Convention and its Committees. There is always a paucity of reliable evidence of the state of public opinion outside Paris. The official sources in provincial France were primarily concerned with recording meetings of administrative bodies and their committees and sub-committees so that, while there are extensive records of the formal and invariably positive response to whatever the latest initiative from Paris was, there is little or no indication of any discussions of other matters, even serious and immediate local problems. In Amiens, for example, for several months since mid-1793 there had been an acute local problem of lodging and feeding large numbers of refugees from Flanders who, together with wounded soldiers from both the French and Imperial armies, had been dumped on the city by the regional authorities, yet the only document in the official archives which directly refers to this problem is a letter from a member of the local *Société Populaire*, protesting at the imposition of yet another 'voluntary' subscription list.[17]

The one source which does offer the potential of finding a more genuine exchange of views, and therefore a truer picture of local feeling, is the correspondence between provincial cities and towns and the various committees in Paris regarding local participation in the Revolutionary Festivals. These produce a very different sort of correspondence from the interminable succession of letters formally eulogising the latest political initiative of the Convention. This was first acknowledged by Buchez and Roux who, in their *Histoire Parlementaire de la Révolution Française* in 1838, singled these letters out as being more indicative of genuine local feeling than the usual formal responses to any official papers from the Convention.[18] Despite the fact that these documents offer a rare opportunity to obtain an insight into the real feelings in the country, they seem to have been very little used by historians for this purpose. It should be emphasised that this evidence is in no wise new or previously unobtainable. Quite the contrary, since it formed the basis both of the work of Vovelle and his students and of Ozouf's detailed commentaries on the provincial aspects of the Festival of the Supreme Being.

One of the most remarkable aspects of the Festival of the Supreme Being was not only the amount of correspondence which it drew from the provinces; it was the nature of the correspondence itself. Well before the actual day of celebration, messages had been arriving addressed to the Convention, the Committee of Public Safety and the Committee of Public Education, all welcoming the upcoming festival in the warmest terms. Correspondence between the provinces and central government in Paris was normally conducted in the stilted 'official' language of Revolutionary rhetoric, a language designed almost as much to obfuscate as to inform. What is so noticeable about many of the documents relating to the Festival of the Supreme Being is how the content cuts through the officialese, to give a real sense of an awakening of national solidarity. The specific coupling in the declaration of 19 Floréal (8 May 1794) of the two propositions that the nation accepted, not only the existence of a Supreme Being, but also the immortality of the Soul, had never before been hinted at, let alone formalised in an official statement by a revolutionary government.

There is some debate on the real meaning of the messages; these expressions of joy and hope were, after all, happening at the height of the Terror and in a society where, in many areas, the practice of religion, even if not actually forbidden, was at best difficult and often dangerous. It has been argued by those historians who support the more established thesis on the import of the Festival that the tenor and content of such documents show nothing more than the automatic reaction of provincial worthies fearful of being seen as out of step with what was being decreed in Paris. Against this must be set the actual language of reports from all parts of the nation. In the report from Amiens the City Council speaks of giving 'the impression of a large family coming together in piety'.[19] Lyon reported that 'All hearts were suffused with tender feelings of brotherhood'[20] while in Angers local people had 'contested for the honour of taking part'.[21] This is certainly not the sad, monotonous language with which Ozouf characterised these documents. These are merely some examples typical of many more quoted in Chapter 4, all of which demonstrate the general feeling of joy and hope engendered by a combination of an acceptable ceremonial of worship of a Supreme Being, and the reaffirmation of the immortality of the soul which France had now officially committed itself to recognise.

Against this, Vovelle, firstly in his major work on de-Christianisation published in 1974,[22] and later in his *1793, La Révolution contre l'Église: De la Raison à l'Être Suprême*, published in 1988, uses the same archives to define a very different set of concepts and their consequences. Drawing on his personal research at both national and local level, as well as a considerable number of detailed regional studies he led with his postgraduate students,[23] he produced work which concentrates on the socio- and geo-political impact of the spread of de-Christianisation, to the detriment of the examination of any other dimension, going so far as to refer to the Festival in a later work as mere 'Smoke and mirrors'.[24]

The purpose of this book is therefore to look again at the enormous amount of available evidence, not only centrally in Paris but also in departmental and civic archives throughout France. I believe that this demonstrates clearly that the Festival of the Supreme Being, far from being an event characterised by sterile compulsion, only of importance as part of the evidence of Robespierre's failure to take total control of the Revolution, was on the contrary an intensely participatory experience. It is this amazing outpouring of feelings from the whole nation which leads me to the belief that these documents are far from being the response of people or organisations afraid to speak out against central government. The overriding effect is that of a clear feeling that the idea of recreating some form of national morality, especially when seen to be linked to widely expressed sentiments of unity, was very much in resonance with the feeling in the nation, especially outside Paris.

What is unclear is what these unprecedented crowds were really celebrating on the great day. There is considerable evidence from contemporary sources both inside and outside Paris that there was a general and widespread expectation that the day of the Festival of the Supreme

Being could also see the proclamation of some form of general amnesty, the end of the Terror and even perhaps the beginning of the Republic of Virtue. Some of the participants would undoubtedly have been hoping that this Festival, held as it was on the day of the feast of Pentecost in the old calendar, was a sign that some form of real religious toleration was returning to public life. Others, while accepting that the removal of atheism as an official facet of public life was on balance positive, frankly saw no great difference between a Goddess of Reason and a Supreme Being; neither was real, neither was part of the public consciousness, neither had any impact on everyday life. The 'consoling idea' of immortality had its positive aspects, but was that all that was on offer? No-one seemed to be seriously working towards the apparent need to fill the missing religious element in people's lives, and this new moral system, unlike a real religion, seemed to be totally lacking in the essential ingredients necessary for its successful continuation. Unlike a 'real' church there was no rulebook, no uplifting or edifying stories to be heard, no martyrs and saints to look up to; even the martyrs of the Revolution were sidelined. There were no pastors or community leaders, no spokesmen were visiting the Paris *sections* or the provincial Republican Clubs to imbue them with the necessary fervour any new cult needs to survive. Equally, none of the official slogans offered those two vital elements of any religion: the long-term prospect of salvation and the short-term prospect of charitable assistance.

While it is undoubtedly stirring to have a great festival which unites the whole of the nation in joyful celebration, it is quite another to follow it up and lay the groundwork for the basic ideology behind the celebrations to become an intrinsic part of national life. It might have been expected that, following the success of 20 Prairial, these questions would be properly addressed, and that the new belief system would be incorporated into the life of the nation as quickly and as deeply as possible, although in view of the general lack of organisational ability throughout the various committees, it was perhaps not altogether surprising that it did not happen. The result was inevitable; in the absence of any strong commitment to the continuation of the worship of the Supreme Being, it would be the negative comments of Robespierre's political opponents which would sound loudest. Despite their assertion that they were not attacking the idea of the Supreme Being as such, these comments led inescapably to the whole idea being considered as being nothing more than a vehicle for the self-aggrandisement of its chief advocate, Robespierre. What happened to the Cult of the Supreme Being after 20 Prairial, why it failed, why it disappeared almost without trace, is both baffling and fascinating.

Notes

1 'Il est cependant une sorte d'institution qui doit être considérée comme une partie essentielle de l'éducation publique, je veux parler des fêtes nationales ... donner à leur réunion un grand motif moral et politique, et l'amour des choses honnêtes entrera avec le plaisir dans tous les cœurs'. (Robespierre, 'Rapport sur les idées religieuse et morales, 18 Floréal Year II' (7 May 1794))
2 'une famille de vingt-cinq millions de frères devancer ensemble la naissance du jour pour élever son âme et sa voix vers le Père de la nature'. *Moniteur*, 23 Prairial Year II (11 June 1794), Vol. 20, p. 701.
3 'De toutes les fêtes célébrées depuis le commencement de la Révolution aucune n'a été exécutée avec plus d'harmonie, de fraternité et d'ensemble.' *Moniteur*, 23 Prairial Year II (11 June 1794), Vol. 20, p. 702.
4 'La beauté du jour, la fraîcheur des décorations, la franche gaîté du peuple, l'unanimité des sentiments exprimés par toutes les attitudes tous les mouvements tous les discours des citoyens, enfin la cordialité et l'ordre qui ont régné dans tout le cours de la cérémonie en ont fait la plus belle fête dont le souvenir puisse être perpétué dans les fastes de la révolution'. (*Moniteur*, 23 Prairial Year II (11 June 1794), Vol. 20, p. 702)
5 See Chapter 6 for specific quotations from Vilate *et al.*
6 E. Hamel, *Histoire de Robespierre d'après les papiers de famille, les sources originelles et des documents entièrement inédits* (Paris, 1865).
7 This theme can be seen running throughout the nineteenth century from F.A. Mignet, *Histoire de la Révolution française depuis 1789 jusqu'en 1814* (Paris, 1827), T. Carlyle, *The French Revolution; A History* (London, 1837) and P.-J.-B. Buchez and P.-C. Roux, *Histoire parlementaire de la Révolution française: ou Journal des assemblées nationales depuis 1780 jusqu'en 1815* (Paris, 1838) and on through J. Michelet, *Histoire de France, Vol. VI, La Révolution* [originally published 1847–52], P. Villaneix, ed. (Paris, 1974) to Charles Nodier, *Souvenirs de la Révolution et de l'Empire* (Paris, 1850), and in the works of Quinet and Louis Blanc through to Jean Jaurès, *Histoire socialiste de la Révolution française* [originally published 1901], A. Soboul ed. (Paris, 1972).
8 'Je me refuse à personnifier la Révolution Française dans ce pieux calomniateur et dans ce mystique assassin.' A. Aulard, 'Aux apologistes de Robespierre', *La Justice*, 28 September 1885.
9 'Culte de la Raison, culte de l'Être suprême, ce fut pour l'opinion, surtout en province, la même chose ... Ainsi, avant le 18 floréal, en adorant la Raison on se vantait d'adorer Dieu; après le 18 floréal, en adorant Dieu on se vantait d'adorer la Raison.' A. Aulard, *Histoire politique de la révolution française: origines et développement de la démocratie et de la république 1789–1804*, 5th ed., 2nd reprint (Paris, 1921), p. 493.
10 For an account of some aspects of the violent confrontations of the Bicentenary celebrations see M. Agulhon, 'Faut-il avoir peur de 1789?', *Histoire Vagabonde*, 2 (1988): 244–61.

11 'tout ce qui est donné à voir et à entendre, ce qui est promené et transporté, ce qui est chanté, sculpté, mimé, proclamé, inscrits dans les fêtes.' M. Ozouf, 'Le renouvellement de l'imaginaire collectif', in *Les Fêtes de la Révolution: Colloque de Clermont-Ferrand, juin 1974*, J. Erhard and P. Viallaneix, eds (Paris, 1977), p. 303.

12 'il y a entre l'approche des historiens et l'approche de toute une partie de nos collègues littéraires, une lecture et un codage différent ... Deux lectures inconciliables, me semble-t-il. Il n'y a pas de compromis possible. L'une disparaît là où l'autre s'impose.' M. Vovelle, 'Sociologie et Idéologie', in *Les Fêtes de la Révolution*, Erhard and Viallaneix, p. 478.

13 'La fête de l'Être Suprême, est-ce une ingénieuse trouvaille, ruse malintentionnée, destinée à asseoir la fortune des possédants (Daniel Guérin), ou ruse bien intentionnée vouée à réconcilier avec la Révolution le catholicisme patriote (Mathiez)? Est-ce au contraire l'aboutissement d'un projet religieux, l'épanchement d'une âme naturellement mystique (Aulard)? Bref, Robespierre en instituant cette fête s'est-il montré fin politique, ou vrai dévot? Stratège ou pontife?' (M. Ozouf, *La Fête Révolutionnaire, 1789–1799* (Paris, 1976), p. 173)

14 Examples are publications on their local Festivals of the Supreme Being of the Historical Societies of Nancy in 1900, St Malo in 1908, Angers in 1916 and Calais in 1924.

15 See also S. Hazareesingh, 'Preface', in *Célébrer la nation: Les fêtes nationales en France de 1789 à nos jours*, R. Dalisson (Paris, 2009).

16 'des procès-verbaux parfois frustes, toujours monotones'. Ozouf, *La Fête Révolutionnaire*, pp. 27–8.

17 A.M. Amiens, Archives Révolutionnaires I/I,2.

18 Buchez and Roux, *Histoire parlementaire*, Vol. 33, p. 163.

19 'une grande famille réunie par les sentiments de la piété filiale'. A.M. Amiens, 1.D.10.9, p. 82.

20 'la douce fraternité embrasait tous les cœurs'. A.M. Lyon, 1.C.651107, p. 5.

21 'se disputer l'honneur de marcher'. A.M. Angers, 1.D.5, p. 88.

22 M. Vovelle, *Religion et Révolution, la déchristianisation de l'an II* (Paris, 1976).

23 In the bibliography of *1793, La Révolution contre l'Église*, Vovelle acknowledges contributions from a total of fifteen unpublished postgraduate works, eleven from his own students and four more presented under other supervisors, and further doctoral students have amplified the regional research work since the original publication.

24 'Mystique et illusion'. M. Vovelle, *Les Images de la Révolution* (Paris, 1988).

1

Towards a new republican morality

Any attempt to follow the development of Robespierre's thinking, leading finally to the speech of 18 Floréal (7 May 1794) and proclamation of the festival in honour of the Supreme Being on 20 Prairial Year II (8 June 1794) has to try to answer two main questions. The first is whether progress in his thinking on the importance of the problem which the lack of any acceptable national moral system through the early years of the Revolution had created can be traced. The second is why he chose a Revolutionary Festival to launch his vision of a new attitude towards religion, rather than attempting to renovate the failing Constitutional Church to incorporate his ideas or simply replacing it with a new, but this time viable, version of a faith-based state church.

Robespierre, in common with the other 'men of virtue' who were the driving force of the Revolution, used a specific form of language when discussing public and private morality.[1] Any examination of Robespierre's speeches and writings shows his constant use of the word 'virtue' when discussing morality. In his speech establishing the Cult of the Supreme Being he used it a total of fifteen times, many more times than the sum of his combined references to the Supreme Being, the Divinity, the Creator, Nature or God. For Robespierre, virtue was all; his speeches and writings are imbued with it, and it is the word he uses again and again whether speaking of politics, religion, patriotism or public morality. This vision of a new moral authority from which Revolutionary France would advance towards the final goal of the truly virtuous state did not come from the deliberations of a committee of academic philosophers, it came from Robespierre's personal conviction that such a system was vital if the Revolution were to continue towards this goal. He endlessly extolled virtue: a quality which he regretted as no longer being the civic selflessness of antiquity, but reduced to something which was constantly and unavoidably diluted by the subjective nature of contemporary republican political morality.

Robespierre himself had always been clear as to his ultimate aim; nothing less than the establishment of the Republic of Virtue. He was equally aware of the fact that any such visionary ideal was increasingly weakened by the combination of the disappearance of a valid system of public morality, the growing power of the atheists and de-Christianisers, the difficulties in the practice of religious observance, and the failure of the Constitutional Church to fill the vacuum created by the disestablishment of the state church in August 1789. One constant problem, when attempting to assess why Robespierre chose a particular course of action during his political career, is that of trying to separate the moralist from the man of action, to try to evaluate his motives without falling into the popular concept of him simply as the butcher of the Terror, the cold and unfeeling dictator steeped in innocent blood. Robespierre himself always insisted that he was neither a philosopher nor a mystic; he was essentially a political animal and, when at the peak of his powers, as he was in the late Spring and early Summer of 1794, he was a politician to his fingertips, as evidenced by his actions in the Committee; a man capable of making swift decisions based on a rapid evaluation of information received, allied with an intuitive ability to seize the moment.[2]

Robespierre had a very singular and personal sense of rightness of action, both public and private, and this led him to an almost circular concept of morality. For him, an action could be classified as 'good' for no other reason than that it arose from 'good' principles, and if it was then performed by a 'virtuous' man the circle was complete. If these criteria were fulfilled, any action, however stark, however apparently unfeeling, however heedless of any claims of friendship or of the solidarity owed to close associates must, by definition, be in and of itself 'virtuous', and therefore something from which only good results could flow. It was this particular view of the moral imperative which gave rise to the popular vision of Robespierre as a man driven solely by reason, personally cold and unfeeling and with a total lack of any humanity.[3]

It was again this unyielding assurance of the rightness of his own moral purpose which allowed him, apparently without qualm or emotion, to accept the necessity to execute not just open opponents like Hébert and Chaumette but once-close colleagues, such as Danton, with whom he had wept at the loss of his wife, and one of his oldest and closest friends and supporters, Camille Desmoulins. Robespierre's public and private life was firmly underpinned by the political and moral principles he assimilated from his reading of Rousseau, Montesquieu and Locke, to which he added an idealised vision of the glories of Athenian democratic thought under Demosthenes, and the stern public morality of the early Roman republic. This strict and unbending ethical construct was the rock on which he built his vision of public life and it was this rigid morality which would finally force him to the conclusion that it was both his right and his moral and political duty to attempt to impose his personal ethical base as the 'official' morality of the Revolution. Only then could the Revolution continue towards the ultimate aim of making the Rousseauvian dream of the Republic of Virtue a reality.

There is little evidence of Robespierre's actual religious beliefs before 1784. He was admittedly a scholar at the College of Louis-le-Grand on a nomination from an ecclesiastic in Arras, but the person concerned seems to have been acting more as a family friend than with any view of a later ecclesiastical career for the young Robespierre. With his fellow scholars he would have been expected to attend Mass regularly and take at least some part in the greater festivals of the church. The only account of his time at Louis-le-Grand is that written by the deputy principal at that time, one of his most noted vilifiers, the Abbé Proyart.[4] Writing under the pseudonym of Leblond de Neuvéglise, Proyart claims in his *Life and Crimes of Robespierre* that any faith Robespierre may have had was soon lost and that he gave up Easter communion as soon as he could. Proyart is hardly a reliable source but this does agree with Robespierre's later remarks in his speech of 1 Frimaire (21 November 1793) that he was 'a fairly bad Catholic since his schooldays'.[5] There is however compelling evidence that from a young man Robespierre had clear views on both private and public, or political, morality. On the question of political morality, the definition which he gave in his '*Plaidoyer*' of April 1784, and repeated in his essay '*Sur les peine infamantes*', published in 1785, clearly lays down the principle he was to follow all his life: 'The necessary mainspring of republics is virtue, ... which is nothing less than love of law and of one's country, and whose very nature requires that all special interests, all personal relationships, should give way to the general good.'[6]

In a speech to the Jacobin Club on 2 January 1792, Robespierre stressed his allegiance to the principles of public morality, and it was this speech which led to his being called the Incorruptible. Referring to the unpopularity of his view on war, he said: 'Two opinions have been raised in this assembly, one encompasses all the aspects which flatter the imagination, all the shining ideas which arouse enthusiasm ... the other is based on cold reason and hard fact. To please, one must defend the first, to be useful the second, in the certainty of displeasing those who may cause you harm; I stand for the second.'[7] On 26 March of the same year during a speech to the Jacobin Club opposing the proposed declaration of war, Robespierre, while showing no signs of following any particular spiritual path other than the generalised Deism of Rousseau, publicly accepted that there is something outside Man which can act as an inspiration towards public and private virtue when he said 'I myself uphold those eternal principles by which human frailty can find strength to make the leap to virtue.'[8] Later in the same speech when he referred to 'Providence' striking down the Emperor Leopold, he was immediately attacked by the Girondin Guadet, an associate of Brissot, for propagating superstition. Robespierre, instead of ignoring the accusation, launched into an apparently unprepared defence of Deism, despite some serious murmurings from his audience. 'To invoke the name of providence and offer the idea of an eternal being who specifically influences the destiny of nations, and who, it seems to me, specially watches over the French Revolution, is not a dangerous idea, it is a heartfelt belief, one I need to hold.'[9]

Although the general theme of morality is never far from his mind, his concentration on it as the single most important facet of public life occurs after the autumn of 1793. Between November 1793 and May 1794, Robespierre took every opportunity to speak on the general theme of morality, although it was not until after the establishment of the Terror in his speech of 5 February and the subsequent struggle with Danton and his followers that the first indication of his intention to offer some form of ethical system appeared. During 1793 not only Robespierre but also other Jacobins, who had become concerned about the fast-growing progress of the destruction of religion, began to express openly their anxiety at the way that in several parts of France the de-Christianisers, apparently acting on their own and without reference to the capital, were effectively ignoring, if not actively opposing, the centralising authority both of the Convention and of the Committee of Public Safety. When Chaumette ordered the inauguration of a Festival of Reason to be held in Notre Dame de Paris on 20 Brumaire, Year II (10 November 1793), and persuaded the Convention to decree that all churches throughout France should become Temples of Reason, Robespierre realised that the time had come when he must speak out. He must have now felt himself strong enough to openly oppose the rising tendency towards atheism and to show publicly his increasing distaste for the activities of the de-Christianisers; a decision which was also fuelled in no small measure by his personal disgust at the manner in which that particular festival was conducted.

From this point onwards Robespierre began to take every opportunity to express publicly his moral and spiritual position and his open support of religious toleration, a position in which he was originally backed by Danton and Cambon, both of whom would add their voices to his by speaking in the Convention during November and December 1793 in support of the guaranteed liberty of all citizens to practice their religion. The first major instance of him speaking publicly on this theme was at a meeting of the Jacobin Club held on 1 Frimaire (21 November 1793). Robespierre was due to speak immediately after a speech by Momoro in support of the anti-clerical position advanced by Hébert and Chaumette in which they maintained that the worst enemies of the Revolution were still the clergy. In the event, Momoro chose to speak on a completely different subject. Robespierre did not however recast his speech in order to respond to the new subject raised by Momoro; he delivered a speech which opened up the whole debate on the process of de-Christianisation and the necessity, as he saw it, to respond to the underlying feeling in the nation of the need for some generally acceptable system of public morality to replace the previous faith-based system. In this speech Robespierre had three main themes; beginning with an outright attack on atheism and its supporters, he then defended both the right and the principle of freedom of worship, proceeding, to the probable surprise of his listeners, with a defence of the unexpressed feeling of a considerable proportion of the nation for the need of the consolations of religion, and finishing by offering a statement of his own position and beliefs.

He began by dismissing Hébert's openly expressed fear of the resurgence of the old religion, asserting that most of the remaining priests were far too busy seeking lucrative posts as municipal administrators and as secretaries or even presidents of *Sociétés Populaires*, to be in any position to offer any real threat to the Revolution. He then made a direct attack on the organisers of the Festival of Reason: 'What right have they to attack freedom of worship in the very name of Liberty and attack bigotry with a new bigotry? By what right do they denigrate the genuine homage paid to truth with a series of ridiculous caricatures?'[10] He proceeded to warn the atheists that any attack on the right of priests to hold services openly, far from having the desired effect, would only make them more determined to celebrate their religion, since what is not permitted to be done openly, will inevitably be done clandestinely.

It is at this point that Robespierre, for the first time in his public speeches, uses the term 'Supreme Being', reminding his hearers that this name was specifically included in the preamble to the constitution of 1793, which repeated the words used in 1789, when it was formally stated that the proclamation of the Declaration of the Rights of Man was made 'in the presence of the Supreme Being'.[11] He then proceeded to attack the heart of the argument, not, as might have been expected given his usual style, by a combination of illustrations from the lives of the heroes of ancient Athens or republican Rome nor with quotations from Rousseau and Montesquieu, but with the confident assertion that he was speaking in the name and in the language of the people. It is in their name that he dismisses atheism as aristocratic and therefore counter-revolutionary, while asserting that the idea that the existence of some form of higher power, whose mission is to protect the weak and the innocent and to punish wrongdoing, is truly republican.[12]

He concluded his speech with a passage which would have found an immediate resonance in many of his listeners: 'Since my schooldays I've been a fairly lukewarm Catholic: I have never been a lukewarm defender of humanity. This makes me even more attached to the moral and political ideas which I have suggested. If God did not exist we would have had to invent Him.'[13] He appears to have taken considerable trouble to select a combination of phrases which his audience would immediately recognise, including the quotation from Voltaire with which he concluded. Even more, the statement that he considered himself 'a fairly lukewarm Catholic' would have immediately struck a chord with the majority of his hearers, many of whom would probably have used exactly the same phrase to define their moral position at some time or other in their lives.

Robespierre continued to speak in favour of some measure of rapprochement between the Revolution and organised religion during December 1793. Earlier in the same year Robespierre had formally proposed to the Jacobin Club that it should expel all bankers and financiers from the organisation as being unfit to be considered as true revolutionaries. When this came up for ratification at the meeting of 26 Frimaire (16 December 1793), the members present decided to take the exclusion further and extend the ban to all members of the clergy. A leading protestant pastor, Bernard, well known as a committed republican, made a plea for justice for both constitutional and protestant priests who, like himself, had embraced the ideas of the Revolution, and begged the meeting to reconsider its decision. Robespierre, who was not expected to speak, made his way to the tribune and made an extempore speech supporting Pastor Bernard and defending those members of the clergy who had embraced the Revolution. He spoke movingly of those members of the lower orders of the clergy who had suffered in the name of liberty since 1789, men who he considered as true patriots: 'men who are part of the Revolution through a continuous stream of sacrifices'.[14]

Pastor Bernard retained his membership and Robespierre received an effusive letter of thanks from Chabot, a constitutional priest then in the Luxembourg prison: 'after many tears of despair your magnificent speech at the Jacobins moved me to tears of joy'.[15] It seems that Robespierre was again taking the opportunity to remind his listeners of the continued existence of a latent pool of belief within the nation, which they would disregard at their peril.

In his speech to the Convention on 17 Pluviôse (5 February 1794), on the subject of the moral principles which must guide the policies of the national convention in the internal government of the nation,[16] Robespierre continued to hammer home the concept that the 'virtuous men' have triumphed and they will now unwaveringly impose their authority on the nation. In this speech Robespierre uses the word 'virtue' no fewer than twenty-nine times. After establishing his view that 'the time has come to identify clearly the aim of the Revolution and the final position we want to attain',[17] he goes on to assert that the only acceptable government is that offered by a democratic republic. He proposes his vision of this using almost the identical definition referring to Montesquieu's *Esprit des Lois* which he had used in his essay of 1784: 'the wellspring of republics is virtue, by which I mean political virtue, which is nothing less than the love of law and of the *patrie*'.[18]

After setting out his vision of the republic and emphasising the necessity for those guiding it to be imbued with virtue and, in consequence, pure in all their actions, he comes to the crunch: virtue alone cannot guard the republic from the combined onslaught of its external enemies and internal traitors, it must be given the necessary power to defend itself. In the most famous and often the most misunderstood phrase of this speech he offers the logical and terrible conclusion that the only way to arm virtue is to join to it an implacable force, that of terror:

> If the mainspring of popular government during peace is virtue, the mainspring of popular government in revolution is both virtue and terror; virtue without which terror is disastrous, terror without which virtue is powerless. Terror is nothing but justice fast, hard and remorseless; it is therefore a quality of virtue; it is less a particular principle than the consequence of the overriding principle of democracy, when applied to the most pressing needs of the *patrie*.[19]

There was nothing new in the proposition that virtue or goodness cannot stand alone without the support of some power to sustain it. Robespierre's choice of words suggests that he might possibly have been referring to Pascal's *Pensées*, a work which would have been one of the major theological and moral textbooks both of his own education and probably that of the majority of the members of the Convention. Although Pascal himself would surely have been horrified by the idea of the use of terror to support virtue, he had used a very similar phrase a hundred years before Robespierre, suggesting the necessity of ensuring that justice has the support of the civil power to assure its successful application: 'Justice without power is helpless, power without justice is tyrannical ... justice and power must be brought together; and to do so either that which is just must be powerful, or that which is powerful must be just.'[20]

Throughout the remainder of the speech Robespierre concentrates on forcefully reminding the members of the Convention that they must ensure this purification. Again he reverts to his original contention that only the practice of public virtue can save the Republic: 'What is the cure for all these ills? We know of none save the enhancement of that mainspring of republicanism, virtue.'[21] He urges the Convention to signify their acceptance of his analysis and accept the task of facing their internal enemies, as they had already accepted the same principles when facing their external enemies. This is not the Robespierre of Frimaire, with his nod towards the Catholic faith. In this speech there is no sign of any concept of a Deity, no words like God or Eternal; the moral tone is as inflexible and as harsh as the proclamation of the need for the Terror.

On 18 Germinal (7 April 1794), two days after the execution of Danton, Couthon told the Convention that the Committee of Public Safety would present 'A plan for a festival; dedicated to the Eternal Being, whose consoling existence the Hébertistes have not been able to eradicate from the public perception.'[22] There was no further public reference to this project until Robespierre stood before the Convention on 18 Floréal (7 May 1794), nor does any mention of this proposal appear, in either official or private papers, during the period between Couthon's statement and Robespierre going to the tribune of the Convention to present his 'Report on religion and morality' over a month later.[23]

Why Robespierre chose this specific moment to make his proposal that the Republic formally adopt a new national belief system is far from obvious. His decision as to the timing of his initiative must relate, in some way, to his personal assessment of the political and moral state of the nation in the late spring of 1794. Obviously there could be no question of any reversion to the Catholic faith as practised under the *Ancien Régime*. Any such suggestion would have given his opponents the opportunity to charge him with treachery to the Republic and its ideals, a charge strong enough to give them a high probability of mounting immediately a successful coup against him on the floor of the Convention. Any proposed new moral code would therefore need to be something which had clear and acceptable aims. To replace the Catholic morality which the early years of the Revolution had so thoroughly destroyed, and do so with a system based clearly, visibly and firmly on republican and revolutionary principles, Robespierre would have to propose something which would meld his personal assessment of the political reality with his vision of the ultimate society and his personal distaste for the process of de-Christianisation. It seems fair to say, from the evidence of his speeches, that he saw de-Christianisation as a major threat to the Revolution. His reading appears to have been that, if its advocates were to succeed, the result of the formation of a republic based on atheism would mean political anarchy, the loss of central governmental control and the ultimate breakdown of the state. His speeches from November 1793 onwards demonstrate his increasing drive to express this evaluation publicly, presumably with the aim of preparing the way for a later declaration of an acceptably republican moral ethos.

Between Couthon's mention of the idea to the Convention in April and the moment when Robespierre mounted the tribune to address the Convention on 18 Floréal (7 May), there is no documentary evidence of any debate or discussion with anyone else, neither on the ideology he intended to propose, nor on the manner in which the nation was to celebrate this new 'religion'. One must assume that there was at least some general discussion in Robespierre's intimate circle, not least for David and Chénier to have prepared in such detail the arrangements, including the text of all the hymns, which were read to the Convention immediately after Robespierre's speech. There is however no mention either in Robespierre's notes or in the *Mémoires* of any of the members of the Committee of Public Safety who survived Thermidor relating either to the question of public morality or specifically to the proposed Festival of the Supreme Being. Why Robespierre would have kept this immensely important project a secret, even from many of his close supporters, is a question which has never been adequately answered. In the heady days of plot and counter-plot within and without the Convention, it is certainly conceivable that it was a combination of his own political acumen and warnings from some of his intimates which would have led Robespierre to fear that any rumour of such a radical proposal would inflame yet further the opposition to him among certain elements in the Convention.[24]

It is possible that he feared that the rejection of any form of de-Christianisation would provide ammunition for an attack on him by the militantly atheist members of the Convention. It is also far from clear whether he, or his intimates, were genuinely aware of the level which the plotting between disaffected members of the Committee of Public Safety, led by Barère, and the leaders of the Committee of General Security led by Vadier,[25] had already reached. It might equally have been that he was already aware of the rumblings in the Convention, against what some members were claiming was his intention to become sole ruler of France, and knew that any indication of support for a new moral code based on a religious foundation would only give them further ammunition against him. The available evidence indicates that he came to a decision that only a moral code based on the acceptance of the existence of some form of Higher Power, coupled with the promise of immortality, could advance the nation towards his vision of the ideal Republic entirely on his own.

While it is true that Rousseau was his favourite source for moral quotations, politically he was much more a follower of Montesquieu and Locke than of the Sage of Ermenonville. He would probably have accepted that, in applying the values of Rousseau's Social Contract, although the concept of 'virtue' was paramount, practical politics, even when based on such lofty ideals, were likely to be more opportunistic than moral. There is also no firm evidence that he really believed it would be possible to impose on society what Furet called 'Robespierre's absurd principle',[26] an idealised system where there would be transparency and interdependence between history, political action and public morality. The open question remains whether Robespierre consciously believed that the imposition of some recognisably 'religious' system would counteract what he saw as the potentially disastrous result of allowing the continuation of atheism and de-Christianisation.

While he was writing his speech of 18 Floréal, he would have been labouring under the totality of the intellectual baggage which he carried, which not only included Rousseau, Montesquieu and the Enlightenment, but also the inescapable spiritual baggage of one brought up in the regular performance of the rites and rituals of the Catholic faith. The first question in the general catechism of the Catholic Church, which would have been as familiar to Robespierre as it was to the vast majority of French people over twelve in 1794, is 'Who made me?', to which the answer is 'God made me'. A man like Robespierre who continuously referred to himself as being 'of the people' would have been acutely sensitive to those who needed to meld their own strong faith-based view of morality with their political support of the Revolution. Even if the answer was different from the traditional affirmation of the existence of the Christian God, even if the moral power was to be called the Eternal, the First Cause, the Creator of Nature or the Supreme Being, there must still be an answer offering the vision of a believable higher authority to which people could relate. Robespierre seems to have believed himself to be close to fulfilling this need and in tune with the majority sentiment in several important areas. These included the majority rejection of atheism and the distaste for the excesses of the de-Christianisers; and recognition of the need for some acceptable, yet clearly republican, replacement of the pre-revolutionary moral signposts. This must be combined with the idea of some form of authority figure, at once superior yet approachable, who would, at the same time, confirm the validity of the concept of the immortality of the Soul.

By May 1794 the Convention gives an impression of being a seething mass of intrigue, within which it was clear that the atheist faction was increasingly vocal in its opposition to Robespierre. Whatever the background, it is clear that the speech of 18 Floréal was sprung on a Convention totally unprepared for anything like what was delivered. The name of the speech, which would have figured on the order paper, is 'A report on moral and religious ideas', which would probably have indicated to the members that they were due for another long homily on political virtue and public morality. What they heard was, in the context of the state of France at the time, mind-blowing.

It began, simply enough, with an introduction in which Robespierre says 'We are going today to suggest that you reflect on those great truths which are vital for the happiness of mankind, and to propose to you such measures as flow naturally from them.'[27] The careful use of the idea of reflection, rather than imposition, implies that the Convention was to be asked merely to think about morality in general, rather than give approval to any new and unexpected measures, and that anything they would be asked to approve would spring naturally from these 'great truths'. He continued with two relatively innocuous propositions at which nobody could take offence. The first is that 'The world has changed, it needs to change again', the second that 'The revolution is half finished; we need to complete the other half.'[28] He follows this by the introduction of the main theme of his speech with the phrase 'The basic foundation of society is morality.'[29] It might have been expected that he would then launch into the question of public morality, but instead of developing this theme, there follow several minutes of what might be considered standard Robespierrean rhetoric; attacks on external and internal enemies, on Bourbons and Capets, on George III and Pitt, on Danton and Hébert.

He then introduces a new theme, not just 'virtue' but something much deeper, the idea of the consolation and elevation of the spirit, a process which leads inexorably to the thesis that there must be some sort of higher power involved in human destiny. It is at this point that he begins a direct attack both on the 'arid doctrine' of atheism, and the equation of it with love of one's country, using language which must have caused his listeners to sit up, not least because he departs from the generalisation of 'vous' to the particular of 'tu', attacking each protagonist of de-Christianisation and atheism directly. 'Who nominated you to tell the people that God does not exist anymore, you who are passionate about this arid doctrine but not passionate about your country? What do you hope to gain by persuading Man that his destiny is determined solely by blind fate which bears down indiscriminately on evil and good; that his soul is nothing but a puff of wind, blown away at the gates of the tomb?'[30]

The cat was not quite out of the bag yet but, as he continues his 'report', it becomes more and more clear that Robespierre is moving towards avenues of thought which no-one could have expected. Firstly, he is inviting each and every member of the Convention, as an elected representative of the Revolution, to re-think their position on religion; secondly he is inviting them to join him in an estimate of the need for the re-establishment of some form of belief system, a system no longer based on the thinking of the *Ancien Régime* but firmly anchored in the culture of the Revolution. Discarding the claims of philosophers and of previously established organised religions, he is about to offer to his hearers the possibility of replacing the old discredited morality with a new code of public and private ethics. This would be a code based firmly on revolutionary and republican virtue, one that reaches out to the ultimate prize, the triumph of the Republic of Virtue. He does not immediately define this new credo; to begin with he asks his hearers to keep an open mind:

> Think only of the national good and the interests of mankind. Every institution, every doctrine which comforts and elevates souls should be welcomed while those that degrade and corrupt them should be rejected. Bring back to life and raise up all the noble and great moral ideas which people have tried to erase; bring together, by the joy of friendship and the bonds of virtue, those who were being separated.[31]

He accepts that his hearers may consider such thoughts mere dreams, yet these dreams are necessary to the Revolution, because even if they are only dreams they are still an intrinsic part of the purest thoughts of Man: 'if the existence of God and the immortality of the soul were nothing but dreams, still they would be the most beautiful of all the conceptions in human thought'.[32]

Nevertheless, before he can finally present his idea of the Supreme Being as something totally in keeping with true republican virtue, he needs to remove any lingering doubts as to what exactly he is asking the Convention to sign up to. 'There is no question of debating any specific philosophical position nor to debate whether any particular philosopher can be considered virtuous, whatever his views, or even despite them, due to his native wit or superior reasoning. It is a question of seeing atheism as covering the whole nation and linked to a national conspiracy against the Republic.'[33]

Finally he can produce his proposition, quoting directly from his own speech of 1 Frimaire: 'The concept of the Supreme Being and of the immortality of the soul is a continuous call to justice, which makes it both social and republican.'[34] He emphasises again that the legislators cannot dismiss these theories merely as the vapourings of philosophers or theologians, these 'dreams' are real and they should look to use them. In case his listeners were beginning to fear that he was re-introducing Catholicism, Robespierre is at some pains to assure them that there is no pretence at introducing a sanitised republican form of Christianity; there will be no priests in the new recognition of the Supreme Being, indeed he even suggests that this entity might perhaps more properly be called the Creator of Nature. This is the point at which he introduces the final theme, the need to bring the nation together in a great festival not just to honour this Creative spirit, but to make the people themselves joyful and for them to be uplifted, not made miserable by another arid festival to Reason. He uses one of his favourite quotes from Rousseau: 'Bring men together and you improve their lot', adding: 'because men brought together try to please each other and they can only please each other with things which render them worthy of respect.'[35]

Unlike every major festival which has gone before, this is not to be a festival solely, or even mainly in the capital; every commune shall have its own *Fête*. This is Robespierre the consummate politician, who, as he always claimed, is at one with the needs and desires of the people. He recognises the need for something really big to replace the great pre-revolutionary national feast-days, something which will resonate in the hearts of the entire nation. This is not to be just a celebration of the Revolution or the republic; this is to be a national celebration of life itself. Carefully, without actually invoking the latent feelings for the old religion in the general population, he offers the possibility of celebrations at least as good as the ones they had enjoyed under the *Ancien Régime*. He then suggests some of the heroes and heroic acts which might be celebrated, invites the Convention to ignore the sour grapes of the corrupt and unfeeling, and proceeds to his peroration, 'Let us not get drunk on our own success. Let us be pitiless in our defeats, modest in our triumphs, and establish among us peace and happiness through wisdom and morality. This is the real goal of our work; this is the most heroic and the most difficult of tasks.'³⁶

The proposition which Robespierre finally placed before the members of the Convention on 18 Floréal (7 May 1794) incorporated a series of basic tenets which would have been as familiar to the members of the Convention as they would be to the educated public at large. The new 'religion' combined Rousseau's basic thesis that every nation has an absolute need for some form of moral authority to look up to, with the addition of Robespierre's personal and highly idealised vision of ancient Greek and Roman civic virtue. Robespierre reiterated his original claim made the previous November that the acceptance of the principles of the existence of a Deity and of the Immortality of the Soul was a continuous call to justice and something which makes it both social and republican. He finished with a call to the Convention to set out the new vision for the nation: 'The people of France acknowledge the existence of the Supreme Being and of the immortality of the Soul.'³⁷

The Convention duly agreed, and voted for the national festival in honour of the Supreme Being to be held a month later on 20 Prairial (8 June 1794). There are two important clauses in the decree which stand out from anything previously passed by the Convention. These note that the reason for the institution of the smaller *fêtes* is to 'Remind man to think of the Divinity and his own dignity', but they also specifically re-confirmed the official line on the question of the freedom to worship: 'Liberty of worship is confirmed as in the decree of 18 Frimaire', a freedom which, although guaranteed ever since the Declaration of the Rights of Man and frequently restated, was still more honoured in the breach than the observance.

The Convention did not only establish the national Festival of the Supreme Being, it also reconfirmed the national festivals of 14 July, 10 August, 21 January and 31 May. Robespierre also proposed the addition to the official festivities of the Republican calendar of no fewer than a further thirty-five *fêtes* to be celebrated locally throughout the nation on tenth-days over the year. The list of who these *fêtes* were to honour is almost a parody of the recurring themes in the speeches of Jacobin politicians. One could believe them to be the product of a late-night session by members of the Committee of Public Safety or more likely by Robespierre's inner circle, with everyone, as the glasses went round, being invited to propose a suitable subject for republican celebration. The actual subjects chosen are The Supreme Being and Nature; Humanity; The French Nation; Great Humanitarians; The Martyrs of Liberty; Liberty and

Equality; The Republic; World Liberty; Patriotism; The Hatred of Tyrants and Traitors; Truth; Justice; Modesty; Glory and Immortality; Friendship; Frugality; Courage; Honesty; Unselfishness; Stoicism; Love; Marriage; Fatherhood; Motherhood; Filial Piety; Children; Youth; Maturity; Old Age; Misfortune; Agriculture; Industry; Ancestors; Posterity; and finally, Happiness.[38]

Having decided to promulgate a new national republican morality, Robespierre would have been faced with the question of how best to launch it. Any attempt to link it directly to any form of organised religion would play straight into the hands of the de-Christianisers. Any open relationship with the Catholic Church would have been fatal to the project; not only would there have been its immediate condemnation by both the atheists and the moderates in the Convention, such a massive *volte-face* would have been deeply suspicious to those still practising their faith throughout the nation. The possibility of establishing it as some sort of adjunct to or extension of the Constitutional Church was equally a non-starter, considering not only the general disinterest in that organisation but, even more importantly with a national launch needed, the patchy cover the Constitutionals offered nationally.

While he could count on any new initiative from the Convention being hailed automatically as a great and wonderful idea by the committed Jacobins and the placemen in the Provinces, his brother Augustin's letters were making him aware that in many areas the behaviour of the local Jacobins was so bad that it was generating increasing hatred of the government, and any initiative welcomed by them would risk automatic rejection by the rest of the people.[39] He must have been very conscious that it was vital that he should reach out to this large silent majority outside Paris, many of whom still practised their faith. This was the great undeclared constituency, these were the ones who not only had to accept his vision of a new morality, but had to do so with such enthusiasm as to ensure that the new vision he was offering would become accepted as the natural successor to the old faith-based system of national morality.

This was the problem which Robespierre must have considered when debating with himself how exactly to launch his vision of a new republican and revolutionary moral code. Whatever route he chose had to be one which could be carried across the whole of the nation; for this great change in the ethos of the Revolution there could be no question of a major launch in Paris and then relying simply on provincial administrations following suit. This must have led to him considering the possibility of using a new form of Revolutionary Festival, one which would require the celebrations to be truly national. Not only were festivals popular in that they allowed rare public holidays and general celebrations, their ethos embodied one of the cardinal principles of the Revolution that the population should be educated, encouraged and enthused to carry out their functions as citizens of the Republic. Since the first festival, the *Fête de la Federation*, held in July 1790 to celebrate the first anniversary of the storming of the Bastille, festivals had taken on an increasing importance in the political and cultural life of the nation. These festivals continued with both major annual events and lesser special events, such as the one in honour of the taking of Toulon throughout the early years of the Revolution. The largest and most successful festival so far was the *Fête de la Réunion* in August 1793, which had combined the belated celebration of Bastille Day with the proclamation of the new republican constitution.[40]

Robespierre clearly believed that the positive feelings engendered by a great and truly national festival would help immeasurably to ensure the successful launch of his vision of the new morality. Given these factors, the use of a national festival, which could be relied upon to arouse immediate interest in the whole population, would seem an obvious choice. Robespierre also had available at his call the three most important people needed to ensure success in the complicated process of organising a national festival. These were the painter and designer Jacques-Louis David, the Pageant Master of the Revolution, who had been responsible for all the successful Revolutionary Festivals since 1791; the National Architect, Hubert, who had overseen all the engineering works for those festivals;[41] and the poet and dramatist Marie-Joseph Chénier, the unofficial poet laureate of the Revolution and author of the majority of the Revolutionary anthems sung at the festivals. David was also a member of the Convention and Chair of the Committee of Public Education, the body which would be responsible for the organisation of any festival held in Paris, and as such would also have had direct access to Robespierre.

Hubert and Chénier, who had family links by marriage, were committed supporters of Robespierre, although Chénier's position had recently become more complicated by the fact that his elder brother, the poet Marie-André Chénier, was at that moment in prison awaiting execution. Robespierre could also call on the services of France's leading composers, Gossec and Méhul, who had supplied music for previous festivals and had provided the music for Chénier's republican hymns. The services of these specialists would also allay any fears Robespierre might have regarding the correct detailed organisation of such a national event. He had before him the example of how disastrous the attempted launch of a new morality by a badly organised festival could be. The ill-prepared attempt by the de-Christianisers, led by Chaumette and

Hébert,[42] to impose atheism on France with the *Fête de la Raison* held in the cathedral of Notre-Dame de Paris on 20 Brumaire (10 November 1793), when they tried to upgrade what was originally conceived as merely a local event held in one area of Paris into a national event, without proper preparation and under impossible time constraints, was generally accepted to have been a failure.[43]

With this organisation behind him, when Robespierre made his speech on 18 Floréal, not only did he have the moral and political arguments carefully prepared, he also had a fully detailed specification of a great national festival both from the point of view of pageantry and of popular participation, ready to lay out for the approval of the Convention. The Festival of the Supreme Being, to be held nationally on 8 June 1794, would be the greatest of all the Revolutionary Festivals, one in which the people would not just be spectators of all the rites and rituals, they themselves would be the actual performers. The grandeur of the occasion would represent the apogee of David's pageantry, remaining unsurpassed even by the great military pageants of the Empire, whose cultural legacy still affects public festivals in France.[44]

At the time, Robespierre seemed to have pulled off the impossible trick, to reconcile all sides. As will be seen, the national response to the Festival at all levels shows clearly that the idea was in tune with an apparent need among a large part of the population who were still searching for something which would replace the old festivals of Pentecost and the *Fête-Dieu*. Even militant atheists such as Sylvain Maréchal, who was opposed to religion in any form, could and did embrace the idea of a Cult of a Supreme Being with marked enthusiasm, considering it to be a profoundly Republican idea.[45]

Notes

1 For an in-depth discussion of Revolutionary moral language see M. Linton, *Choosing Terror: Virtue, Friendship, and Authenticity in the French Revolution* (Oxford, 2013).
2 See G. Labica, *Robespierre: Une politique de la philosophie* (Paris, 1990).
3 There is further interesting analysis of Robespierre's stature as a philosopher of political life at the time of the Revolution in Labica, *Robespierre*.
4 L. de Neuvéglise, *La vie et les crimes de Robespierre* (Augsburg, 1795).
5 'J'ai été dès le collège un assez mauvais catholique', Robespierre, *Œuvres*, Vol. 9, p. 443.
6 'Le ressort essentiel des républiques est la vertu ... c'est à dire la vertu politique, qui n'est autre chose que l'amour des lois et de la patrie.' Robespierre, *Œuvres*, Vol. 1, p. 21 and pp. 203–9.

7 'Des deux opinions qui ont été balancées dans cette assemblée, l'une a pour elle toutes les idées qui flattent l'imagination, toutes les espérances brillantes qui animent l'enthousiasme … l'autre n'est appuyée que sur la froide raison et sur la triste vérité. Pour plaire, il faut défendre la première; pour être utile il faut soutenir la seconde, avec la certitude de déplaire à tous ceux qui ont le pouvoir de nuire; c'est pour celle-ci que je me déclare.' Robespierre, *Œuvres*, Vol. 8, pp. 74–5.

8 'Je soutiens, moi, ces éternels principes sur lesquels s'étaie la faiblesse humaine pour s'élancer dans la vertu.' Robespierre, *Œuvres*, Vol. 8, p. 233.

9 'Invoquer le nom de la Providence et émettre une idée de l'être éternel qui influe essentiellement sur les destins des nations, qui me paraît à moi veille d'une manière toute particulière sur la révolution française, n'est point un idée trop hasardée, mais un sentiment de mon cœur, un sentiment qui m'est nécessaire.' Robespierre, *Œuvres*, Vol. 8, p. 235.

10 'De quel droit viendront-ils troubler la liberté des cultes au nom de la liberté, et attaquer le fanatisme par un fanatisme nouveau? De quel droit feraient-ils dégénérer les hommages solennels rendus à la vérité pure, en des farces éternelles et ridicules.' Robespierre, *Œuvres*, Vol. 10, p. 196.

11 'dans la présence de l'Être suprême', Robespierre, *Œuvres*, Vol. 10, p. 259.

12 'J'ai déjà dit que je ne parlais ni comme individu ni comme un philosophe systématique, mais comme un représentant du peuple. L'athéisme est aristocratique. L'idée d'un grand Être qui veille sur l'innocence opprimée est toute populaire. Le peuple, les malheureux m'applaudissent. Si je trouvais des censeurs, ce serait parmi les riches et parmi les coupables.' Robespierre, *Œuvres*, Vol. 10, p. 196.

13 'J'ai été dès le collège un assez mauvais catholique: je n'ai jamais été un défenseur infidèle de l'humanité. Je n'en suis que plus attaché aux idées morales et politiques que je viens de vous exposer. Si Dieu n'existoit pas, il faudroit l'inventer.' Robespierre, *Œuvres*, Vol. 10, p. 197.

14 'des hommes qui sont attachés à la Révolution par une suite non interrompue de sacrifices', Robespierre, *Œuvres*, Vol. 10, p. 259.

15 'après bien de larmes de désespoir, ton sublime discours aux Jacobins vient de m'en faire verser de consolation', Robespierre, *Œuvres*, Vol. 3, p. 243.

16 'Les principes de morale politique qui doivent guider la Convention nationale dans l'administration intérieure de la République.' Robespierre, *Œuvres*, Vol. 9, pp. 350–66.

17 'il est temps de marquer nettement le but de la Révolution, et le terme où nous voulons arriver', Robespierre, *Œuvres*, Vol. 9, p. 350.

18 'le resort essential … c'est la vertu: je parle de la vertu publique … de cette vertu qui n'est autre chose que l'amour de la patrie et de ses lois', Robespierre, *Œuvres*, Vol. 9, pp. 350–66.

19 'Si le ressort du gouvernement populaire dans la paix est la vertu, le ressort du gouvernement populaire en révolution est à la fois la vertu et la terreur: la vertu, sans laquelle la terreur est funeste: la terreur, sans laquelle la vertu est impuissante. La terreur n'est autre chose que la justice prompte, sévère,

inflexible; elle est donc une émanation de la vertu; elle est moins un principe particulier, qu'une conséquence du principe générale de la démocratie, appliqué aux plus pressants besoins de la patrie.' (Robespierre, Œuvres, Vol. 9, p. 357)

20 'La justice sans la force est impuissante: la force sans la justice est tyrannique ... Il faut donc mettre ensemble la justice et la force; et pour faire cela que ce qui est juste soit fort, ou que ce qui est fort soit juste.' B. Pascal, *Les Provinciales, Pensées et opuscules divers*, G. Ferreyrolles and P. Sellier, eds (Paris, 1999), S.135, Pensées V.

21 'Quel est le remède de tous ces maux? Nous n'en connaissons point d'autre que le développement de ce ressort général de la République, la vertu.' Robespierre, Œuvres, Vol. 9, p. 364.

22 'Un projet de fête décadaire dédiée à l'Éternel, dont les Hébertistes n'ont pas ôté du people l'idée consolante.' *Moniteur*, Vol. 20, p. 151.

23 'Rapport sur les idées religieuses et morales', Robespierre, Œuvres, Vol. 9, pp. 443–65.

24 For more detailed discussion of the atmosphere of conspiracy surrounding the Convention see P.R. Campbell, T.E. Kaiser and M. Linton, eds, *Conspiracy in the French Revolution* (Manchester, 2007).

25 Marc-Guillaume-Alexis Vadier, leader of the Comité de Sureté Générale and one of the main movers in the Thermidor conspiracy against Robespierre.

26 F. Furet and D. Richer, *La Révolution française* (Paris, 1978), p. 144.

27 'Nous venons aujourd'hui soumettre à votre méditation des vérités profondes qui importent au bonheur des hommes, et vous proposer des mesures qui en découlent naturellement.' Robespierre, Œuvres, Vol. 9, p. 443.

28 'Le monde a changé, il doit changer encore'; 'La moitié de la révolution du monde est déjà faite; l'autre moitié doit s'accomplir.' Robespierre, Œuvres, Vol. 9, p. 443.

29 'Le fondement unique de la société civile, c'est la morale.' Robespierre, Œuvres, Vol. 9, p. 444.

30 'Qui donc t'a donné la mission d'annoncer au peuple que la Divinité n'existe pas, ô toi qui te passionnes pour cette aride doctrine, et qui ne te passionnas jamais pour la patrie? Quel avantage trouves-tu à persuader l'homme qu'une force aveugle préside à ses destinées, et frappe au hasard le crime et la vertu; que son âme n'est qu'un souffle léger qui s'éteint aux portes du tombeau?' Robespierre, Œuvres, Vol. 9, p. 451.

31 'Ne consultez que le bien de la patrie et les intérêts de l'humanité. Toute institution, toute doctrine qui console et qui élève les âmes, doit être accueillie: rejetez toutes celles qui tendent à les dégrader et à les corrompre. Ranimez, exaltez tous les sentiments généreux et toutes les grandes idées morales qu'on a voulu éteindre; rapprochez par le charme de l'amitié et par le lien de la vertu les hommes qu'on a voulu diviser.' (Robespierre, Œuvres, Vol. 9, p. 451)

32 'si l'existence de Dieu, si l'immortalité de l'âme, n'étaient que des songes, elles seraient encore la plus belle de toutes les conceptions de l'esprit humain', Robespierre, *Œuvres*, Vol. 9, p. 452.

33 'il ne s'agit pas ici de faire le procès à aucune opinion philosophique en particulier, ni de contester que tel philosophe peut être vertueux, quelles que soient ses opinions, et même en dépit d'elles, par la force d'un naturel heureux ou d'une raison supérieure. Il s'agit de considérer seulement l'athéisme comme national, et lié à un système de conspiration contre la République.' Robespierre, *Œuvres*, Vol. 9, p. 452.

34 'L'idée de l'Être suprême et de l'immortalité de l'âme est un rappel continuel à la justice; elle est donc sociale et républicaine.' Robespierre, *Œuvres*, Vol. 9, p. 452.

35 'car les hommes rassemblés chercheront à se plaire, et ils ne pourront se plaire que par les choses qui les rendent estimables', Robespierre, *Œuvres*, Vol. 9, pp. 456–7.

36 'Défions-nous de l'ivresse même des succès. Soyons terribles dans les revers, modestes dans nos triomphes, et fixons au milieu de nous la paix et le bonheur par la sagesse et par la morale. Voilà le véritable but de nos travaux; voilà la tâche la plus héroïque et la plus difficile.' Robespierre, *Œuvres*, Vol. 9, pp. 457–8.

37 'Le peuple français reconnaît l'existence de l'Être suprême et l'immortalité de l'âme.' Robespierre, *Œuvres*, Vol. 9, p. 461.

38 'A l'Être suprême et à la Nature. Au Genre humain. Au Peuple français. Aux Bienfaiteurs de l'humanité. Aux Martyrs de la liberté. A la Liberté et à l'Egalité. A la République. A la Liberté du Monde. A l'amour de la Patrie. A la haine des Tyrans et des Traîtres. A la Vérité. A la Justice. A la Pudeur. A la Gloire et à l'Immortalité. A l'Amitié. A la Frugalité. Au Courage. A la Bonne foi. Au Désintéressement. Au Stoïcisme. A l'Amour. A la Foi conjugale. A l'Amour paternel. A la Tendresse maternelle. A la Piété filiale. A l'Enfance. A la jeunesse. A l'Âge viril. A la Vieillesse. Au Malheur. A l'Agriculture. Á l'Industrie. A nos Aïeux. A la Postérité. Au Bonheur.' Robespierre, *Œuvres*, Vol. 9, p. 462.

39 Augustin Robespierre complained on several occasions to his brother that local Jacobin notables were imprisoning and even executing anyone who questioned their conduct. For more detailed data see Augustin's letters of February and March 1794 in G. Michon, *Correspondance de Maximilien et Augustin Robespierre* (Paris, 1928) and for more specific accounts of Augustin's travels, see M. Young, *Augustin: The Younger Robespierre* (London, 2011).

40 The delaying of the celebration of the anniversary of the Bastille in 1793 until its combination with the *Fête de la Fédération* in August of the same year is discussed in more depth in Chapter 3.

41 During this period the title 'Architect' meant that the person concerned had completed a course of studies as both an architect and as a civil engineer.

42 Pierre-Gaspard Chaumette was a convinced atheist who, with Jacques-René Hébert (publisher of Le Père Duchesne), were the leaders of the radical de-Christianising faction.
43 See M. Ozouf, *La Fête Révolutionnaire, 1789–1799* (Paris, 1976), pp. 157–67.
44 For a further detailed discussion of the influence of the Festival of the Supreme Being on later Republican Festivals, see also O. Ihl, *La fête républicaine* (Paris, 1996), S. Hazareesingh, *The Saint-Napoleon: Celebrations of Sovereignty in Nineteenth Century France* (Oxford, 2005) and R. Dalisson, *Célébrer la nation: Les fêtes nationales en France de 1789 à nos jours* (Paris, 2009).
45 S. Maréchal, *Tableau historique des événements révolutionnaires, depuis la fondation de la République jusqu'à présent, rédigé principalement pour les campagnes* (Paris, An III), p. 133.

2

The national response to Robespierre's proclamation[1]

Robespierre had made his move, but the real measure of success or failure of his attempt to reset the moral agenda of the Revolution would depend on the response from outside the capital. In this the Festival of the Supreme Being showed several major differences against any other festival since 1790. The first, and most evident of these was that in previous festivals any local celebration by a city, town or commune had been a question of choice; choice of whether and how to participate and, to some extent, choice of when to do so. Here, for the first time, it was specified that the whole nation must take part, not how and when it suited them but on a day and at a time clearly specified in advance. By contrast the extent of national participation in the previous major festival, the *Fête de la Réunion*, in August 1793 had been limited to the presence, by invitation, of two representatives from the regional assembly of each *département*.

The second was that the actual details of the celebrations were not left entirely to the individual local authorities; they would have to operate within a very specific set of parameters laid down by David and attached to the Decree establishing the Festival. Obviously there would be some divergences to allow for local conditions but the local organisers were specifically required to follow these guidelines. In the end, as will be seen later, many local politicians did take it upon themselves to vary quite considerably from David's template. Another point of difference was that within that template were included instructions for a level of musical participation never before specified. Finally, and most difficult of all for the organising bodies outside the capital, the time frame was extremely tight. For the major festivals of 1791 and 1792, the type of celebration and the dates were well known in advance so there were no problems. For other elective participatory festivals the local authority had often been able to stretch the time limits to accommodate their own capabilities. For the Festival of Reason, officially to be celebrated on 20 Brumaire (10 November) the details from Paris were generally so late in arriving that those areas which chose to celebrate also had to pick their moment. Now the date was immutable, and preparations had to be put in train urgently for any hope of success.

Everything would therefore depend on the reaction of the people in the provinces, since the official bodies in Paris only had to make the usual welcoming noises, to pass resolutions and to submit letters approving any initiative from the Convention. The provincial administrations had not only to welcome formally the new Festival, they had also to organise it physically in their own locality. Following the speech of 18 Floréal, the leaders of public opinion outside Paris, particularly those in the *Sociétés Populaires* and the Jacobin Clubs, were faced with the need to give an immediate response to something totally unexpected, and for which they were completely unprepared. Because of the problems of effective and rapid communication between the provinces and Paris, the time constraints were even more acute than normal; there was not only the need to respond formally to the speech of 18 Floréal, the local authorities also had to put into immediate motion the practical measures necessary to ensure the proper celebration of the new Festival. It would be these immediate responses which would indicate to Robespierre, and to the Convention, the level of public acceptance and support for the decree.

It is precisely because of its particular characteristic of intense national participation that the Festival of the Supreme Being offers two areas of documentation which can be of real help in attempting to gauge the level and tenor of popular response. Firstly, there are the official replies generated by the actual decree and David's detailed specification for the conduct of the Festival. Secondly there are the unexpected unofficial responses generated by the nature and substance of the subject of the Festival; unexpected because this type of response had never appeared before. Finally there are the reports on the conduct of the great day itself in the various localities, some in the press, others in formal or informal reports by organisations and individuals. The fact that Robespierre's initiative produced by far the largest national response to that of any Revolutionary Festival is also a considerable advantage. In contrast to Chaumette's Festival of Reason in November 1793, which generated just under 800 official responses,[2] over 1,600 were received for the Festival of the Supreme Being.[3] Not only were there on this occasion more replies from the provinces, they were also essentially different from those in response to previous festivals. This time there were not only the regular formalised letters of congratulation from the placemen in local administrations or the activists in the local Jacobin Society. The replies included submissions directly from members of the public, in the form of hymns and prayers addressed to the Supreme Being, or poems and speeches intended for declamation during the local celebrations. These documents, so very different from the usual stilted official responses, offer clear evidence of the depth and quality of feeling engendered by the proposed Festival. The reaction to the idea of worship of the Supreme Being also indicates that the problems of religion and religious observance were far nearer the surface than might have been assumed either from the passivity of the response to the ongoing campaigns of de-Christianisation or from the proclamation of atheism implicit in the invitation to celebrate the Cult of Reason.

The question is whether the documents relating to the Festival of the Supreme Being genuinely give a more real insight into the experiences of the people as a whole than, for example, those relating to the two previous major festivals, the *Fête de la Fédération* in July 1792 and the *Fête de la Réunion* in August 1793. It is precisely because of the array of local sources available that the study of the genuine public response to the Festival which this local documentation allows draws inescapably to a new evaluation of the importance of the great event of 20 Prairial in the nation as a whole. The documentation available in provincial archives and other sources on the national response to Robespierre's proposal for a new form of national worship offers this fresh insight, primarily because of the special characteristics which set the Festival of the Supreme Being apart from any other Revolutionary Festival. As many commentators have argued, all public spectacles have a basic underpinning of public participation, yet in both pre-Revolutionary and early Revolutionary Festivals this was normally limited to the general public being passive participants, simply spectators, while the real celebrations were performed by selected groups or individuals, much in the manner of a congregation taking part in a church service in a secondary or semi-passive role.

David's specification for the celebrations in Paris, which were the template for the whole country, emphasised Robespierre's insistence on massive public participation. In contrast to previous festivals, this time the celebrants were to be the whole assembly, not merely the chosen few; the people were to be the performers and not merely the audience.[4] The manner and language of Robespierre's proclamation also required that not only the leaders of public opinion, but the whole population should face up to the problem of the potential re-establishment of a level of public worship which the Decree creating the Festival of the Supreme Being brought with it. The people of France were no longer expected simply to respond to a political imperative handed down from the centre; they were expressly invited to accept the re-introduction of a form of organised national worship, based on a visibly Deist figure, in sharp contrast to the negativism of the de-Christianisers or the unapproachability of a Goddess of Reason.

This addressed the core of the problem of the acceptance of the public practice of religion, as originally guaranteed in the Declaration of the Rights of Man. It also seems to have awoken an immediate response in the provinces where the middle classes, among whom the influence of Rousseau and the Enlightenment was far outweighed by their inherent conformity to the old morality, were still very much exercised by the problem of how to transform the pre-revolutionary faith-based moral system into something which, while still retaining the force of moral suasion which the old religion had given, would be acceptable within the new Revolutionary ethos. The suggestion that there would be the re-emergence of a comforting system of national morality was generally greeted positively, even in some cases with joy, as the whole nation drew together with Paris in the preparations for a truly national celebration. The fact that the religious question was still a live issue, despite the efforts of the de-Christianisers, was noted by Mathiez in Angers, a city with a counter-revolution with strong religious overtones on its doorstep, where, 'the struggle against bigotry and the priests of the Vendée has not extinguished the feelings of belief in their souls'.[5] The opening paragraph of the letter which the municipal authorities of Orleans sent out to all citizens, detailing the arrangements for the Festival, states it unequivocally: 'The law calling on you to celebrate a festival to the Supreme Being has done no more than express openly those feelings which have never left you.'[6]

As the documents arrived from Paris, the active members of local *Sociétés Populaires* and Jacobin Clubs needed to begin organising the new Festival immediately. During Year II the membership of these societies had changed from the original majority membership drawn from the professional and merchant classes, who had often deliberately set the requirements for membership as high as possible so as to minimise recruitment from the artisanal and lower classes. In many areas, these original cadres now found themselves with a significant proportion of new members from these hitherto excluded areas.[7] Robespierre would have been only too well aware that, when the copies of the decree arrived at Town Halls, it would be the reaction from the new membership of the Jacobin Clubs and the *Sociétés Populaires* which would be vital to the success of his plan. There would, of course, be the standard replies, couched in the overblown rhetorical language with which provincial republican orators welcomed every word from Paris, but its real success would be clear were there also to be genuine pleasure visible. There could be a real national surge in favour of the new ideology provided that those members of the provincial middle classes who had been keeping a deliberately low profile for the last two years, possibly still hoping for some form of reconciliation between their faith and the Revolution, were to emerge from the shadows to welcome the new initiative. Another possible contributory factor was that, as early historians of the Revolution agree, there was a strong expectation, certainly in Paris, that Robespierre would use the occasion of the Festival to declare some sort of national amnesty and with it the end of the Terror.[8] If this hope really existed in the mind of those preparing to celebrate the festival, it would be a strong factor in determining the success of Robespierre's initiative.

There were different phases in this public response to the decree; the first was the immediate reaction to the proclamation of the Cult of the Supreme Being, followed by the response to the idea of the *Fête* itself. This is clearly demonstrated in the documents received by both the Convention and the Committee of Public Education, directly in response to the copies of Robespierre's speech. There were two further phases, firstly communications relating to the manner in which the various cities and communes intended to organise the celebrations of 20 Prairial, followed by the documents received by the Convention and the Committee after the celebrations, describing local and regional reaction to the events of 20 Prairial itself. It is, however, quite impractical to attempt to classify the pre-celebration documentation according to a specific cut-off date. Logically, one would wish to place all this type of documentation into a single group comprising those documents received by the Convention and the Committee before the Festival itself on 20 Prairial, assuming that documents received after this date would refer to the celebrations per se, and not to the run-up to them.

Unfortunately this is not possible. The problems of communication within France were such that considerable delays inevitably occurred between the Convention sending out the official papers, their reception in a distant town or city, and the time needed for the municipal or other official body to study them, discuss them in open meeting and draft a suitable reply. There would then be a further lengthy delay before the response reached the relevant committee or secretariat in Paris. There was yet another complication in that, because of the timescales mentioned above, the documentation regarding the Cult of Reason, which should have effectively disappeared with the execution of Chaumette over a month earlier, was still occupying the minds of official bodies in many of the more distant areas of France. Examination of the documents received by the Committee of Public Education shortly after the proclamation of 18 Floréal show that it was still receiving large numbers of letters relating to events of several months earlier. For example, in the two days immediately following Robespierre's speech, the Committee received formal letters from the communes of Gien in the Loiret and Verneuil in the Cher, in which each of these two local administrations reported that they had, as ordered, changed the name of their principal church to the Temple of Reason. In the same communication they offered their congratulations to the Convention on its decision to promote the worship of Reason.[9] As late as 3 Prairial (22 May), official confirmation was still being received from the Doubs, the Ain, the Côte-d'Or and the Gard that the local churches had been transformed into a Temple of Reason, rather than into a Temple of the Supreme Being as required by the decree of 18 Floréal.[10]

Naturally, the first to receive copies of the official publication of the proclamation of the new Festival were the official bodies in Paris and the Île de France. The first recorded reception by the Convention of a formal reaction to the proclamation was only six days after the speech itself, when the administration of the city of Paris, who, according to the record had already received the formal document from the Convention printers in time for its meeting on the evening of 22 Floréal (11 May), came to the bar of the Convention on 24 Floréal (13 May), to offer their formal congratulations and assurances of solidarity.

The timescale for the reception of the documentation sent out from Paris to the provincial cities varied considerably. While the administration in Lille was already receiving suggestions from its committees for the official plan for the celebrations on 30 Floréal (19 May),[11] in Strasbourg the Council did not see the documents from Paris until 1 Prairial (20 May);[12] in Angers it was 4 Prairial (23 May),[13] in Amiens 5 Prairial (24 May)[14] while in Bordeaux the papers were only seen by the Municipal Council on 7 Prairial (26 May) when they were personally presented to them by the new *Représentant en Mission*, Jullien, after his arrival in the city.[15] With these timescales operating in the larger and more important cities, one can only imagine when the documentation regarding the *Fête* was received in the more remote areas. The village of Belvès in the Dordogne reported to the Committee of Public Education in a letter dated 21 Prairial (9 June), that it only got the papers on the 19th, just in time for the *Fête* to be held on the next day, and this letter was itself only received by the Committee on 24 Messidor (12 July), over a month after the Festival.[16]

The Convention and the Committee of Public Education continued to receive submissions from the provinces, both in the shape of formal reactions to Robespierre's original proposition, and in more informal submissions, usually in the form of proposals for hymns or prayers, from the various towns and villages throughout France, until well after the date of the *Fête* itself. As with the earlier crossings of messages relating to the Cult of Reason up to the end of Prairial, the two types of documentation, pre- and post-celebration, became mixed together with messages regarding the assassination attempt on Robespierre of 3 Prairial (22 May) and acknowledgements of receipt of other pieces of legislation or of general correspondence.

Detailed official accounts of the event in the major provincial centres began to arrive in Paris soon after the celebrations of 20 Prairial, followed later by further documents from provincial, departmental and cantonal registers describing the festivities in smaller towns and communes, right down to village level. The diversity of the actual celebrations in different areas, and the light which these detailed accounts of the festivals throw on the different emphases in the celebration of the *Fête* throughout provincial France, especially perhaps those held in the frontier towns, as against those aspects chosen for emphasis during the main event in Paris, is of capital importance in any attempt to establish the true nature of the national cultural picture, as are the differences between the formalised *adresses* of congratulations and detailed descriptions of the holding of the *Fête*, together with both official and unofficial reactions to the celebrations.

The final category to be studied is that of the individual personal commentaries which were published, sometimes immediately after the Festival celebrations, sometimes many years later, by people who were present at one of the festivals either as participants with an active role in the official side of the celebrations, or purely as spectators. The majority of these accounts are from people who were at the main event in Paris; regrettably, there are few similar eyewitness accounts of events held in the provinces. These comments offer striking differences in their emphasis on specific aspects of the perceived importance of the manner in which the Supreme Being touched the lives of individuals and communities, and together with the comments from eyewitnesses are of immense importance in the final evaluation of both the immediate and the lasting cultural effect of the *Fête*. These post-celebration documents are discussed in more detail in Chapter 6.[17]

This chapter is concerned with the first of these three phases; documents which may be conveniently divided between, on the one hand, the national reaction to Robespierre's proposal in the form of *adresses* received by the Convention, and, on the other, the receipt of proposals for hymns and prayers submitted to the Committee of Public Education.

These were usually received before the date of the event, and help towards the general analysis of the national pre-festival reaction to the proposition of the Cult and the Festival of the Supreme Being. The documentation divides into two basic types: firstly, the 'official' *adresses* normally directed at the Convention or to the Committee of Public Safety from Municipal or Departmental administrations and the network of *Sociétés Populaires*, and secondly the more unofficial submissions, sent directly to the Committee of Public Education. These consist of items submitted by public and semi-official bodies, some of which were examples of speeches or essays supporting the concept of the Supreme Being; more often these were submissions received from individual private citizens proposing hymns, prayers, poems or eulogies. These were often sent in as an example of what was to be used in their own locality, sometimes even in the hope of them being accepted as contributions to the celebrations of the *Fête* in the capital. It might be expected that there would have been considerable detailed comment in the press, yet, in the event, both the Parisian and the provincial press generally limited themselves to reprinting the text of Robespierre's speech and the Decree of 18 Floréal.[18] In contrast to the very full coverage by the Parisian press of the actual celebrations, there were very few direct comments in the provincial press, even such fervent admirers as Butenschön in Strasbourg contenting themselves with partially or fully reprinting the text (although in his case he translated the more striking parts of it into German) and urging their readers to study it carefully.

It was customary for documents such as new laws and decrees from the Convention and the Committee of Public Safety to be received by the provincial administrations in packages of several at a time. This is clearly shown by many entries in the minute books of departmental and municipal authorities, noting the arrival of three, four or even more such sets of documents in one shipment. However, the proclamation and decree of 18 Floréal were considered so important that after the printing of the speech and decree by the official printers on 19 Floréal, copies were sent immediately by fast courier from Paris, so that responses began to be received by the Convention and the Committee of Public Education within a shorter period than was customary. This is true both of the formal *adresses* which were sent to the Convention, usually by either the *Société Populaire* or the Administration of a city, town or district, and the more literary efforts sent in by individual citizens, or presented as essays or as *adresses* from local literary or cultural bodies, often offering proposals regarding the forms of celebration to be followed in their communes, or reporting on speeches made or papers presented in support of the new Cult.

Robespierre would have been only too well aware that, when the copies of the decree arrived at Town Halls, and, even more importantly, at the Jacobin Clubs and the *Sociétés Populaires*, all over France a genuinely positive reaction would be vital to his plan. Of course there would be the standard replies, couched in the overblown rhetorical language with which provincial republican orators welcomed every word from Paris, but would there, this time, be genuine pleasure visible amongst the boilerplate oratory? How dangerous would be the potential level of general euphoria which the idea of the *Fête* could raise throughout the country, and would those who had been keeping a deliberately low profile for the last two years, still hoping for some form of reconciliation between their faith and the Revolution, emerge from the shadows to welcome the new initiative? Would they now be expecting Robespierre to use their support to do something like proclaiming a general amnesty, if not the complete end to the Terror, and how could he use this new solidarity to finally crush the de-Christianisers? The immediate responses to the Decree of 18 Floréal would give a strong indication of the final answers to some of these questions. Robespierre knew that within a few days his ally, Payan, would lead a delegation from the Paris commune to the Convention to welcome and praise the initiative, and that he would be closely followed by other delegations to the Convention from the *Sociétés Populaires* of the Paris *sections* and from nearby communes from the Île-de-France, all of whom could be relied upon to make speeches welcoming his initiative, as they did automatically with all new initiatives from the Convention. What was far more important and interesting would be the reaction of the more distant towns and cities where his personal standing, despite his careful nurturing of links with provincial Jacobin Clubs from his time as Secretary, was more debatable. This was where success or failure would lie; the reaction of the different areas would finally determine whether not only the Festival but also the underlying proposal of a new republican morality was accepted throughout the nation.

As far as the formal *adresses* are concerned, the first to offer congratulations to the Convention was, as was to be expected, the administration of the city of Paris, which presented itself at the bar of the Convention on 24 Floréal (13 May) to offer formal congratulations on the speech. The record in the minutes of the Convention is couched in typical officialese:

> The administration of the commune of Paris was admitted to the bar [of the Convention]: it congratulated the national Convention on its decree of 18 Floréal and, keen to eliminate all remaining traces of superstition and to

underpin those religious ideas which serve as the basis of public morality, it has decreed that on all temples dedicated to public use the words Temple consecrated to Reason, be effaced and replaced by the inscription To the Supreme Being.[19]

This was the first of many similar items to be selected by the Convention for 'Honourable mention and insertion in the official minutes with the response from the President [of the Convention] and their distribution to all municipalities.'[20]

Payan, the National Agent of Paris, appeared at the bar of the Convention the next day.[21] He was followed by other delegations from the *départements* and towns of the Île-de-France while, at the same time, the first letters began to arrive from the provinces. All of these fulsomely praised Robespierre for proposing the new Cult and expressed their anticipation of the *Fête*. These 'official' responses directed specifically to the Convention have been analysed in depth by various scholars. Vovelle underlined the massive popularity of the Festival of the Supreme Being as against that of Reason; his figures show the total number of addresses received by the Convention in support of Chaumette's proclamation of the Cult of Reason in Brumaire (November 1793) as a total of 768. These were spread over a far longer period than was the case of the 1,500-plus responses received in relation to the Supreme Being,[22] so that the Supreme Being not only collected more votes than Reason had received over a period of ten months but did so in a much shorter time frame.[23] The geographical distribution of these responses for the two cults demonstrates, as might be expected, a very similar picture, with the majority of formal submissions coming from the major population regions of the Île de France, the towns along the great river axes of the Seine and the Rhône and the major population areas of the Rhône-Alpes, Bordeaux and the Marseilles-Aix conurbations.[24]

In 1994, Whitworth published a much more detailed analysis of the 'official' responses received by the Convention.[25] He analysed a total of 1,617 responses, sent to the Convention between Floréal and Fructidor of Year II (mid-April to mid-September 1794), which he divided into two categories. The first covers 1,100 documents which specifically mention the decree establishing the Cult of the Supreme Being, and use the actual words 'Supreme Being' in their text, while the remainder have a looser reference to the object of the response, often utilising the words 'God' or 'The Eternal' in place of 'Supreme Being'.[26]

This analysis distinguishes between dated and undated submissions; it shows that although the overall spread of dates of reception of both types of *adresses* covered the period from 22 Floréal (11 May) as far as 23 Fructidor (9 September), well after the events of Thermidor, the highpoint for dated documents was the period between 5 and 10 Prairial (24 and 29 May), during which period 34 per cent of the total was received by the Convention, while the largest reception of undated documents was between 10 and 20 Messidor (28 June to 8 July). This analysis confirms the point made earlier regarding the problems of communication, dated *adresses* tending to be from the larger municipalities and therefore received earlier in Paris. According to Whitworth's analysis, despite such events as the assassination attempt of 3 Prairial and the promulgation of the *Loi du 22 Prairial*, there were overwhelmingly more official *adresses* received by the Convention during the period of Prairial and Messidor directly referring to the proclamation of 18 Floréal than there were referring to these other major events. It is also noticeable how many of the *adresses* which were received after 3 Prairial specifically praised the Supreme Being for having averted the attempted assassination of Robespierre.[27]

Apart from the written submissions, many of the *sections* of Paris, as well as several communes reasonably near to the capital, followed the example of the Paris administration by sending delegations to the bar of the Convention to express personally and directly their support for the new Cult. The *Moniteur* reports that on 29 Floréal (18 May) the Convention received a delegation from the Jacobin Society of Paris, who offered the following remarks: 'the whole of France supports your decree; the sun shines on this unanimous rising of an entire people honouring a God ... Citizen representatives, be always as you have shown yourselves before the world, the representatives of a great and magnanimous nation, of a people who place morality at the heart of patriotism.'[28] This particular delegation was considered important enough to merit not only the usual expressions of 'honourable mention in the minutes', but, according to the *Moniteur*, also direct replies. First to speak was the President of the Convention, Carnot, who said: 'To deny the existence of the Supreme Being is to deny the existence of Nature ... Calling upon the Supreme Being is to call to one's side the whole spectacle of Nature, the manifestations which soften pain, the hope that consoles suffering humanity.'[29] He was followed by Couthon, acting, as so often, as Robespierre's mouthpiece:

> The Jacobins and the benches [of the Convention] today thank you, bless you for having formalised by a decree that sacred truth which the just man invariably finds in his heart 'The people of France acknowledge the existence of the Supreme Being and of the immortality of the Soul' (cheers)

... they well know, these monsters who preach atheism and materialism ... that the surest way to kill the Revolution would be to take away from man the hope of a future life and replace it with the desolation of nothingness![30]

The Convention received a further six delegations on 30 Floréal. One represented the administration of the commune of Versailles, with the other five representing individually the Paris *sections* of Mutius-Scaevola, Marat, Popincourt, Bonne Nouvelle and the Commune de Mont-Marat.[31] Yet even with the 'official' reactions, all was not sweetness and light; parts of France which had been particularly affected by the de-Christianisation efforts of such *Representants en Mission* as Fouché were visibly unimpressed by the new morality. In its issue of 2 Messidor the Paris newpaper, *L'Abréviateur universel*, reported the uproar in the Jacobin Club in Paris on 23 Prairial when Robespierre told the meeting:

> In Nevers, Chaumette's doctrine was openly proclaimed; the decree which ordered the celebration of the Festival of the Supreme Being was trampled underfoot. On receiving the news of this happy event which has saved liberty by putting it under the protection of integrity, they said: 'the Convention has been led astray by moderates, as for us, we will not change our direction or our feelings and will hold to our principles'; they continue to proclaim atheism and immorality (cries of indignation).[32]

Apart from these official responses sent to the Convention itself, the records of the Committee of Public Education also show a flood of communications relating directly to the proclamation of 18 Floréal. In these cases it was not only letters of support; since this body was seen as being the centre of intellectual activity, it also became the natural target for all the would-be poets and rhymesters who rushed to offer prayers and hymns to be used on tenth-days in the run-up to the final celebrations, as well as on the occasion of the *Fête* itself. The highest density of this type of submission coincides almost exactly with the influx of official responses to the Convention as established by Whitworth. While there was a steady stream from late Floréal onwards, 21 per cent of the total submissions were received by the Committee between 5 and 19 Prairial, a total of four sets of Prayers, eleven Hymns, three sets of odes and seven copies of speeches made or to be made either directly on the subject of the Supreme Being or allied with pronouncements on Revolutionary Morality in general.[33] These were intended to be used in different local celebrations on 20 Prairial throughout France, although presumably their authors hoped that if they were lucky, they might even make it to the main event in Paris.

The inflow did not stop with the day of the *Fête*. If we extend the time frame to the meeting of the *Comité d'Instruction publique* on 7 Thermidor, their last meeting before the events of 9 Thermidor, Table 1 at the end of this chapter shows that a total of 117 documents, all containing items proposed for use at the *Fête* had been received, including 17 sets of prayers and invocations to the Supreme Being; 39 hymns to the Supreme Being; 14 sets of odes, poems and couplets in praise of the Supreme Being; 17 speeches either on the subject of the Supreme Being alone or on the effect the Supreme Being would have on public morality, as well as 30 sets of documents relating either to the manner in which the *Fête* was to be celebrated locally, or as detailed reports on how it had actually been celebrated.

From the minutes of the Committee, it would appear that upon arrival each of the documents was first scanned by the Secretary, Arbogast, and then passed on to the member responsible, originally the Abbé Grégoire. Later on, when Grégoire was heavily involved in two other major projects,[34] these documents would have been passed to his replacement, Villars, constitutional Bishop of Mayenne. The minutes do not extend as far as detailing what Grégoire or Villars actually did with the documents concerned, and the documents themselves are not included in the files in the Archives Nationales. Fortunately most of the contributors also published their literary efforts locally so that we do have a flavour of the quality of verse offered. In Calais, the *Agent National* Pigault Maubilliarcq, in addition to giving the main speech before the Temple of the Eternal himself, composed no fewer than five hymns, with a total of twenty-two verses especially for the occasion.[35] In Metz the local bard, Citizen Angelot, described as 'employed in the temples of humanity', produced a hymn which so impressed the local *Société Populaire* that the President, Trottebas, ordered that 2,000 copies be printed and distributed free throughout Lorraine.[36] Some of the hymns talked of adoring God in a republican manner or, as one from Nancy suggested, without hypocrisy.[37] They obviously met the need to combine Republican fervour with relief at the newly found ability to offer worship to an unseen Being. It is perhaps worth noting that many of the unnamed local poets had no problem using the word 'God'. This type of relatively uncomplicated verse, which could easily be sung to a well-known tune during the celebrations, both characterises the efforts of the amateur poets who joined in the national outburst of literary creativity, and emphasises the level of popular participation in the local celebrations.

The Committee also received a considerable number of proposals for speeches to be made at the festivities as well as essays or memoranda submitted to a local society or administrative body by a local worthy. One submitted to the Committee by the commune of Douai, over the joint signatures of five members of the municipal administration, provides a good example of the pretentious language in which these offerings were couched:

> The moment has come to prove to our enemies and to those opposed to our Revolution that the monster of Atheism, vomited up by a faction opposed to the general wellbeing, has not taken root with us, this we solemnly declare. We recognise a Supreme Being. Who among us would be so stupid as to deny His existence? We also acknowledge the immortality of the Soul, and add to our duties those of striking down bad faith and tyranny, of punishing tyrants and traitors, of giving succour to the miserable, to respect the weak, to defend the oppressed and not to be unjust towards anyone. Let our enemies pale, let them see what such strength means, let us show them the witness of our Profession of Faith.[38]

The figures are a clear demonstration of how the concept of a 'new religion', based on the dual concept of the existence of some form of approachable entity who could be visualised both as an obvious replacement for a benevolent and retributive God, together with the logical extension into the second concept, that of the immortality of the soul, struck an immediate chord with the French people. In this sense, the time constraints on the responses to the proclamation of 18 Floréal, mentioned earlier in this chapter, seem almost not to have come as a shock to the movers and shakers of public opinion in the provinces, but to have helped concentrate the thoughts already present in the minds of many of them. The establishment of the worship of a Supreme Being did not strike them as some abstract philosophical idea which had fallen on them out of a clear blue sky. It seems to have been more a matter of general relief that the problem which they had so far been carefully avoiding was now settled in a satisfactory Revolutionary and republican manner. The empty space in the national vision of morality was being filled, and in a manner which could be not only easily, but even gratefully accepted. Atheism and its offshoot, Reason, had proved themselves to be unpopular and unacceptable replacements for a national morality, which had always been based on the proposition that right living and justice would be rewarded. A dry and arid system in which all human endeavour merely disappeared on death into what Danton referred to as 'The Void', had no chance of success over one which promised not only some form of continuation of sentiment but, quite specifically, the prospect of either reward or, if needed, retribution, even after death. The underlying strength and appeal of the concept of the Supreme Being was simple, as simple as the basic faith, catholic or protestant, previously expressed by the majority of the population before the Revolution. Good would be rewarded and evil punished, if not in this life then at least after death, a proposition which, as the volume and style of the responses clearly demonstrates, effectively received immediate popular national support.

As will be seen in the next chapters, this massive national support transformed itself on 20 Prairial into the greatest of all Revolutionary Festivals, one whose level and intensity of public participation would never be matched.

Table 1 Submissions made to the *Comité d'Instruction publique* regarding the Festival of the Supreme Being between 23 Floréal and 7 Thermidor Year II

Date	Prayers	Hymns	Poems	Speeches	Reports	Total
23 Floréal				1	1	2
29 Floréal				1		1
5 Prairial	2					2
7 Prairial			1			1
9 Prairial			1		1	2
11 Prairial	1	3				4
17 Prairial		4		1		5
19 Prairial	1	4	1	4		10
21 Prairial	1	4	2	1	3	11
23 Prairial	1	2	1	1	3	8
29 Prairial	1	3		1		5
1 Messidor			2		3	5
4 Messidor	1	3	1		2	7
15 Messidor		1		1		2
19 Messidor	1	1		1	4	7
23 Messidor	2	1			2	5
25 Messidor		2	1		2	5
27 Messidor	3	3		2	1	9
29 Messidor		2			4	6
1 Thermidor					2	2
3 Thermidor		6	3			9
5 Thermidor	3		1	3		7
7 Thermidor					2	2
TOTALS	17	39	14	17	30	117

Source: Archives Nationales.
AF / II / 17 / 117/40, 41.
AF/ II / 17 / 118/5, 6, 9, 10, 15, 18, 20, 21, 33, 49, 53, 72, 79, 81, 88, 89, 94.

Notes

1 This chapter contains material previously published in J. Smyth, 'Public experience of the Revolution: the national reaction to the proclamation of the Fête de l'Etre Suprême', in *Experiencing the French Revolution*, D. Andress, ed., SVEC 2013:05 (Oxford, 2013). This material is reproduced by permission of the Voltaire Foundation, University of Oxford (www.voltaire.ox.ac.uk).
2 M. Vovelle, *1793, La Révolution contre l'Église: de la Raison à l'Être Suprême* (Paris, 1988), p. 162.
3 Vovelle, *1793, La Révolution contre l'Église*, p. 8. John Whitworth in his 'L'envoi des adresses à la Convention en réponse au décret du 18 floréal: une étude des archives parlementaires', *Annales historiques de la Révolution française*, 298 (1994): 201–68 gives the final total figure as 1,617.
4 For in-depth discussion of the performed and the performative in the Revolutionary ethos see also S. Maslan, *Revolutionary Acts: Theatre Democracy and the French Revolution* (Baltimore, 2005) and M.-H. Huet, *Rehearsing the Revolution: The Staging of Marat's Death* (Berkeley, 1982), pp. 27–45.
5 'la lutte contre le fanatisme et les prêtres de la Vendée n'avait pas éteint dans les âmes l'esprit religieux', A. Mathiez, 'Robespierre et le culte de l'Être Suprême', *Annales Révolutionnaires*, 1910, p. 208.
6 'La loi qui vous appelle à célébrer une fête à l'ÊTRE SUPRÊME, n'a fait qu'exprimer des sentiments qui n'ont jamais été effacés dans vos cœurs.' *Le Conseil général de la commune d'Orléans à ses concitoyens le 15 prairial, an 2* (Orléans, n.d.).
7 See D. Guérin, *La lutte des classes sous la 1ère République, 1793-1797* (Paris, 1968).
8 This is a point specifically made by Nodier and Ruault, both of whom claim to have been a spectator at the event, while Michelet's report of the event is claimed to be based on the memories of his father. It also features in the works of Carlyle, Buchez and Roux and others.
9 A.N. AF.II.17.117.
10 A.P., Vol. 90, pp. 531–5.
11 A.M. Lille L.1254/1.
12 A.M. Strasbourg 1.MW.93, p. 523.
13 A.M. Angers I.D.5, p. 76.
14 A.M. Amiens, Archives Révolutionnaires 1.D.10.9, pp. 65–6.
15 A.M. Bordeaux I.18.64.
16 A.N. F.17.1065.5.
17 See Chapter 6, 'Contemporary comments on the festival', pp. 127–45.
18 The full speech or major extracts appeared in the local press in many cities of which Angers, Orleans, Bordeaux, Marseille and Strasbourg are examples.
19 'Le conseil-général de la commune de Paris est admis à la barre: il félicite la Convention nationale sur le décret qu'elle a rendu le 18 floréal; et jaloux de faire disparaître tous les signes de la superstition et de propager les idées religieuses qui servent de base à la morale publique, il a arrêté que, sur les

temples destinés aux fêtes publiques, on effaceroit ces mots, *Temple consacré à la raison*, et que l'on y substitueroit cette inscription: *à l'Etre Suprême*.' (A.P., Vol. 90, p. 329)

20 'La mention honorable, l'insertion au bulletin de cette adresse, son impression ainsi que la réponse du président, et l'envoi aux municipalités.' A.P., Vol. 90, p. 331.
21 *Moniteur*, Vol. 20, p. 525.
22 Vovelle, *1793, La Révolution contre l'Église*, pp. 186–9 and Planche 14, p. 283.
23 Vovelle, *1793, La Révolution contre l'Église*, p. 187.
24 Vovelle, *1793, La Révolution contre l'Église*, Planches 11 and 13, pp. 282–3.
25 Whitworth, 'L'envoi des adresses à la Convention'.
26 Whitworth, 'L'envoi des adresses à la Convention', Tables 1 and 2.
27 Whitworth, 'L'envoi des adresses à la Convention', p. 264.
28 'le peuple Français tout entier se lève pour sanctionner votre décret; le soleil éclaire ce lever unanime de tout un peuple qui rend hommage à l'existence d'un Dieu ... Citoyens représentants soyez toujours tels que vous avez paru aux yeux de l'univers, les représentants d'une nation grande et magnanime, d'un peuple qui a voulu que la moralité fît l'essentiel du patriotisme.' *Moniteur*, Vol. 20, p. 492.
29 'Nier l'Être suprême c'est nier l'existence de la nature ... Invoquer l'Etre suprême c'est appeler à son secours le spectacle de la nature, les tableaux qui charment la douleur; l'espérance qui console l'humanité souffrante.' *Moniteur*, Vol. 20, p. 492.
30 'Les Jacobins et les tribunes viennent aujourd'hui vous remercier, vous bénir d'avoir consacré par un décret cette vérité sainte que le juste retrouve toujours dans son cœur 'Que le peuple français reconnaît l'Être suprême et l'immortalité de l'âme' (on applaudit). Ils savaient bien, ces monstres qui ont prêché l'athéisme et le matérialisme ... que le moyen le plus sûr de tuer la révolution était d'enlever aux hommes toute idée d'une vie future, et de les désespérer par celle du néant!' (*Moniteur*, Vol. 20, p. 492)
31 A.P., Vol. 90, pp. 454–9.
32 'A Nevers le système de Chaumette a été proclamé avec impudeur: le décret qui ordonne la célébration de la Fête à l'Etre suprême y a été foulé aux pieds; en recevant la nouvelle de cet heureux événement qui a sauvé la liberté en la mettant sous la sauvegarde de la probité, on y a dit: 'la convention a été trompée par des modérés; pour nous nous ne changerons pas de conduite et de sentiments et professerons les mêmes principes; alors on a continué de prêcher l'athéisme et l'immoralité"' (Murmures d'indignation). (*L'Abréviateur universel*, Issue 535, p. 2138)
33 See Table 1, Submissions to the *Comité d'instruction publique*.
34 Grégoire was involved in the drafting of a new Law regarding the status and responsibilities of Instituteurs, in addition to chairing the Committee's linguistic survey of France.
35 G. Tison, 'La Fête de l'Être Suprême à Calais, 20 prairial, an II', in *Société historique du Calaisis. Bulletin Septembre–Octobre 1924* (Calais, 1924) notes that

it was the same Pigault Maubilliarcq who received Louis XVIII on his triumphal entry into Calais at the Restoration, and composed a special anthem for the occasion.
36 *Hymne à l'Être suprême* (Metz, n.d.).
37 *Commune de Nancy: Ordre de Marche de la fête à l'Etre Suprême* (Nancy, n.d).
38 *Le people français reconnaît l'existence de l'Être suprême et l'immortalité de l'âme* (Douai, n.d).

3

The celebrations in the capital

The proclamation had been made; now the actual work of organising the Festival with all its complex constructions and detailed movements of materials and people could begin. Obviously the celebrations in the capital were to be the most spectacular of all, and the plan of his design for the Festival which David presented to the Convention immediately after Robespierre's speech of 18 Floréal (7 May) begins with a passage of purple prose to set the mood. 'Scarcely has dawn broken when the sound of martial music is heard from all quarters, bringing a delightful awakening from sleep. At the rising of the friendly star which enlivens and colours Nature, friends, brothers, wives and husbands, the young and the old, and mothers embrace and vie with each other to beautify and celebrate the feast of the Divinity.'[1] It was now up to David and Hubert, the National Architect, to provide a suitable background for such an extraordinary celebration.

By the late 1780s Paris had become the second largest city in Europe after London, with an estimated permanent population in 1789 of 650,000. By comparison, the next three largest cities in France had populations of 150,000 for Lyons, and 100,000 each for Marseilles and Bordeaux. Since 1789, the further steady movement of workers into the capital both from the surrounding areas and from further afield is estimated to have raised the permanent population of Paris to nearly 690,000, and many of the Parisian *sections* now contained large immigrant communities of relatively recent provenance.[2] Some *sections* in the north of the city had a strong representation of stonemasons, largely from Normandy; in the central areas there was an influx of out-of-work silk workers from the Lyon area, and several areas south of the river saw the arrival of migrant building workers from the Limousin.³ The need for these newcomers to find work also meant that there was an immediately available pool of manpower, which could provide the labour needed for the construction work required for the Festival.

Despite the lack of any actual records of meetings to discuss the upcoming *Fête*, it must be assumed that on some occasion well before his speech of 18 Floréal, Robespierre would have held at least general discussions with David to establish the design parameters for the spectacle and ensure that everything presented, whether tableaux, pageants or the proposed organisation of the actual procession, met his political and cultural objectives. David's detailed plan was clearly fully prepared for Robespierre's speech to the Convention, and it seems unlikely, given Robespierre's normal meticulous attention to detail, that he would have allowed David to draw up such a detailed plan, complete even to the selection of the words and music of the hymns to be sung during the ceremonies, unsupervised. David had unquestionably given ample proof both of his revolutionary zeal and of his personal loyalty to Robespierre, but it would be reasonable to expect that Robespierre would at the very least have made notes of any such discussions, although it is possible that they were among Robespierre's papers destroyed after Thermidor. There must also presumably have been preliminary discussions on financial and practical problems between David and his atelier, Hubert, and the unofficial Poet Laureate, Marie-Joseph Chénier; Hubert in the construction of the pageants, and Chénier working with the leading composers of the Revolution, Gossec and Méhul, to produce the necessary hymns and anthems.

Robespierre's objectives were made very clear in the decree establishing the new Festival; firstly, it was to be a celebration specifically designed to culminate not in a political event, but in an act of homage to the Supreme Being; secondly, it was to change the emphasis from all previous festivals in that the celebrations were to be based on the fullest possible participation of the public; and thirdly, it was to be a truly national event. This festival was not just to be celebrated in Paris, with the option of celebrating left to other cities; it was to be celebrated on the same day and at the same time in every city, town and village in France. Even so, the significance of the grandeur of the celebrations in the capital was paramount; the fact that the detailed ceremonial in Paris was laid out as a template for the rest of the nation to follow, strengthened the Jacobin message of the pre-eminence of the capital and of the centralisation of executive power. By creating a spectacle of such magnificence that no provincial city could even hope to approach it, there would be not only admiration of the wonders which were to take place in the capital, but also an implicit recognition of the centralisation of legislative and executive power. This was to be by far the most politically important and most carefully organised event of its kind that France had ever known, and consequently the celebrations in the capital had to be larger, noisier, more ornate, more imposing, in short grander and of more consequence than anything previously experienced.

David chose to use a modification of the two-site concept which he had used for the *Fête de la Réunion* the year before. He drew on the painful lessons learned from that festival by selecting two centres, the Jardin National (the Tuileries), and the Champ de la Réunion (the Champ de Mars), which were much closer to each other than the two centres used in the celebrations of 1793, when the excessive length of the processional route, traversing the whole of Paris from the Bastille to the Champ de la Réunion, had caused severe problems. Another major change was the clear distinction between the formal nature of the first part of the ceremonies at the Jardin National, and the populist nature of the proceedings at the Champ de la Réunion. The first part, held immediately outside the meeting place of the Convention, would emphasise the official aspect of the festivities, with its formal speeches and the destruction of the statue of 'Hideous Atheism', not by the people, but by the President of the Convention – in the event Robespierre himself – with only the official guests invited to participate in this part of the proceedings. In the same way the music here would be furnished by the official choirs and orchestra, with no public involvement. The celebrations at the Champ de la Réunion, on the other hand, would involve only one short speech, followed by hymns sung by the whole assembly with the proceedings culminating in the mass act of worship of the Supreme Being.

At the Jardin National, while the speeches and statue burning were going on at one end of the gardens, those taking part in the procession would be marshalled into their positions at the other end. The public participation would then begin with the procession, which involved people from each of the forty-eight *sections* of the capital, making its way from the Tuileries, through the Place de la Révolution, across the Seine and arriving at the Mountain constructed at the Champ de la Réunion. This was to be the time at which public participation was at its peak; the hymns were to be sung or chanted by the different elements of the population chosen to be present on the Mountain, rather than by the choirs alone. In the final act of the ceremony, selected elements of the people would make the gestures of homage to the Deity and defence of the Republic. The youths would draw their swords, the nursing mothers would hold their babies up towards the Sun, visible proof of the Supreme Being looking with favour on his chosen nation on what it was hoped would be a glorious summer's day.

The problems experienced during the procession in the *Fête de la Réunion*, coupled with the recent difficulties caused by the breakdown of organisation even at the much smaller *Fête de la Raison* in the confined space of the cathedral of Notre Dame the previous November, would have made both David and Robespierre determined that there would be no repeat of these in the new Festival. This was to be not only the largest, but, even more importantly, the most politically sensitive public celebration yet staged. The extremely detailed nature of David's plan has led many commentators to argue that the considerable over-elaboration, verging on control mania, in these exceptionally precise instructions, must inevitably have caused a loss of spontaneity in the final results. There is certainly ample evidence that both David and Robespierre shared a tendency towards over-elaboration, and if one adds to this Robespierre's known personal tendency towards excessive detail, there is some merit in this accusation. It is however equally reasonable to point out that, from the point of view of both David and Robespierre, it was imperative that the lessons in maintaining control of the crowds at a large public manifestation, painfully learned from previous *fêtes*, should be carefully applied to this new and complex undertaking. Their experience of Revolutionary Festivals since 1790, especially the problems which had arisen during the two festivals held in the previous year, would have underlined this.

The chaotic arrangements during the procession to the Champ de la Réunion in August 1793 must have been the subject of some discussion within David's own team, before the specifications for the Festival of the Supreme Being were finalised. The problems are self-evident, and any director of a village pageant trying to control even a short uncomplicated procession composed of amateur actors in holiday mood would immediately appreciate them. The chaos which had arisen during the long and inadequately controlled procession through the streets of Paris in 1793 would be the same, magnified many times, and it is reasonable to assume that it was David's determination to avoid the recurrence of these problems which drove him to insist on the issue of full and detailed instructions. These were duly drawn up, with the intention of establishing the tightest possible control so that each and every participant would know exactly what they were to do and precisely when, where and how they were to do it. The Convention duly ordered them to be printed and distributed to each of the forty-eight Parisian *sections*.[4]

These instructions list the names of all the marshals, referred to as '*Citoyens Artistes*', who were to be responsible for the correct ordering of the procession and, above all, its proper comportment en route between the departure from the reporting points in the Jardin National and the arrival of each part of the procession at the Champ de la Réunion. They begin by instructing Citizens Fromageat and Julien, assisted by three members of the Jacobin Society, to get the band of the Army of the North, who were to lead the procession, with its associated military unit, in place at the Pont-Tournant exit to the Tuileries with the first of the marching *sections* immediately behind them. The *sections* were to march generally in alphabetical order, starting with the representatives of the *Section des Arcis*, then those of the *Section des Amis de la Patrie* and so on through the alphabet, until the *Section de l'Unité* closed the march. In between the *sections* were military units, fire-fighters, groups of drummers and a selection of military bands. The procession was divided into two halves, so that, after unit 28, the *Section des Lombards*, there was a group carrying a tricolour ribbon forming a square within which marched the members of the Convention, with Robespierre, as President, at their head. After the members of the Convention, the processional order began again with unit 29, *Section de la Maison-Commune*, until the final unit 48, *Section de l'Unité*, followed by a carriage carrying the children from the Institute for the Blind, and a military band which closed the procession. Figure 1 shows the final chosen route of the procession.

Any attempt to assess how successful the organisation was on the day is complicated by the absence of a formal official report. Normal practice would have been for this to be drafted then presented for detailed comment to the Convention, followed by its incorporation in the official record and its printing and distribution throughout the nation. The day after the *Fête*, it was agreed that an official record of the events of the previous day should be incorporated in the minutes,[5] but, in fact only Robespierre's two speeches at the Jardin National were inserted into the record of the day's proceedings,[6] and for a detailed description of the events at the two sites we are forced to rely on the sometimes contradictory testimony of unofficial commentators, which are discussed in more detail in Chapter 6.[7]

The organisation and construction of the pageants for the *Fête* got under way when two decrees were issued on 26 Floréal. The first of these empowered Hubert to get things moving: 'The Committee of Public Safety orders the Committee of Public Education to take all necessary measures to ensure the execution of the decree regarding the National Festival due on 20 Prairial. Citizen Hubert will be in charge of this Festival

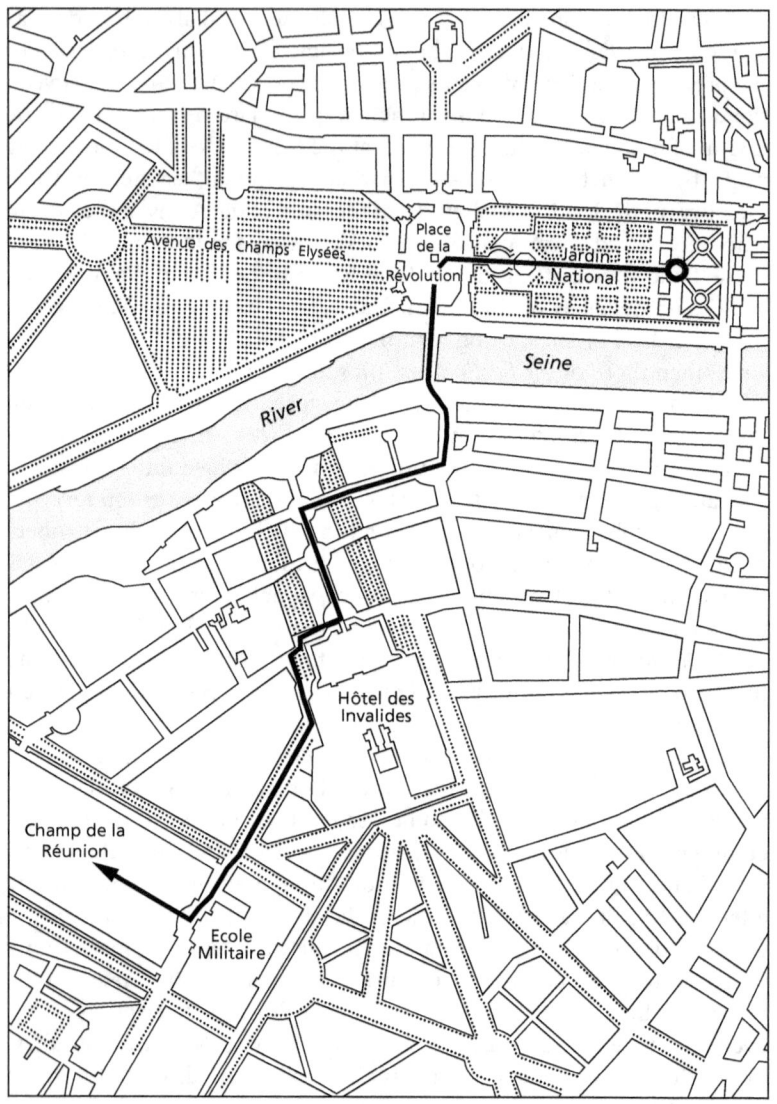

Figure 1 The route of the procession in Paris

and all expenses shall be charged against the funds put at the disposal of the Committee in the same manner as for all other public expenses for which it is responsible.[8] A second decree of the same date established the first tranche of funding, ordering the release from the Paris municipal budget of the sum of 100,000 livres, to enable the start of the groundworks needed to begin the constructions required for the *Fête*. Many of the detailed reports on how this particular festival was funded, not only in Paris but also in some of the major provincial cities, are available from detailed documentary evidence in both national and departmental archives and a fuller discussion of how both the capital and provincial communities funded their celebrations is the subject of Chapter 5.

Given the complexity of the constructions he intended to use, David needed a considerable period of preparation for his team. While some of the building work was available either as plans, or even actual units, from previous *fêtes* – for example, David's favourite representation of the Republic as Hercules on his pillar, intended as a centrepiece at the Champ de la Réunion, was now a stock item brought out for all festivals – the majority still had to be designed and built specially for the occasion. The large double statue at the Jardin National, with its external statue of Hideous Atheism and internal statue of Wisdom, was a new concept, having figured in none of the previous *fêtes*. By far the largest and most complex item however was the Mountain to be constructed at the Champ de la Réunion. Nothing of this size appears ever to have been attempted before for any festival. The only previous use of a Mountain as the centrepiece of a festival had been the one built in Notre Dame for Chaumette's Festival of Reason the previous November, but this had been quite small, since it had to fit inside the upper nave of the cathedral, and only needed to be large enough to carry a small Greek Temple with a single occupant, the Goddess of Reason.

David's design for the Mountain, to be built in the centre of the Champ de la Réunion, was originally intended to be large enough to carry on its slopes the entire National Convention, the musicians and singers of the Opera, a military band, and several hundred old men and youths, together with a group of nursing mothers and their babies drawn from each of the forty-eight *sections* of Paris. In addition, the whole structure was to be topped by a platform, big enough to hold a large Tree of Liberty and the President of the Convention, who would stand there to lead the assembly in their adoration of the Supreme Being. Although the Mountain had to be large enough to encompass all these participants, it would also need to be low enough for the President's voice to carry to the crowds below. A high top platform might have worked with a thunderous orator like Danton, or a trained actor like Collot d'Herbois, but would have been unrealistic for Robespierre, given his light and slightly squeaky voice. Hubert could have been forgiven if his heart sank when he saw the full details of the designs and pageants needed. From 8 May, the day when the Convention accepted David's proposal, to the day of the *Fête* itself, he and his construction gangs had just thirty days to build and install these complex theatrical sets.

The organisational problems of the *Fête* were played out on different levels between May and June: there was the actual construction of the various pageants, the organisation of the mass public participation, and the background activities of the politicians, specifically those involved in the Committee of Public Safety and the Committee of Public Education. The financial records of the Festival in the national archives show an interesting mix of construction companies and individual artisans whose expertise was required for the manufacture and installation of David's designs. There were representatives from every conceivable trade; architects, masons, carpenters, painters of all types, sculptors, locksmiths, blacksmiths, paperhangers, gardeners, haulage contractors, office staff, general labourers, site security, even a boilermaker, and Hubert lost no time in setting his main contractors and their work gangs in motion on both sites.

The two sites required different types of preparation, since the Jardin National was not going to be the subject of such major works as the Champ de la Réunion, nor were the structures required anything like as large or as complex. The main requirements at the Jardin involved covering the ornamental lake in front of the Convention building and the installation of the double statue of Atheism covering Wisdom. There was also an extension of the apron in front of the buildings, to allow adequate space for the orator to address the assembly and to provide stands for members of the Convention and distinguished guests. Public access was relatively simple since it was specified in the general instructions that only official guests and those who were actually marching in the procession to the Champ de la Réunion were to enter the gardens and the marchers were to make their way there before the beginning of the formal part of the ceremonies. Since they were not to play any part in these ceremonies, and were confined to their marshalling points, no set structures were needed for them, as they would not be organised in any formal manner until they formed up for the procession (see Figure 2, 'The *sections* assemble in the Jardin National for the procession'). The official plan required the public to enter by one of the three access gates to the gardens from the eastern, or city side. These are the gates leading respectively from the Manège, the Pont-Nouveau and the Pavillon de l'Unité, all of which allowed free access both to the gardens themselves and to the area in front of the Convention. The fourth (western) gate, via the Pont-Tournant, which led directly to the Place de la Révolution, was to be reserved for the departure of the procession from the Jardin, across the Place de la Révolution and on to the new bridge across the Seine, then to the Champ de la Réunion for the second set of ceremonies.

In view of the very tight timescale imposed, it is probable that the twin figures of Atheism and Wisdom at the Jardin National would have been constructed as a fairly simple interior support structure, such as a wooden frame weighted by brickwork, on which the figure of Wisdom would be modelled by members of David's atelier. It is logical to assume that this would have been done on site, rather than in an atelier, to avoid the obvious problems of moving a large and not very solid object through Paris, then getting it into place in the gardens in front of the Convention.

Figure 2 The *sections* assemble in the Jardin National for the procession

To have carved a statue of Wisdom in stone of the size required – from the evidence of the contemporary illustrations of the event, the figure would have been about two or two-and-a-half times life size[9] – would have required more time than was available. There was also the very considerable problem of materials. Building materials, and especially stone of any sort, were at a premium in the capital; also the statue of Wisdom would have had to be made quickly, so as to allow enough time for the statue of Atheism to be overlaid on it. Again, although we have no specifically detailed description of the manufacture of either of the figures, it seems likely that the interior statue was probably made of plaster, overlaid with fireproof clay, on a reasonably solid framework. The second and external statue would probably have been made of papier-maché, impregnated with some easily flammable solution, such as naphtha, on a light and combustible frame so that, when ignited by Robespierre at the conclusion of his speech, it would have burst immediately and satisfactorily into flame, revealing the interior statue.

This supposition is strengthened by the inclusion in the detailed accounts for the work at the Jardin National of specific payments to the papermakers, Jacquemart et Bernard, and the general merchant, Morrisson, for paper and naphtha and of a further large sum paid to one Aubert, described as a '*tapisseur*', whose work was probably not so much the paperhanging the word implies but the cladding of the inner statue with the impregnated papier-maché.[10] David used the sculptors Regnier and Massa, together with members of his own atelier, to finish the internal statue on site and oversee the papier-mâché specialists doing the rough work on the statue of Hideous Atheism, before completing the final detailed modelling work themselves. The figures for the various contractors show that in the Jardin National more than half of the total account was paid to the staging and carpentry contractors, with two painting contractors, one of whom is referred to as a scenery painter, also working on the statues.[11]

The Champ de la Réunion was the site of the largest civil engineering works, needed in order to construct the Mountain. There had been a very considerable amount of ground preparation work (costing over 250,000 livres) done on this site the year before in preparation for the *Fête de la Réunion*,[12] so the basic civil works needed to prepare the site would have been relatively uncomplicated. This work seems to have been carried out by the workforce of the Paris municipality, who then gave way to the outside contractors. The chief contractors engaged in the actual construction of the Mountain were carpentry and brickwork companies; the three main scaffolding contractors submitted bills for a total of some

213,000 livres, while the account of the principal brickwork contractor was for 104,000 livres.[13] In the event, the actual construction fell short of this over-ambitious project, and on the great day there was not enough room to accommodate the whole Convention, to the publicly expressed annoyance of several members, including some of Robespierre's most vociferous opponents, such as Lecointre, Bourdon de l'Oise and Merlin de Thionville. It is not easy to establish from the list of contractors who was actually working on which site, but it is reasonable to assume that the majority of the masons, groundworkers and construction workers would have been occupied with the Champ de la Réunion. Unfortunately, the method of construction is again imprecise, since there appear to be no engineering records or detailed manufacturing or construction drawings available for study. There are various artists' impressions of the actual construction, one of which is used as the cover of this book, but none are sufficiently accurate to be used as a reliable guide to the exact size of the Mountain.

However, recent research in the National Archives has thrown up a document of considerable importance in establishing the general parameters of the Mountain. This is a detailed quotation from a painting contractor, Chevalier, for his work on the Mountain in which he specifies the number and sizes of the staircases and platforms. He also made sketches both of these items and of other structures originally specified but later discarded, such as a small Grecian temple. His estimate for the repainting of the column supporting David's statue of Hercules brandishing his club also gives an indication of the size of the unit, which further assists in calculating the overall height of the Mountain.[14] Working from this set of data it is now possible to estimate more accurately the overall size of the Mountain as having been approximately 120 feet long and 60 feet wide, rising to a height of some 30 feet in a series of platforms, above which was placed the platform carrying the Tree of Liberty, giving an overall height at the topmost platform of about 40 feet.[15] One can get a good idea of the type of construction required by using the accounts sent by the various contractors; almost 80 per cent of the total funding for the work at the Champ de la Réunion was for work undertaken by the two main staging and carpentry contractors.[16] A further large sum went to Citizen Morrisson, described as a '*serrurier*'. Rather than the work of a modern locksmith he would most probably have been responsible for the on-site provision of considerable quantities of fasteners (nails, screws and bolts) as well as more complex items of metalwork such as hinges, plates and corner pieces which the carpenters would have needed to hold together the staging which formed the various levels of the Mountain. The document

Figure 3 The Festival of the Supreme Being on the Champs de la Réunion

from Chevalier confirms that it was a relatively simple construction, basically timber staging with timber platforms and some retaining walls; the whole then embellished with cladding of papier-mâché and cartridge paper, duly painted. On completion the surroundings were grassed over and plants and flowers brought in, as much to hide the semi-finished works as to give the structure visual appeal. Figure 3 gives one of the most famous impressions by Demachy of the general panorama of the site.

From the end of Floréal and during the first twenty days of Prairial, Hubert was working against a very tight deadline to try to finish the constructions in time. From the beginning, it was necessary for the work to proceed almost on a round-the-clock basis with the workmen often forced to continue by candlelight. There is a scrap of paper in Hubert's handwriting, attached to a letter to the Committee of Public Education dated 6 Prairial, in which he requests money from the Committee for the provision of candles for carpenters and paperhangers who were required to work at night.[17] As the date of the *Fête* grew near and it was still unclear whether the deadline would be met, Hubert sought the direct intervention of the Committee of Public Safety, who issued the following decree on 11 Prairial (30 May): 'The Committee of Public Safety, relying on the patriotic zeal of the workers employed in the preparations for the National Festival, due to be celebrated on the 20th of this month, decrees that all work shall be completed by noon on the 19th Prairial. This decree shall be posted on all festival sites.'[18] The effect on the workforce of having this particular piece of paper plastered up on every site can well be imagined, particularly the sites in the Jardin National, whose workers could possibly hear the noise of the crowd if not the actual fall of the blade on the nearby Place de la Révolution. In fact by working around the clock until the early morning of 20 Prairial, although not completed as well as Hubert would have liked, the work was finished in time for the ceremonies to take place.

The actual timing of events is a little vague, in that the only specific indication of starting times is in the unofficial details for the *sections*. These refer to the sound of drums waking everyone up at 5 a.m. in time for them to decorate their houses, after which they would proceed to their *section* office to await the call to the procession. Then at 8 a.m. a cannon would be fired to call the delegates to their marching positions.[19] Other accounts speak of the crowd growing in the Jardin National from the early morning with the official guests congregating at the statue at the Convention end, while the delegates from the *sections* of Paris assembled at the other end of the gardens to form the procession. It would seem that the actual ceremonies were due to begin at 9 a.m., although this is not completely clear from the records.

There is even more confusion if the account of Joachim Vilate, written after Thermidor as part of his campaign to clear himself of charges of supporting Robespierre, is taken into consideration. The details of this are set out in more detail in Chapter 6 but it is clear that his detailed account, which has Robespierre making everyone wait for several hours, is pure fabrication.[20] Vilate's account does however confirm the appearance of Robespierre, as seen in the prints showing him leading the members of the Convention, dressed in a dark suit with the sash and plumes of a *Représentant en Mission*. Michelet famously asserted that Robespierre chose to wear a light blue silk suit rather than the 'official uniform' of dark blue with red collar, designed by David for the members of the Convention, a statement which has long been accepted as a fact, and continuously repeated by other commentators.[21] In fact, no formal uniform had been approved for the members of the Convention, who decided at their meeting of 17 Prairial (5 June) that, since they were still waiting for a debate to decide on their official dress, there would be no time to have uniforms made for all of them anyway. They would attend the Festival in the dress of 'Representatives of the people to the Armies and the Départements'.[22] This meant that members of the Convention would wear dark clothing, over which would be the tricolour sash with the tricolour plumed *panache* on their headgear.

Robespierre's speeches at the Jardin National concentrate on the Supreme Being rather than the general theme of public morality. There is, however, the question of Robespierre's actual reference to the Divinity, his use of various terms to characterise the new protector of the nation. In all his three speeches during the festival, Robespierre began to use a series of descriptive names for the new object of veneration, by the people of France. Following his use of more general names for the idea of a Divinity in his speech of 7 May, in his two speeches at the Jardin National on 20 Prairial, Robespierre moves away from generalities and uses nomenclature which more fully addresses the divine aspect of the Supreme Being. There is an in-depth study of the use of these names by Duprun,[23] based on their relationship to the six classical versions of the Name of God, the so-called 'Divine Names' originally defined by Denis the Areopagite[24] in the first century AD. Duprun's study however relates only to the two speeches at the Jardin National, but if the expressions used in the speech of 18 Floréal are added it can be seen that while Robespierre refers to the Supreme Being a total of seven times, he also uses the word 'God' six times, and the word 'Divinity' twice. By contrast, in his speeches in the Jardin National on 8 June he changes his language very considerably. Despite the fact that the context is much more about

Table 2 Analysis of the different names for the Supreme Being used by Robespierre in his speech of 18 Floréal to the Convention and in his speeches at the *Fête* on 20 Prairial

Form of name	No. of times used speech of 18 Floréal	Speeches during the *Fête*
God (*Dieu*)	6	1
Divinity (*Divinité*)	2	3
Creator of Nature (*Auteur de la nature*)	0	1
Being of Beings (*Être des êtres*)	0	2
Great Being (*Grand Être*)	0	1
Supreme Being (*Être supreme*)	7	2
Creator of our being (*Auteur de notre être*)	1	0

divine aspects of the Supreme Being the use of the word 'God' has been dramatically reduced. The word 'Divinity' is still favoured but for the rest a whole series of names, very much on the lines of those popular with the thinkers of the Enlightenment, including Creator of Nature, Creator of our being and Being of Beings are offered.[25] Table 2 shows clearly the marked differences of emphasis between the original speech and those of 20 Prairial.

It would seem that in his speeches on 20 Prairial Robespierre was being very careful in his choice of the attributes with which he wished to invest the object of the ceremonies, sharply reducing the use of 'God', while increasing the use of 'Divinity', even at the expense of 'Supreme Being'. He also introduces two new descriptions; Being of Beings and Great Being, neither of which he used in his speech to the Convention. The third new name, Creator of Nature, is reserved for the ceremony at the Champ de la Réunion. Since the ceremony at the Jardin National was not as publicly accessible as that at the Champ de la Réunion, his choice of what names to use may well have been made after a careful assessment of the effect on the members of the Convention and the official guests, as well as his estimate of the mood of the members of the *sections* waiting in the Jardin to begin the procession. One can see the residue of his Catholic training in his choice of phrase; the use of the ideas that since the assembly is honouring, if not actually worshipping, the Supreme Being, although there are no prayers as such, there is a form of prayer being offered, and there is a definite feeling that some sort of new belief system is being proclaimed. One can easily understand how, with words like these, ordinary people could have grasped at the hope that this was to be the beginning of the revival of some measure of toleration of the public expression of the old faith. With only very slight changes, this would almost have done as a sermon by a liberal ecclesiastic; the Creator is honoured, his justice and mercy are praised; only the name is changed.

Standing in front of the Convention, facing the double statue, Robespierre gave the first of the two speeches in which he exhorted the people to join in praise of the Supreme Being while enjoying the day under His benevolent gaze, a speech which emphasises the theistic nature of the ceremonies.

> Frenchmen and republicans, it is your duty to purify the nation they have soiled and bring back the justice they have cast out. Since both liberty and virtue are from the bosom of the Divinity; neither can exist amongst men without the other. Do you, the great-hearted people, wish to crush all your foes? Then practice justice and offer the Divinity the only acceptable form of worship. Let us today, under His gaze show our genuine happiness. Tomorrow we will again combat vice and tyranny, today we demonstrate to the world what republican virtue is, and so honour the divinity even more.[26]

There is considerable confusion about what happened next. According to David's detailed instructions this was the moment at which the choir of the Opéra would sing Marie-Joseph Chénier's hymn *'Source de vérité qui outrage l'imposture'* to music specially composed by Gossec. The *Mercure Français* confirms that Chénier's hymn was sung, while the *Auditeur National* merely speaks of 'beautiful music ... played to rapturous applause'.[27] In fact, according to the majority of commentators, what the choir actually sang was a completely different hymn by Desorgues, *'Père de l'univers, suprême intelligence'*, to the same music. The story as related by several musicologists, particularly Constant Pierre and Pierre Hédouin, is that Robespierre took exception to some references in Chénier's original text. At the time of the great festival Marie-Joseph Chénier, although a committed Jacobin, was at personal loggerheads with Robespierre, firstly because Robespierre had taken exception to his latest play *Timoleon* publicly and forced him to burn it before the Committee of Public Safety, and secondly because Chénier was actively campaigning for the release of his brother, the poet Marie-André Chénier from the St Lazare prison, from which he managed to smuggle out his 'Iambs', a series of anti-Jacobin satirical poems.

Pierre and Hédouin offer two different sources for the story; Pierre quotes the composer Zimmermann,[28] who claims he had it direct from Sarrette himself,[29] while Hédouin offers a more detailed account which he received from Pauseron, whom he describes as Gossec's 'favourite pupil'.³⁰ According to Hédouin, Robespierre summoned Sarrette, the newly appointed Director of the Institut national de la musique, on 15 Prairial (3 June), five days before the ceremonies were to take place, and questioned him on the state of the music for the *Fête*. Sarrette showed him Chénier's hymn to the Supreme Being which Robespierre read; he took grave exception to the penultimate verse which referred to God-making power which causes sadness and pain. Robespierre apparently felt that this was a thinly disguised attack on him personally. He also wanted the hymn sung not by the choir of the Opéra, as had been arranged, but by the whole assembly. According to Hédouin he insisted that a different set of verses to the music composed by Gossec be produced. Sarrette, who must have assumed that Robespierre had at least read the hymn before David included it in his printed instructions, now faced the problem that, with only four days to go before the *Fête*, he had to provide a whole new text and probably a new score as well. The story takes on an even more improbable aspect, as Hédouin continues: 'Luck came to Sarrette's rescue. At 6 o'clock the next morning Théodore Desorgues arrived at Gossec's house to ask him to set some words he had written to music. It so happened that they matched the piece already composed perfectly.'³¹ The following day a much relieved Sarrette dispatched musicians from the Institut to each of the forty-eight *sections* to teach them the new hymn. Improbable as it may seem, there is other evidence to support this story. In the music section of the Bibliothèque nationale, at the Palais Garnier, there is a copy of the music including Chénier's original text, but with the revised text by Desorgues inserted in pencil above it. There is also a separate account from the official printers of music who submitted two accounts, one for the original printing of the Chénier Hymn and the second, for a further 180 livres, for the 'Engraving and printing of the Hymn by Citizen Desorgues'.³² The National Archives also have copies of the Letters of Authority, issued to Sarrette's representatives to the various *sections*, countersigned or notated by the representative of each *section*.³³ In the end, Robespierre's will prevailed and it was Desorgues' words which were used at the Jardin National.

After this musical interlude, Robespierre walked down to the statue of Hideous Atheism and was handed the lighted torch. One can only imagine Hubert, David and the team of sculptors holding their breath when Robespierre held the flame to the exterior figure. Would it ignite, would it burn clearly, leaving the white statue of Wisdom clearly visible? There would certainly have been no time to do a dry run, no rehearsal; it all had to work first time. In the event, it did burst satisfactorily into flame, although, according to most commentators, the statue of Wisdom was fairly heavily scorched in the process. The official report on the proceedings in the *Gazette Nationale* on 25 Prairial states that the statue of Hideous Atheism was burned by the President and as Wisdom shone forth to the people in all her splendour, the Jardin National rang with shouts of joy. In the slight fog from the burning statue of Atheism, Robespierre made his second speech assuring the people that:

> This monster, spewed on France by her kings has disappeared into the Void and with it all the crimes and misery of the world! Wisdom is what our enemies wanted to banish from the Republic. Being of Beings we have no need to offer you false prayers, you know your creation, neither their needs nor their most secret thoughts are unknown to you. Hatred of bad faith and tyranny burn in our hearts together with the love of justice and of our country, we shed our blood for mankind; this is our prayer, this is our sacrifice this is the faith we offer.[34]

One of the most useful contemporary sources of information on the activities on 20 Floréal is the detailed report on the festival which two citizens, Bontemps and Barry, who were present at the celebrations as delegates from the Guillaume Tell *section* of Paris later submitted to their own sectional committee.[35] According to them

> On the walls of the two sides of the amphitheatre the following inscriptions could be read, heartening the people and frightening the despots:
> The people of France acknowledge the existence of the Supreme Being and the immortality of the Soul
> If you are pure enough to long for a God, you will find one in your heart
> To honour God and to punish kings is the same thing
> The Divinity has condemned tyranny, the people of France carry out his orders[36]

These slogans, all of which make direct reference to Robespierre's speech of 18 Floréal, are noticeably different from those which would be seen later in the day at the Champ de la Réunion. The slogans in the Jardin National are suitably theistic, in view of the content of the speeches on this site. They would hardly have been out of place in a religious festival of the *Ancien Regime*, with a brief introduction of the more revolutionary and republican sentiments present in Robespierre's speeches. As will be seen, the slogans used at the Champ de la Réunion were of a more general nature tending towards a more holistic view of public morality rather than the theme of the specifically divine nature of the Supreme Being which comes out from the two speeches in the Jardin Public.

The mood, already joyful, would have been still further lightened as the people prepared, under the direction of the marshals and in accordance with the instructions issued by the Municipality, to take their places in the procession with the bands and the military units to begin the march to the Champ de la Réunion. Marker-posts had been erected in the gardens to provide assembly points for each part of the procession, which formed up, with its head at the Pont-Tournant exit to the Place de la Révolution, and its different groups snaking around the gardens to its tail at the Tuileries end. There was a certain amount of confusion since the Convention also issued an Order of Procession which was printed as a completely separate set of instructions from those issued by the Paris administration.[37] These instructions were subject to further minor amendments by both the Municipality and the Convention. Each time such a variation was made one printer or another would issue another version. This meant that in the days immediately preceding the festivities the *sections* had before them not only the original official instruction from the official printers, but also two further versions printed by unofficial printers, each of which was issued over Hubert's signature.

One of those printed without formal consent of the Convention does contain the hymn by Deschamp and Bruny, '*O Dieu puissant, invisible à nos yeux*' which the children of the blind school were to sing during the procession.[38] The other version, which bears the notification that it was printed 'By order of the Convention',[39] repeats the details of the procession but includes the original Hymn to the Supreme Being, Chénier's '*Source de vérité*', probably because it was published before Sarrette's interview with Robespierre. This second version also set out the actual route to be followed by the procession, as finally agreed by the Convention in their session of 19 Prairial, the day before the celebrations. The procession was to leave the Jardin National and proceed to the Place de la Révolution, where it circled round the Statue of Liberty which had replaced the equestrian statue of Louis XV in the centre of the square, left the square by the southern exit and crossed the Seine by the new Pont de la Révolution, after which it continued along the banks of the Seine, across the Place des Invalides and along the Avenue de l'Ecole Militaire to enter the Champ de la Réunion.[40]

The authorities were naturally concerned with making certain that access to the processional route was clear and without any major obstacles. The first problem was that as the head of the procession emerged from the Jardin National, it would immediately be confronted by the guillotine. This engine had led a peripatetic existence, moving between the Place de Grève and the Place de la Réunion (ex Place du Carrousel), with one day only at the Place de la Révolution for the execution of Louis XVI. It was finally re-erected at the Place de la Révolution in May

1793, when the Convention moved from the Salle de Manège to the Salle des Machines and took exception to having the infernal engine immediately outside their front door.[41] As the site of the guillotine was on the eastern side of the square, close to the Pont-Tournant exit from the Jardin National, this would not only have cast a damper on the proceedings, it would also have presented a serious physical obstacle, so the day before the procession the guillotine was dismantled and removed. According to indications in the Paris police archives, the Fire Brigade and the municipal cleansing department then combined to remove as much stain as possible from the cobbles. The passage across the Seine was by the new bridge, originally designed in 1786 and opened in 1791 as the Pont Louis XVI; renamed Pont de la Révolution in 1792. The roadbed of this bridge was laid in 1790, largely from stone and rubble reclaimed from the ruins of the Bastille. Although there is no record of the individual songs and speeches made in the procession during the march, it would be surprising if the orators among the delegates from the *sections* had not made great play of the happy thought that here were the People, marching as free citizens while crushing the ruins of tyranny under their feet.

The city authorities were equally concerned that the dispersal route after the ceremonies should be kept free of any hindrances. According to the instructions for dispersal, the crowd was to proceed from the Champ de la Réunion into the Rue de Bourgogne and along the Rue Dominique[42] to the Esplanade des Invalides, where they would disperse to their various *sections*. To ensure this route was clear, members of the City Architects department, accompanied by a Police Commissioner and a gang of workmen, were dispatched to check on it.[43] During their investigation one of these inspection groups discovered a building described as a lean-to, against the wall of the Maison de la Révolution in the Rue de Bourgogne, precisely where it would most disturb the passage of those leaving the Invalides area. From the report it appears most likely that this was the shebeen of an illegal vendor of alcohol, a type of unauthorised drinking den common in the less intensely populated areas of the capital, especially in areas south of the river where there were large pockets of immigrant building labourers.[44] Being unable to establish who owned it or what it was doing there, the inspectors had their crew of labourers pick it up bodily, and dump it in a convenient open space. The same inspectors also issued notices to the owners of two fences in bad repair in the Rue Dominique, warning them that if the necessary repairs were not undertaken immediately, these would be done by the Public Works department, and charged at premium rates. They also made the inhabitants of that street clear up the footway, make two other walls safe and remove piles of gravel and general rubbish which had been allowed to accumulate. On a second inspection, the representative of the Architects department and the Commissioner of Police submitted a joint report that the work had been duly carried out and the dispersal route was clear of obstacles.[45]

On arrival at the Champ de la Réunion, the men proceeded to the rear of the Mountain, on the river side, the young persons encircled the Mountain, while the chosen group of fathers and grandfathers with their sons and grandsons, together with the nursing mothers with their babies, took up their positions on the Mountain itself, along with members of the Convention and the Opéra orchestra and chorus. To ensure the correct execution of these instructions, marshals were waiting at the foot of the Mountain for the arrival of the procession to ensure that everybody was correctly placed to take their proper part in the ceremony of homage to the Supreme Being.[46]

According to contemporary sources,[47] it was during the actual procession that some of the most severe personal attacks on Robespierre were launched. As President of the Convention, Robespierre was to march at the head of that body but, whether deliberately or not, he finished up marching alone and at some distance from his fellows. This opportunity to attack him directly and personally was seized upon by his opponents, since any remarks made in the open air would not give Robespierre the same facility of denouncing them as if they had dared to express the same sentiments in the Convention or at the Jacobin Club. The clearest account is that by Marc-Antoine Baudot, the representative of the Saône-et-Loire, who wrote in his *Notes Historiques*, re-published by Edgar Quinet's widow in 1893:

> There were more than eight people in the ranks between myself and Robespierre; I heard all the curses. They came from Thirion, from Montaut, from Ruamps and above all from Lecointre de Versailles, who more than twenty times called Robespierre 'Dictator! Tyrant!' and threatened to assassinate him ... among those cursing Robespierre during the procession I would especially single out Thirion, Ruamps, Montaut, Duhem, Lecointre de Versailles and Baudot.[48]

These members of the Convention had good reason to both dislike and fear Robespierre. Thirion, Lecointre and Ruamps had been associated with the *Indulgents*; Robespierre had forced Duhem's exclusion from the Jacobin Club on 22 Frimaire, and had openly treated Montaut, a *ci-devant* Marquis noted for his extremist views, with disdain. Later, on 11 Thermidor, Lecointre published a *mémoire* in which he boasted of his intention to have had Robespierre assassinated during the *Fête*, naming his co-conspirators as Barras, Fréron, Courtois, Garnier de l'Aube, Rovère, Thirion, Tallien and Guffroy.[49] In his description of the festival, Ruault says in a letter dated 2 Messidor (20 June) 'that madman Lecointre de Versailles had formed the intention of sacrificing in the name of God and the Country the great president on the day of the Festival in the Champ de Mars, on the altar raised to the Patrie'.[50] If Robespierre was affected by these insults he showed no reaction at the time. It was only in his last speech to the Convention on 8 Thermidor that he ever referred to the insults offered him on the day of the Festival.

On arrival at the Champ de la Réunion, the marshals took charge of those members of the public who had been selected to ascend the Mountain and showed them which steps they should use and exactly where they were to stand. The Mountain, now flanked on the one side by the oxcart laden with examples of French industry and agriculture, and on the other side by David's favourite statue of Hercules with his club, mounted on a column, was soon covered with people. As has been mentioned previously, David had seriously underestimated the size of construction needed for the number of participants who were supposed to be accommodated on the Mountain. In the event there was just enough space for a sufficient number of people to take their places on the Mountain to allow the ceremonies to proceed, largely as originally intended, although several members of the Convention, to their obvious annoyance, could not be accommodated. Robespierre led the assembly in the adoration of the Supreme Being from his position on the top platform, next to the Tree of Liberty which carried the motto: 'Look after me with care and your children will reap my fruits and bless you in my shade.'[51] Since this was positioned right at the top of the Mountain, it would probably have been invisible to the majority of the celebrants and, given Robespierre's light voice, it is doubtful whether those on ground level heard what was being said.

The orchestra played a specially composed piece after which they led the assembly in another hymn to the Supreme Being. This time without any objection from Robespierre, Marie-Joseph Chénier's *'Dieu puissant, d'un peuple intrépide'* was sung by the choirs and the whole assembly to the tune of the *Marseillaise*. According to Bontemps and Barry, during the singing of the first verse the elders and the armed adolescents on the Mountain swore an oath never to sheath their swords until they had destroyed all enemies of the Revolution.[52] A further verse was then sung by the nursing mothers during which they held their babies up towards the Sun, at which point, according to David's specifications, the whole assembly was to be united in the adoration of the Supreme Being, as He was seen to be smiling down on his chosen nation. The Mountain was decked not only with flowers and leaves but just as in the Jardin National, slogans were displayed around it. These are listed by Sylvain Maréchal in the pamphlet he prepared for distribution in the provinces as:

> Only justice can make all men equal
> The people of France look to the liberty of the world
> No man can fake virtue
> There is no point in removing kings if you don't follow a virtuous life
> Ignore the priests, let's just be virtuous
> The revolutionary is a hero of common sense and truthfulness
> Liberty is the reign of justice
> Frenchmen and women, cherish Liberty, bought at the price of the blood of your brothers, your friends, your husbands; use the power which nature has given you to spread Republican virtue
> Do not get drunk on success; be terrible in defeat, modest in triumph[53]

These slogans which show a considerable difference from those used at the Jardin National, seem more suited to the populist nature of the ceremony at the Mountain. Unlike the earlier slogans, there is also, in several cases, a direct homage to Robespierre, in that they are either actual or slightly modified quotations from his speeches. For example, the slogan which begins 'Ignore the priests …' is a variant of a phrase in Robespierre's speech of 18 Floréal; 'Ignore the priests, let us return to God.' It is also noticeable that there are far fewer references to any aspects of the Divine than in the first phase of the celebrations, and the vaguely theistic political rhetoric is largely replaced by sentiments inciting people to the practice of virtue, morality and probity.

During the celebrations at the Mountain Robespierre came in for further verbal attack. One of the most famous was, according to Michelet, spoken by an unnamed *sans-culotte*: 'The devil! He isn't happy to be the master, he wants to play God!'[54] Gorce ascribes the same words to Thuriot[55] while Vilate ascribes a very similar remark, 'It's not enough for him to be High Priest, he wants to be God!' to Bourdon de l'Oise.[56] The other equally famous remark is generally ascribed to another of Robespierre's opponents, Merlin de Thionville, 'the Tarpean rocks are right by the Capitol', obviously intended to remind Robespierre of the fate which had awaited unpopular legislators in Republican Rome.[57] This time, Robespierre certainly heard the insults, even if he chose not to respond immediately. Guillaume quotes from a note in Robespierre's private papers on the behaviour of Bourdin de l'Oise in which he accused Bourdin of expressing gross sarcasm and indecent references to the proclamation of the Supreme

Being and of telling other members of the Convention that the people 'scorned this decree'.[58]

Having got this mass of humanity in place and the ceremony duly completed, the next logistical task was to get them away again. This is where the detailed instructions fell short; for this part of the operation they are neither as precise nor as clear as they were for the previous parts of the day. The instructions from the Convention merely say that the forty-eight *sections* were to leave in the same order in which they had arrived and proceed to the Place des Invalides, where they were to disperse.[59] Although this might sound like a recipe for general confusion, it seems from the accounts available to have worked well as there are no specific comments from those present at the time to indicate that there were any major problems. The Police archives also have no reference to any crowd problems immediately after the ceremony, so it must be assumed that the *sections* left the Champ de la Réunion by the central exit, proceeded along the Rue Dominique, to the Invalides from where they dispersed back to their own areas. The members of the Convention returned to their building by the route by which they had come, but, since the public galleries were closed and no official session was possible, they also dispersed almost immediately.

This was far from being the end of the celebrations, however. Many of the *sections* had arranged some form of entertainment, often a Civic Banquet, where everyone brought along food and drink to share with their fellow citizens, and in many cases the evening continued with speeches, music and dancing. These street parties also gave every local Pindar an opportunity to declaim his verse publicly, or hear it sung lustily to a well-known air by his fellow-citizens, every would-be Demosthenes to make his patriotic oration to an admiring crowd. These local poets and orators, many of whom had sent their contributions to the Committee of Public Education in the hope of having them incorporated in the official festivities, would be the star turns of the evening.

There can be no doubt as to the success of the day as far as the organisation and the Festival itself were concerned. Every contemporary commentator, even such vilifiers of Robespierre as Vilate and Ruault, was full of praise for the celebrations themselves and expressed general approval of the idea of honouring a Supreme Being. The weather had been perfect, an ideal summer day. The *sections* too clearly enjoyed themselves, both in the formal events of the day and later in their more informal local celebrations. It would seem that Robespierre, despite the public attacks on him by some members of the Convention, could be pleased with the spectacle of the population of the capital apparently accepting wholeheartedly their joining together to honour the Supreme Being. At that level, it is clear that the day had been a complete success, everyone had enjoyed themselves and the idea of the Supreme Being, as a potential national belief system, was up and running. Yet it is one thing to have a great festival which, for a brief span, apparently unites the whole nation in joyful celebration, and quite another to lay the groundwork for something which, if successful, would become an intrinsic part of national life.

While it might have been expected that, following the success of the great festival the new belief system would be incorporated into the life of the nation as quickly and as deeply as possible, this simply did not happen. The vilifying comments of Robespierre's political opponents, despite their assertion that they were not attacking the idea of the Supreme Being as such, led inescapably to it being seen merely as the vehicle for the self-aggrandisement of its chief advocate and any hope of a new national morality, based on the acceptance of the presence of the Supreme Being, disappeared almost as quickly as it had appeared.

Notes

1 'L'aurore annonce à peine le jour, et déjà les sons d'une musique guerrière retentissent de toutes parts, et font succéder au calme du sommeil un réveil enchanteur. A l'aspect de l'astre bienfaisant qui vivifie et colore la nature, amis, frères, époux, enfants, vieillards et mères s'embrassent, et s'empressent à l'envi d'orner et de célébrer la fête de la Divinité.' A.P., Vol. 90, p. 141.
2 R. Monnier, 'L'Image de Paris de 1784 à 1794: Paris, capitale de la Révolution', in *Les Images de la Révolution française*, M. Vovelle, ed. (Paris, 1989), p. 73.
3 R. Cobb, *The Police and the People: French Popular Protest 1789–1820* (Oxford, 1970), pp. 228–30.
4 '*Instruction Particulière pour les commissaires chargés des détails de la fête à l'Être Suprême qui doit être célébrée le 20 prairial, conformément au décret de la Convention nationale du 18 floréal l'an deuxième de la République française, une et indivisible. Imprimée par ordre de la Convention*' (Paris, 1794).
5 A.P., Vol. 91, p. 440.
6 A.P., Vol. 91, pp. 441–2.
7 See Chapter 6, 'Contemporary comments on the festival'.
8 'Le Comité de salut public arrête que le Comité d'instruction publique reprendra toutes les mesures nécessaires pour l'exécution du décret sur la fête Nationale du 20 prairial. Le citoyen Hubert dirigera l'exécution de cette fête et la dépense sera nette et payée sur les fonds mis à la disposition de

la commission comme toutes les autres dépenses publiques dont elle est chargée.' A.N. AF.II.67.497.8.
9 See Figure 2 and the engraving, '*Les sections assemblées au Jardin National*', at the Musée Carnavalet.
10 See Table 5, p. 113.
11 See the analysis of the costs of the *Fête* in Paris in Chapter 5.
12 See Table 3, p. 107.
13 See Table 6, p. 114.
14 The author is indebted to Jean-Philippe Cartz, architect and structural engineer, for his calculations to determine the probable dimensions of the Mountain.
15 At the time the metric system had not been adopted and all Chevalier's figures are in *pied* (feet) and *pouces* (inches). The metric equivalent is approximately 40 × 15 × 12 metres.
16 See details in Chapter 5.
17 A.N. F.4.2090. *Hubert au Comité d'Instruction publique, le 6 Prairial*.
18 'Le Comité de salut public comptant sur le patriotisme et le zèle des ouvriers employés aux travaux de la fête nationale qui doit être célébrée le 20 de ce mois, arrête que ces travaux seront terminés le 19 prairial à midi. Le présent arrêt sera imprimé dans de divers lieux où se font les préparatifs de la fête.' A.N. AF.II.67.497.11.
19 *Détails Exacts des cérémonies et de l'Ordre à observer dans la Fête de l'Etre suprême qui doit être célébrée le 20 prairial, d'après le Décret de la Convention nationale du 18 floréal, l'an deuxième de la République une et indivisible* (Paris, n.d.).
20 J. Vilate, *Causes secrètes de la révolution du 9 au 10 thermidor; par Vilate, ex-juré au tribunal Révolutionnaire de Paris, détenu à La Force* (Paris, An III).
21 J. Michelet, *Histoire de France, Vol. VI, La Révolution*, originally printed 1847–52, reprinted P. Villaneix, ed. (Paris, 1974), p. 250.
22 'En attendant qu'il soit fait un rapport sur le costume National, les membres de la Convention Nationale assisteront à la fête Nationale du 20 de ce mois avec le costume de représentants du peuple près les armées et dans les départemens.' *Moniteur*, 19 Prairial, An II (7 June 1794), p. 1056.
23 J. Duprun, 'Les "noms divins" dans deux discours de Robespierre', *Annales historiques de la Révolution française*, 44 (1972): 172–6.
24 St Denis or St Dionysius was the Judge of the Areopagus converted by St Paul (Acts 17:34) who is claimed as the first Bishop of Athens. He shares a feast day of 3 October with St Denis of France with whom he is often confused. Eusebius, *Historia Ecclesia*, Vol. 3, Book 4.
25 *Auteur de la Nature, Auteur de notre être* and *Être des êtres*.
26 'Français républicains, c'est à vous de purifier la terre qu'ils ont souillée, et d'y rappeler la justice qu'ils en ont banni. La liberté et la vertu sont sorties ensemble du sein de la divinité: l'une ne peut séjourner sans l'autre parmi les hommes. Peuple généreux, veux-tu triompher de tous tes ennemis? Pratique

la justice et rends à la Divinité le seul culte digne d'elle; peuple, livrons-nous aujourd'hui, sous ses auspices, aux justes transports d'une pure allégresse; demain nous combattrons encore les vices et les tyrans; nous donnerons au monde l'exemple des vertus républicaines, et ce sera l'honorer encore.' (Robespierre, Œuvres, Vol. 10, p. 482)

27 'une brillante symphonie ... exécutée au milieu des applaudissements', L'Auditeur National, Issue 624, p. 6.

28 C. Pierre, Bernard Sarrette (Paris, 1895) and Les Hymnes et Chansons de la Révolution (Paris, 1904).

29 F. Zimmermann, 'Bernard Sarrette, fondateur du Conservatoire', France musicale, 21 November 1841.

30 P. Hédouin, 'Gossec', in Mosaïque. Peintres-Musiciens-Littérateurs-Artistes Dramatiques: à partir du 15ième siècle jusqu'à nos jours (Paris, 1856).

31 'La providence vint au secours de Sarrette éperdu. Le lendemain à six heures du matin, Théodore Desorgues arriva, conduit par le hasard, chez Gossec et lui proposa de mettre en musique des paroles qu'il avait faites sur le sujet à l'ordre du jour. Or, il se trouva qu'elles allaient parfaitement sur l'air déjà composé.' Hédouin, Mosaïque, pp. 298-301.

32 'Gravure et impression de l'Hymne du Citoyen Desorgues.' See Table 4, p. 109.

33 A.N. F.17.1065.5.

34 'est entré dans le néant, ce monstre que le génie des rois avait vomi sur la France; qu'avec lui disparaissent tous les crimes et tous les malheurs du monde! ... C'est surtout la Sagesse que nos coupables ennemis voulaient chasser de la République. C'est à la Sagesse seule qu'il appartient d'affermir la prospérité des empires; c'est à elle à nous garantir les fruits de notre courage ... Français, vous combattez les rois, vous êtes donc dignes d'honorer la Divinité ... Être des êtres, nous n'avons point à t'adresser d'injustes prières: tu connois les créatures sorties de tes mains; leurs besoins n'échappent pas plus à tes regards que leurs plus secrètes pensées. La haine de la mauvaise foi et de la tyrannie brûle dans nos cœurs avec l'amour de la justice et de la Patrie; notre sang coule pour la cause de l'humanité; voilà notre prière; voilà nos sacrifices; voilà le culte que nous t'offrons.' (Robespierre, Œuvres, Vol. 10, pp. 482-3)

35 'Précis de la fête célébrée à Paris le 20 prairial, l'an 2 de la République française, une et indivisible, rédigé par les citoyens Bontemps et Barry', in Discours prononcés les jours de décadi dans la section de Guillaume Tell (Paris, An II).

36 'Sur la face et les deux côtés de l'amphithéâtre on lisait les inscriptions suivantes, leçons bien consolantes pour les peuples, et terribles pour les despotes:
Le peuple français reconnaît l'existence de l'Être Suprême et l'immortalité de l'âme.
Sois assez pur pour désirer qu'il y ait un Dieu; tu le trouveras dans ton cœur.

Honorer la Divinité et punir les rois, c'est la même chose. La Divinité a condamné les tyrans, le peuple français a exécuté ses arrêts.' (Bontemps and Barry, *Discours prononcés*)
37 A.P., Vol. 91, pp. 425-6.
38 Deschamp, *Véritable Détail de la cérémonie qui doit être célébrée décadi 20 prairial ... Suivi de l'hymne en honneur de l'Être suprême* (Paris, n.d.).
39 *Détails exacts des cérémonies et de l'ordre à observer dans la fête de l'Etre suprême suivis de l'Hymne à l'Être suprême par Chénier et Gossec* (Paris, n.d.).
40 A.P., Vol. 91, pp. 425-7.
41 The guillotine was first erected on the Place de Grève on 22 April 1792 for the execution of criminals. For the first 'political' execution, that of Collenot d'Angremont on 22 August 1792, it was moved to the Place du Carrousel. It then shuttled between the Place de Grève for criminal and the Place du Carrousel for political executions. It made a one-day visit to the Place de la Révolution for the execution of Louis XVI on 20 January 1793, before reverting to its peripatetic existence between the Place de Grève and the Place de la Réunion until 22 May 1793 when it was erected permanently at the Place de la Révolution.
42 Previously and now Rue Saint Dominique.
43 Archives de la Police, Paris, AA.159.247/248. Section des Invalides, An II.
44 See Cobb, *The Police and the People*.
45 Archives de la Police, Paris, AA. 159.247/248. Section des Invalides, An II.
46 *Instruction Particulière pour les commissaires chargés des détails de la fête à l'Être Suprême*.
47 It is generally accepted that while these post-Thermidorean sources are of dubious veracity, they are nevertheless, in the absence of any more reliable sources, worth citing with reservations. See also Chapter 6, 'Contemporary comments on the Festival'.
48 'Il n'y avait entre Robespierre et moi plus de huit personnes de file, j'ai entendu toutes les imprécations; elles partaient de Thirion, de Montaut, de Ruamps et surtout de Lecointre de Versailles, qui appela plus de vingt fois Robespierre dictateur! tyran! et menaça de le tuer ... Parmi ceux qui dirent beaucoup d'injures à Robespierre pendant la procession, je distinguai particulièrement Thirion, Ruamps, Montaut, Duhem, Lecointre de Versailles.' (M-A. Baudot, *Notes Historiques sur la Convention, le Directoire, l'Empire et l'exil des votants* (Paris, 1893), p. 5)
49 *Conjuration formée dès le 5 préréal (sic) par neuf représentants du peuple contre Maximilien Robespierre, pour l'immoler en plein Sénat*. Par L. Lecointre, député de Versailles, Seine-et-Oise (Paris, An II).
50 'Ce fou de Lecointre de Versailles aurait conçu le dessein d'immoler à Dieu et à la Patrie ce grand président, le jour de la fête au Champ de Mars, sur l'autel dressé à cette patrie', N. Ruault, *Gazette d'un Parisien sous la Révolution, Lettres à son frère 1783-1796*, A. Vassal and C. Rimbaud, eds (Paris, 1976), p. 351.

51 'Soyez toujours assez généreux pour me conserver; vos enfans cueilleront mes fruits, et vous béniront sous mon ombrage.' Bontemps and Barry, *Discours prononcés*.
52 Bontemps and Barry, *Discours prononcés*.
53 'C'est la justice qui rend seule les hommes égaux / Le Peuple Français vote la liberté du monde / On n'imite pas la vertu ... / Peuple, c'est peu d'anéantir les rois, si tu ne sais pas respecter les vertus / Laissons les prêtres: retournons à la vérité / L'homme révolutionnaire est un héros de bon sens et de probité / La Liberté est le règne de la justice / Françaises, chérissez la Liberté, achetée au prix du sang de vos frères, de vos amis, de vos époux: servez-vous de l'empire que vous a donné la nature pour étendre celui de la vertu Républicaine / Défions-nous de l'ivresse-même des succès: soyons terribles dans les revers, modestes dans nos triomphes.' (S. Maréchal, *Tableau historique des événements révolutionnaires, depuis la fondation de la République jusqu'à présent, rédigé principalement pour les campagnes* (Paris, An III), pp. 133–8)
54 'Le bougre! Il n'est pas content d'être maître! Il lui faut encore être Dieu!' Michelet, *Histoire de France*, Vol. VI, *La Révolution*, p. 252.
55 P. de la Gorce, *Histoire religieuse*, Vol. 3 (Paris, 1909), p. 503.
56 'Il ne lui suffit pas d'être l'archiprêtre. Il veut être Dieu!' Vilate, *Causes secrètes de la revolution*.
57 'La roche Tarpéienne est près du Capitole.' Reported by several commentators present at the occasion, including Vilate, Baudot and Lecointre. During the early days of the Roman Republic criminals, traitors (and some politicians) were hurled to their deaths from the Tarpean Rocks, hard by the Capitol.
58 'Le jour de la fête de l'Etre Suprême, en présence du peuple, il s'est permis sur ce sujet [le décret qui proclame l'existence de l'Etre Suprême] les plus grossiers sarcasmes et les déclamations les plus indécentes; il faisait remarquer avec méchanceté aux membres de la Convention les marques d'intérêt que le public donnait au président pour tirer contre lui des inductions atroces.' *C.I.P.*, Vol 2, p. 587.
59 *Instruction particulière*, p. 4.

4

The celebrations outside Paris

Every report of the celebrations of the Festival of the Supreme Being outside Paris underlines the wholehearted way in which the ordinary people of France embraced the idea. Practically every city, town, village and even hamlet throughout the nation joined in the celebrations and the clear impression given is that they did so not because of any political imperative; indeed they did so despite the general distaste in the provinces for Jacobin centralisation. The evidence points strongly to the idea that the ethos of this national celebration, based as it was on the proposal to introduce some form of comprehensive national moral code, outweighed any provincial anti-centralist or anti-Jacobin sentiments.

To be successful, every ceremony had to have the total involvement of both the local officials and, even more importantly, the public. Robespierre would have been very conscious of the need for the *Fête* to arouse the republican ardour of the local political administrators, both to ensure their wholehearted participation and to motivate them to draw on every available strand of local cultural talent. For this special festival, it would not be enough to rely on the talents of the activists and the political classes; the concept needed to catch the imagination and enthusiasm of local poets, musicians and orators whose talents would be needed to ensure genuine local participation. It had to fire up the imagination of the people as a whole, to persuade them to become involved in the actual events of the day, not to leave it to local politicians. From the reports available it seems that the combination of the proposition of a comforting system of national morality based on a vaguely theistic Great Being, and the recognition of the importance of the immortality of the human soul, stood a real chance of being greeted positively throughout the nation, following as they did the bleakness of a period which had only offered the hopelessness of a series of negative values such as arid de-Christianisation, Atheism or an unapproachable Goddess of Reason.

The documents which flooded into Paris from the provinces after the proclamation of 18 Floréal, as well as the evidence in local archives, are a clear indication that this is exactly what did happen. It also seems that, despite David's template for the festival in Paris setting the bar very high, the level of achievement to which provincial organisers could aspire also had a positive effect. The records available in Municipal and Departmental archives, detailing the specific individual preparations for the festival, show clearly that the final organisation of each local celebration was very much decided locally. These documents offer an insight into three important areas. Firstly, they demonstrate local reaction to the proclamation; secondly, they set out how each commune made preparations for the great day; and finally, they include detailed reports on the actual celebrations of 20 Prairial. These sources have been used by both sides in the heated arguments which took place during the Bicentenary. Mona Ozouf in her extensive examination of all the Revolutionary Festivals[1] and Michel Vovelle in his major study of de-Christianisation[2] used them differently, ultimately disagreeing violently as to the underlying trope of the festival. However, neither side seems to have accepted the deeper insights these documents offer into the mindset of local people, showing that, on this occasion, they were not merely slavishly following a set of instructions from Paris; they were enhancing and modifying them so as to create their own unique local festival.

There were, of course, exceptions to the general positive response. Some areas had been so thoroughly affected by the guidance of the more extreme proponents of the de-Christianisation process that even a decree from the centre was not sufficient to change their attitude. Such refusals were rare enough to arouse comment and were very much against the national trend. When the administration of Nevers, under the influence of Fouché, informed the Convention that they would refuse to follow the decree of 18 Floréal, their letter was greeted 'with indignation' when it was read out in the Jacobin Club in Paris.[3]

To obtain a reasonably accurate overall picture of how the celebrations were carried out outside Paris, it is helpful to look at the festivities in various locations, firstly some large celebrations in major provincial centres, then those in smaller, but still important towns, and finally the way in which the festival was celebrated in small semi-urban or agricultural communes. Taken together they present a clear picture of a nation coming together in a previously unprecedented manner to celebrate not just the Nation, the Republic or the Revolution as individual concepts but all of these joined together, with the added effect of the benign influence of the Supreme Being. In order to get a flavour of the overall picture outside Paris, five major cities, each of them a major trading centre with road and either fluvial or sea-borne trade routes, will be examined. These are Angers on the Loire, Bordeaux on the Gironde, Lyon (now renamed Commune-Affranchie) on the Rhône, Strasbourg on the Rhine and Amiens on the Somme. Angers, Strasbourg and Amiens were all still involved in major military movements, while Lyon and Bordeaux were emerging from the shadow of federalist rebellion. Each of them also had its own special political, economic and, in the case of Strasbourg, linguistic problems. To demonstrate how the festival was organised in areas much less immediately influenced by war or rebellion, Tours, Orleans and Grenoble have been chosen. Bailleul, a similar size township but at that time acting as host to a large army preparing for the invasion of the Spanish Netherlands, gives a contrasting picture.

The instructions from Paris were very clear; the festivities were to be based on a two-site celebration, with a linking procession from the first to the second site.[4] The speeches and actions at the first site were to lead to the destruction of some representation of 'Hideous Atheism' from which, ideally, a vision of Wisdom clothed in purity would arise, to be followed by a carefully organised procession between the two sites, culminating in the pinnacle of the celebrations, the mass public act of homage to the Supreme Being, led by the chief officials of the area and performed on a symbolic Mountain erected for the purpose. Every one of these various components of the Festival was to be held in the open air, so as to ensure that the general public were not just passive spectators, but active participants, most particularly during the act of homage to the Supreme Being. One major problem for many of the areas outside Paris was whether or how far the very detailed specifications David had laid down could be reproduced in much smaller public areas than those available in Paris. Sometimes the town or city involved, while accepting the overall thrust of the Festival, was forced to make alterations on purely practical grounds. Others, like Bordeaux and Angers, under the direct instruction of a powerful *Agent National* or *Représentant en Mission*, made major changes to the basic design parameters, seriously affecting Robespierre's underlying concept of a mass open-air festival. In extreme cases, there was the deliberate playing down, or even elimination of the culminating act of homage to the Supreme Being.

Despite these local difficulties the majority evidence is one of communal administrations faithfully following David's concept, with major modifications only as far as necessary to suit local practical or financial constraints.[5] It is remarkable how many provincial cities did manage to erect some form of David's double statue of Wisdom overlaid by Atheism, including the ceremonial destruction by fire of the external layer with the emergence of the statue of Wisdom from the flames. In addition, the majority followed, at least in spirit, Robespierre's basic requirement of a mass adoration as the final ceremony. Where some major cities, such as Angers or Strasbourg, seriously modified Robespierre's basic tenet of an open-air mass demonstration of homage to the Supreme Being, or even, as in Bordeaux, eliminated it altogether, they stand out as exceptions to the general rule. It would be fair to say that any local modifications or differences not only reflected the particular capability and commitment of any given commune, but would also demonstrate the different emphasis that each local administration gave to the various aspects of the Festival. Each civic entity offered its own particular vision of the Supreme Being. This approach was sometimes clearly affected by the local political situation; cities such as Lyon or Bordeaux, with their immediate past record as *Fédérés*, would be naturally eager to demonstrate their loyalty to the Jacobin government and the Mountain. Against this, cities like Angers and Strasbourg, each with a major war front on its doorstep, could be expected to transfer the emphasis from the general national wellbeing to the particular problems of an armed struggle.

Of the cities examined, only Bordeaux and Lyon had open public areas large enough to even attempt to replicate David's massive Mountain in Paris, and in the event only Lyon produced an equivalent size of pageant. Another factor which could seriously affect the scale or nature of the celebrations outside the capital was that many provincial towns and cities were experiencing severe financial problems, and the sudden and unexpected imposition of such a major item of expenditure as this festival promised to be could well tip an already fragile situation over into a crisis. One example is Bordeaux, where, even if the City Council had wished to follow exactly the instructions from Paris, they were unable to do so not only because of the attitude of the recently arrived special representative of the *Comité de salut public*, Jullien, who called for major changes to Robespierre's concept, but also because of the serious financial problems they were experiencing.

Although most communes accepted David's twin-site concept, local circumstances often led them to opt for a simplified version. It was quite common for existing civic amenities such as the Maison Commune or the town or market square to be used both as the assembly point for the procession and as the site for the first speeches, usually followed by a procession through the centre of the town to the most suitable open space for the erection of a symbolic Mountain for the final mass homage to the Supreme Being. Sometimes, as in Bordeaux, this was the local Champ de Mars, sometimes, as in Amiens, the open space in front of the cathedral (newly christened Temple of the Supreme Being), while in Angers and several other areas a local park was chosen for the final ceremonies. There was also the practical problem that, in many towns and cities, there simply was not enough open space available for anything like the vast constructions specified in the instructions from Paris. In Nantes, the City Architect, Lamarie, informed his local council that, 'We have had to adapt the scenery proposed to the spaces chosen for the festival ... the Cours and the Place de la Liberté are far from being as huge as the Paris Champs de Mars.'[6] In the end, he, like most local engineers, settled for those aspects of David's instructions which were the most practical for them to follow, given their constraints of time and budget.

One striking difference in the celebrations in the provinces against those in Paris is the widespread use of banners with suitably edifying slogans, carried in front of the different groups in the procession. This had always been a feature of previous processions in the capital but on this particular occasion the use of slogans in Paris was limited to static displays at the actual celebration sites. The use and choice of these banners was another way in which the provincial administrations differentiated themselves from the capital. These slogans, normally preceding such elements of the procession as the adolescents, the old men, the nursing mothers or the nubile girls, were used, in the best revolutionary tradition, to inform, instruct and excite the onlookers, and the choice of slogans often indicated a very different emphasis from those displayed around the Jardin National or the Champ de la Réunion in Paris. Occasionally the slogans on the boards had to do with specific local problems, such as the proximity of an enemy army, as in Strasbourg or Bailleul, or of a nearby rebel force as on the Loire. They could also demonstrate a different approach to the idea of a Supreme Being watching over France, as shown by some of the banners carried in Angers, Calais or Tours. In the more politically or militarily sensitive areas, such as the lower Loire and the North, the lofty sentiments of Paris are largely replaced by more hard-hitting admonitions with a clear local relevance. In areas close to actual conflict zones, there are slogans decidedly more bellicose than those in Paris. One example is Angers where the three military units in the procession marched behind banners proclaiming respectively, 'Truth strides out against thrones', 'Liberty or Death' and the banner displayed by the local volunteers vaunting themselves as 'Children of Mars and Bellona'.[7]

Slogans were also used to demonstrate local adherence to some of the more edifying sentiments of the new republican morality. In St Omer, the nursing mothers proclaimed their responsibility to their babies as 'We will raise them for the nation'.[8] In Angers, the adolescent girls marched behind the uplifting slogan 'Under the torch of marriage we will bear heroes for the nation',[9] while in Compiègne their promise to the combatants was a little more direct, 'We will make them forget all their woes'.[10] For the adolescent youths, slogans were often equally warlike and edifying: in Strasbourg they were the only group with a banner, which simply promised that 'We will follow the example of Barra and Viala'.[11] In Abbeville it was a trifle more mournful, 'We will know how to die for the nation',[12] while in Nancy, direct bellicosity was replaced by more elevating, if turgid, sentiments, 'Fill our hearts with virtue and make us worthy of our civic responsibilities'.[13] In many provincial centres, the local Jacobins, in the shape of the *Société Populaire* or the *Amis du Peuple* obviously felt it incumbent on them to underline both their civic status and their responsibilities as flag-bearers of the Revolution. In Abbeville this part of the procession was preceded by a banner inscribed 'We watch over you'.[14] Tours attempted to raise the tone with 'The man who denies the existence of the Supreme Being deliberately deludes himself',[15] while Calais brought it back to basics with the short and pithy reminder 'We are watching you'.[16]

Not all areas had slogans, and of those that did, not all of them had a slogan for every group. In Strasbourg and Nancy only the youths had a slogan; Calais had a slogan for each of the seven major groups in its procession; in Tours, each of the eight *sections* marching in the procession had its own banner while other towns such as St Omer, Compiègne and Bailleul limited the use of banners to selected groups. Tours was especially distinguished by the lofty, if rather overblown, sentiments carried on its banners. For example, in Calais, the banner borne before the senior citizens had the simple sentiment 'Honour and respect age'.[17] By contrast, in Tours, their banner read 'When we pass on into the bosom of the Supreme Being we will leave our successors happy and free'.[18] There is a similar contrast in the slogans carried before the agricultural labourers; that of Calais was brief and to the point, 'The most practical of trades should be the most honoured',[19] whereas Tours goes perhaps a little far, even for the rhetoricians of the Revolution, with a banner reading, 'O Nature, beneath his humble smock the labourer in thy fertile fields follows thy gracious laws and proclaims thy bounties'.[20]

One of the most remarkable features of the celebrations of the festival outside Paris was the manner in which the vast majority of local authorities managed to get very considerable constructions, or, at the very least, large and imposing pageants, made in an extremely tight time frame. The work in Paris had been partially prepared in David's *ateliers* before the specification were issued, but in the provinces the local city architect or engineer was invariably faced with a much more restricted deadline and often a minimal budget, since central government had made no provision for funding anything outside the capital. To give an idea of the exceptionally tight deadlines the city engineers were working to, Lyon, Strasbourg and Amiens all issued instructions as late as 9 Prairial (28 May), allowing a bare ten days to complete the necessary works, although in Lyon the engineers had the good fortune of being able to re-use the large constructions erected the year previously. In Amiens, although the decree from Paris was received relatively early on 5 Prairial (24 May), final instructions were only issued on 9 Prairial (28 May), after an unsuccessful attempt to get funding from the departmental authorities. In Angers the decree from Paris was received on 4 Prairial (23 May) but because the *Agent National*, Fillon, decided to completely revamp the original proposals which the local administration put forward on 8 Prairial (27 May), the final plan was only released on 14 Prairial (2 June), giving those involved just one week to get everything ready, which totally scuppered Fillon's grandiose proposals for a whole series of statues and platforms in the park. In the end, only a basic platform, more or less in the form of a small mountain, was constructed.

It was to be expected that local politics would have a major impact on decisions as to how exactly to stage the festival, especially where there was the influence of a strong *Agent National* working with a carefully selected town council. It might be thought that cities like Lyon and Bordeaux, which had the most need to prove their loyalty to the Mountain, would have been the most careful to follow David's requirements as closely as possible. In fact only Lyon followed all of David's detailed instructions, including the provision of a statue of Atheism burning to reveal Wisdom. By contrast, the celebrations in Bordeaux were totally transformed from the original ideas set out in the decree of 18 Floréal at the direct instruction of the newly arrived *Représentant en Mission*, Jullien. In Strasbourg the council, under the lead of the newly appointed *Agent National*, Mainoni and his carefully chosen Mayor, Monet, both committed de-Christianisers, had intended to ignore the festival altogether, until forced to act when called to order by the departmental administration. In Angers, when the town council made Robespierre's concept of homage to the Supreme Being the cardinal point of their detailed plan for the festivities, the new *Agent National*, Fillon, rejected their proposals out of hand and imposed his own ideas.

Lyon, since the purging of the city administration after the defeat of the *Fédérés*, was naturally keen to show its loyalty to the Jacobin cause, and would be expected to follow, as closely as possible, the detailed instructions from David, despite the fact that the available pool of labour was heavily committed to the rebuilding of those parts of the city which had been destroyed by the massive bombardments ordered by Fouché and Collot d'Herbois during the revolt. Fortunately the city already had a vast edifice available on the Place Egalité which had been constructed for the *Fête de la Réunion* in the previous year. This consisted of a stairway leading to a platform on either side of which were altars, one to the Martyrs of the Revolution, the other dedicated to the memory of the local hero, Chalier. This meant that it was only necessary for two new constructions to be made: that of the statue of 'Hideous Atheism', placed between the two altars on the Place Egalité, and a Mountain on the Champ de Mars, now renamed Champ de la Montagne. The ceremonies carefully followed the Parisian model with a procession to the first site where the first major speeches were made. The main speakers were Dupuy, the *Représentant en Mission*, Tarpan, the *Agent National* and his deputy Fillieux, and, after several more speeches and the burning of the statue of Atheism, a second procession marched to the newly erected Mountain where a noted local actor, Dorfeuille,[21] read a long speech at the close of which there was a mass homage to the Supreme Being and the singing of Chénier's *Hymne à l'Être Suprême*.[22] There does seem to have been a certain embarrassment in official Lyon with the Deistic nature of the Festival. Figure 4a shows the medallion which the city fathers issued to celebrate the event. This was in essence a reworking of a similar medallion which had been struck to celebrate the *Fête de la Raison* in November 1793 which is shown as Figure 4b. As will be seen the medal issued in November 1793 is inscribed with the words Equality, Liberty, Reason surrounding the Masonic symbol of the all-seeing eye of Horus with the rays of the Sun. Even the new medallion has no direct reference to the subject of the Festival, merely the date and the place, although the Chalier monument has now had the addition of some rays surrounding the central figure, presumably meant to refer to the bounty radiating down from the Supreme Being. This can be seen also in the speech of Tarpan, the *Agent National*, where he refers to 'The Divinity who looks down on us and seeks only our happiness.'[23] The chief official speechmaker, Dupuy, made several references to the underlying Deist concept of the Festival; for example in 'O Supreme Being! Principal of life and happiness, whose children assemble today in your honour.'[24] However, any more specific direct references to God, or to the Author of the Universe or of Nature which were a feature in the celebrations in many other cities are noticeably absent from all the speeches in Lyon. In his speech Fillieux, Tarpan's Deputy, made no direct reference to the

Figure 4a The medal struck in Lyons in celebration of the Festival of the Supreme Being

Figure 4b The medal struck in Lyons in celebration of the Festival of Reason

Supreme Being at all, offering instead a list of republican attributes to be strived for: 'truth, justice, honesty, virtue and wisdom' without any direct reference to the principal subject of the Festival.[25]

In Angers, the political situation had been extremely agitated throughout 1793 and early 1794. As Mathiez noted, despite the City Council having been 'cleansed' it was still divided between moderates and de-Christianisers,[26] and there was a feeling that some kind of religious tolerance was still possible within the Jacobin concept since 'the conflict against fanaticism and the priests in the Vendée had not removed from their hearts the spirit of religion'.[27] When the Decree of the Committee of Public Safety was received on 4 Prairial (23 May), the council nominated three leading Jacobin members to prepare detailed proposals for the celebrations. They reported back four days later with an extensive and carefully considered set of suggestions, following David's template as closely as possible. These were accepted by the council and immediately passed on to the *Agent National*, Fillon, for his approval. Since the council had accepted a proposal clearly in line with the specifications received from Paris, it would be expected that the proposals would be passed.

This was however not to be the case: a week later, on 14 Prairial (June 2), with only a week to go before the actual *Fête*, Fillon presented his own very different proposals. He had made major changes both to the council's plan and to David's original concept. His scheme accepted that the first part of the celebrations should be in the open air, with speeches at the Maison Commune, to meet Robespierre's requirements and 'to strike down fanaticism'.[28] This would be followed by a procession to the first site of the celebrations at the largest public space in Angers, Le Mail. Here he proposed to have erected a Mountain, surmounted by a massive Obelisk on which was a full-size Statue of Liberty. Instead of the statue of Atheism being burned with Wisdom emerging from the flames, there would be a statue of Wisdom spurning Atheism, Federalism, Realism and Fanaticism. The whole was to include a large platform for the speakers and be surrounded by several Trees of Liberty.[29] There was obviously no chance of any of this imposing edifice being erected in the six days available. From the official report on the proceedings it would appear that they finished up with a much smaller platform for the speakers on which the Mayor, Berger, made a speech inviting everyone to acknowledge the republican advantages of belief in a Supreme Being and the consoling idea of an afterlife.

The proceedings, already markedly different from those in Paris, changed again when, after a declamation of patriotic texts by an actor and a young soldier, the procession re-formed and marched to the newly christened Temple of the Supreme Being. For the final part of the ceremonies, instead of being in the open air, the proceedings were inside the Temple itself, thus seriously limiting the number of spectators – precisely the effect Robespierre wished to avoid. Then, in place of the required simple ceremony centred on the public adoration of the Supreme Being, there followed a formal re-dedication of the Temple in a manner highly redolent of the service of consecration of a Catholic church, even down to the lighting of incense at the four corners of the Altar of the Nation. Finally, instead of the mass adoration of the new protector of the Republic, as required in the specific instructions from the Convention, Robespierre's speech of 18 Floréal was read, punctuated by 'hymns, songs, and music suitable for the festival'.[30] After a break for lunch, everyone returned to the Mail, where 'the rest of the day passed off in pleasant amusement'.[31]

The background to the Festival in Strasbourg is coloured by the special combination of political and linguistic problems in that city. After the appointment of Saint-Just and Lebas as *Représentants en Mission* first to the Département of the Lower Rhine and later to the Army, the two major figures of the early Revolutionary years, Dietrich the first Mayor, and Schneider the Public Prosecutor were each removed from office and executed. Saint-Just became the *Représentant en Mission* specifically to the Army of the Rhine, and was replaced in the city itself by Milhaud and Guyardin. They continued the process of de-Christianising and the policy of gallicanisation, attempting to impose French as the only official language. After the elections of 1793, when Strasbourg did not elect a single Jacobin to the City Council,[32] Robespierre sent further commissioners from Paris to purge the council.[33] They were unable to find a Jacobin candidate whom the majority of the electors would support for Mayor, and finally appointed Pierre-François Monet, the francophone Secretary of the local Jacobin Club, and an ardent supporter of gallicanisation, as Mayor, despite his being under the legal age for holding office.[34]

Language was a major problem in Strasbourg: the leading local historian, Claude Betzinger, estimates that in 1789 fewer than 10 per cent of the population of Strasbourg spoke French sufficiently well to be able to use it freely in their everyday life, with a possible further 5 per cent who could cope with official documents in French.[35] The normal language throughout the region was either the High German of the bourgeoisie or the regional German dialect of the common people. By 1794, the total number of French speakers would have been even fewer, since the bi-lingual part of the population was largely the merchant and manufacturing classes, and most of these had left the city after 1792. This created a basic problem which affected the attendance at any Republican Festival, since these were now conducted only in French, and the vast majority of the population of Strasbourg and its surrounding area would have had only an imperfect idea of proceedings in a language they neither spoke nor understood. Another important consideration for the potential acceptance of an idea such as that of the Supreme Being in Strasbourg was the question of religion. Since its annexation from the Empire in 1681, Strasbourg had enjoyed a unique status among French cities, not only conducting its own affairs in its own language, but also being home to the only University in France to be both Germanophone and Lutheran, as opposed to Calvinist, Protestant.[36] Pre-revolutionary Strasbourg had been an exceptionally tolerant society with a majority of Lutheran Protestants; a Catholic minority of about 20 per cent, a small number of Zwinglian Protestants[37] and an important Jewish element.

When Chaumette declared his *Fête de la Raison* in Notre Dame de Paris in November 1793, Monet enthusiastically embraced this idea – he was one of very few provincial mayors to do so – and organised one of the largest festivals outside Paris.[38] As part of the festivities he had a huge red Phrygian bonnet built over the spire of the Cathedral, now renamed Temple of Reason, destroyed most of the statues still left in and on the Cathedral, dismantled the altars and held a special ceremony of abjuration at which all the remaining priests in Alsace, both Lutheran and Catholic, were invited to publicly renounce their orders.[39] The local daily paper, *Der Weltbote*, printed a German translation of part of Robespierre's speech of 18 Floréal and all of David's instructions in its issue of 24 Floréal (13 May), although it was not until 5 Prairial (24 May) that Monet responded with the usual 'boilerplate' address to the Convention marking the arrival of the decrees regarding the renaming of the *Temple de la Raison* to that of the Supreme Being. The Cathedral was renamed on the same day as required; however Monet and Mainoni, the *Agent National*, had already decided to have a different festival at the end of May, to celebrate the defeat of Federalism. This would create a problem of organisation since if both this new festival and the Festival of the Supreme Being were to be held, Strasbourg would have to cope with two major festivals within a fortnight of each other. The result was that any celebration of the Festival of the Supreme Being was quietly dropped and at the meeting of the municipal council on 6 Prairial (25 May), Monet, supported by the *Agent National*, completely ignored any reference to the proposed festival on 20 Prairial, in favour of his proposed festival to be held on 12 Prairial (31 May).[40] Two days later, on 8 Prairial (27 May), a strongly worded letter arrived from the Directorate of the Department of the Lower Rhine ordering Strasbourg to celebrate the Festival of the Supreme Being 'with all due dignity'. The council deputed the Mayor and the Chief Engineer 'to make all the necessary and proper arrangements', although the local archives do not show any records of these being discussed by the whole council.[41]

There were also difficulties in arranging for crowds of the proper size to attend the ceremonies of 20 Prairial. Apart from those Francophone elements of the Army of the Rhine brought in to the city for the occasion, the proportion of the inhabitants of Strasbourg who would actually have understood the speeches and hymns was minimal. From the documents available it would seem that many of the spectators were either bussed in from outlying villages or had been drawn on to the streets for fear of being seen to be insufficiently republican. The crowds were further swelled by the local indigents, lured not only by the promise of free food and drink but also by a special additional distribution of poor relief for any who attended the celebrations. The council also ensured that the two state orphanages brought their children to the *Fête* by issuing them with a special supplement of fifty pounds weight of cheese from the city reserves.[42]

Strasbourg also differed from Paris in its arrangements for the Festival. In addition to the usual groupings, which already included a large military presence, they added workers in the powder mills, women making army tents, and a group representing the friendly revolutionary nations, Switzerland, Poland and the United States.[43] Robespierre's call for an open-air celebration was ignored and the main ceremonies were inside the now totally bare Cathedral where the procession entered and gathered in the nave around a Mountain. This exactly repeated the ceremony for the Festival of Reason, but this time the Mountain was not crowned by a Greek temple containing the Goddess of Reason but by the Altar of the Nation.[44] A hymn was sung after which a piece of music specially composed by the eminent local musician Pleyel[45] was played and an oration against Atheism delivered. After a further speech and more hymns the assembly dispersed and those indigents who had been persuaded to attend retired to their homes where they were given a free meal, while free drink was available at the various Trees of Liberty in the city. The celebrations culminated in the illumination of the Phrygian bonnet covering the spire of the Cathedral. The official detailed report on the *Fête* was made by the Mayor on 28 Prairial to the Council who had it reprinted in large numbers since they believed that it would 'make a strong impression on all virtuous and sympathetic minds' although, since they did not arrange for its translation and publication in German, the number of these virtuous and sympathetic minds would have been rather limited.[46]

In Amiens, the festivities were more subdued than in many other cities. By mid-1794 the local political situation was once again relatively calm after the serious destabilisation of the area in 1793 as a direct result of aggressive de-Christianisation. The permanent concern of the city administration was the problem of housing and feeding not only their own population, but also the large number of wounded soldiers from the French army, who, together with a considerable number of prisoners-of-war, chiefly Flemish soldiers of the Imperial Army, had been dumped on them by the provincial authorities. The situation was so bad that public subscriptions had to be raised to provide the wounded French soldiers with the basic necessities which the commune could no longer finance.[47] A full twin-site celebration was considered far too expensive and it was decided that everything was to be done in front of the Cathedral. To ensure a good turnout and add to the success of the celebrations the indigents, as in Strasbourg, were promised a double payment of poor relief if they attended.[48]

The procession assembled at the Maison Commune and marched the short distance to the open space in front of the Cathedral, now the Temple of the Supreme Being, where a small Mountain, surmounted by a Tree of Liberty, had been raised on a platform remaining in the square from the last festival. The whole celebration was in a fairly minor key, and there was no statue of Atheism, nor was any mass public homage to the Supreme Being arranged. Instead, there was 'a moment of silence and contemplation of the beauties of Nature, after a secret and pure worship of the great Being'.[49] This was followed by hymns, composed by a local poet and sung to the music of popular songs by local actors and musicians, and several formal orations, one of which specifically honoured the Supreme Being. After the final speech by the President of the *Société Populaire*, the procession returned to the Maison Commune, and dispersed to prepare for the events of the afternoon when there was dancing around the Mountain. In the evening there was an open-air ball to raise money for poor relief. This seems to have been a success since local archives show that the musicians got through twenty-six bottles of cider and two carriages were hired to take them home.[50]

Tours was in a very different situation from Angers or the towns on the lower Loire, being at a reasonably comfortable distance from both the events in the Vendée and the activities of the Parisian *sans-culottes*. Situated as it was at the intersection of the major import-export routes to Paris from Nantes and Bordeaux and of the major north-south trading routes for goods moving between the industrial centres of northern France and the southern industrial areas of Toulouse, the south-west and the Limousin, Tours also had some pretension to intellectual eminence through its University and the many religious foundations in the area, and the proceedings of the Festival in this city were distinguished by the style and content both of the banners displayed in the procession and the hymns used during the ceremonies.

The ceremonies at Tours closely followed those laid down for Paris but with a strong use of the *Marseillaise* as the standard air for the hymns used in the ceremonies. After the general assembly a hymn, composed by a local poet, was sung to the tune of the *Marseillaise* and the procession left for the Place du Musée on which was erected a group of statuary representing Atheism, Ambition, Egoism, Pride and Fanaticism which was set on fire to reveal the serene countenance of Wisdom. Another locally composed hymn was sung to the tune of a popular song *Mourir pour la Patrie*, after which the procession re-formed and marched to the Temple of the Supreme Being to the strains of the *Marseillaise*. There, more verses were sung, again to the tune of the *Marseillaise*, and the assembly moved on to the Place de la Nation, where a huge altar had been raised to Nature.[51] After a general hymn, representatives from the groups in the procession of mothers and daughters, fathers and sons, agricultural workers, orphans and senior citizens paid tribute to the Supreme Being on behalf of their peers. This was followed by a final act of mass worship, at the culmination of which 'the odour of the flowers which fills the air rises, with the voice of the people, towards the Supreme Being.'[52] Tours extended the celebrations after the ceremony of adoration, with the presentation of a 'staging of religious and patriotic nature in which the dramatic artistes of the city demonstrated their solidarity with the people and their worship of the Supreme Being.'[53] This combination of religious with patriotic reinforces the sense of the importance Tours, like many other areas, gave to a Festival which was seen by many as working towards the re-integration of the morality of the Revolution with the unspoken yet still present national need for an accepted liberty to practise religion.

Grenoble handed the responsibility for the Festival over to a member of the local Committee of Public Education, Antoine Français, whose individual flair showed how far local organisers could go in modifying the principles so carefully laid down by Robespierre. In a document which he called his *Idée*, Français not only presented his proposals for the celebrations to the City Council but added a long introductory harangue on the merits of festivals in general, and Revolutionary Festivals in particular.[54] He also put his finger on the problem of representing the Divine, of giving shape to the unseen and unknowable: 'Since God can only make Himself known to us in His works, or by the virtues which flow from Him, and which draw us to Him, any representations or symbols by which we seek to show or personify Him must be strictly forbidden.'[55] For

Français, this *fête* was not going to be based on some unknown entity; he totally ignored the words Supreme Being, preferring the words God or The Eternal. In his concept the people of Grenoble would not acknowledge a vague Supreme Being, they would publicly worship God.

The banner which was to lead the procession through the city modified the words of the decree of 18 Floréal to read 'The people of France recognise the existence of God and the immortality of the Soul'.[56] There were no more openly religious symbols: immediately after this banner came the tablets of the Declaration of the Rights of Man, the Book of Laws and the busts of the Martyrs, carried in an open carriage and protected by the figure of Hercules brandishing his club. The rest of the procession was divided into groups, some of which were very different from those in other areas. In addition to the normal groups honouring Agriculture, Industry, Filial Piety and Nursing Mothers, the procession included groups of the wounded, referred to as 'Martyrs for Liberty', followed by a collection of broken chains, crowns and mitres, some piled up in a cart, others borne aloft on pikes, representing Enemies, Traitors and Tyrants. This was followed by a group carrying the banner 'Love', described by Français as representing 'The freshest and purest things that the empire of Flora can offer ... each maiden, dressed in white, carries a basket of flowers from which rise doves. This festival ... accepts only chaste love'.[57]

The procession finally arrived at the banks of the River Isère, on which was a flotilla of boats decked out in republican bunting. On its banks, Français had constructed a Corinthian Temple festooned with garlands, containing the choirs and musicians and bearing the inscription 'Temple of the Supreme Being'.[58] Once inside the temple area, a far more complex ceremony than that which Robespierre had envisaged was held. Every single one of the thirty-six different types of Revolutionary Tenth-day Festival, as laid down in the Decree of 18 Floréal, was represented by an actor carrying a banner or placard to indicate the theme of the particular festival. Once they had all entered into the Temple the ecclesiastical nature of the ceremonies in Grenoble became even more striking as 'From the highest point of the Temple, a speaker will invoke God in the attribute of each group'.[59] Religion had reappeared to stand openly hand-in-hand with republicanism; this was not an act of homage to a Supreme Being, this was a direct invocation of God in all His attributes, a republican reproduction of the litany which would have been chanted at the celebrations of the *Fête-Dieu* under the old regime.

Bailleul, close to the northern border with the Austrian Netherlands, was in a very different position from Tours or Grenoble, being well inside a major war zone. At the time of the Festival it was the temporary home of the Revolutionary army, preparing for the assault northwards, which was to lead to the victory of Fleurus three weeks later, on 8 Messidor (26 June). The Festival here showed a very high level of both organisation and discipline, and was notable for the number of banners and placards carried in the procession and displayed around the Mountain.[60] The procession was led by a banner 'designed to remind people of the reason for the festival', followed by girls bearing flowers and youths carrying a banner which proclaimed them as the 'Hope of the Nation'. Then came the mothers who promised 'to raise our children for the Nation' and the men of military age, marching with linked arms under the motto 'Union is our strength!' They were followed by the unmarried maidens who promised that 'Our delicate hearts can only be inspired by virtue and patriotism'. Finally came the tablets of the law led by the banner 'The despair of the wicked, the deceitful and the treacherous'. When the procession reached the Mountain, new slogans were visible around the orators' platform declaring that:

> The Mountain will save the Nation
> It will crush hideous federalism
> It will throw over the monster of Atheism and its false prophecies
> Pitt, Coburg and their masters shall not prevail against it[61]

Several speeches were made and, after the singing of a hymn to the Supreme Being, incense was burned to cries of 'Long live the Republic, long live the National Convention!' The council was rightly proud of its efforts and voted to have the proceedings of the day set down in print and 300 copies sent to all interested parties locally and nationally.

The Festival was celebrated with as much pomp as could be managed, often with local embellishments, in practically every village and hamlet throughout France. Records are available in many Departmental Archives of these celebrations, and many local historians took the opportunity presented by the Bicentenary to produce detailed reports of their local *fête*. From all of these, four have been selected, not only to demonstrate the republican ardour of the village in question, but also to give some insight into the little local difficulties with which the civic officials or the *Agent National* sometimes had to contend.

To the south of Paris, in the Île de France, the commune of Sceaux, having renamed itself successively Bourg-Egalité then Sceaux-l'Unité, entrusted the organisation of its festival to a rather shady character who referred to himself as 'Palloy the Patriot'.[62] Palloy seems to have aspired to out-do David in the grandeur of his operation; every house was to be painted with a red cap with a tricolour cockade and all old flags and bunting were to be taken down and replaced with new. Each of the thirty-four streets in the commune was to have its own signboard, detailing one of the thirty-six special tenth-day festivals, enumerated by Robespierre in the decree of 18 Floréal, with the last two banners To Posterity and To Happiness being displayed next to the official party at the Mountain. No detail was omitted, every major participant was named and instructed in their duties, and the whole day finished with a civic banquet at which 'All citizens are invited to bring their meal and to be seated, without ceremony, one beside another as it happens.'[63] The available documentation regrettably does not confirm whether any element of this grandiose scheme was actually followed through.

Not far from Sceaux is the commune of Mennecy.[64] It had made its revolutionary mark on 16 Brumaire (6 November 1793) when, as described by Aulard, a delegation of its inhabitants appeared at the bar of the Convention dressed in ecclesiastical attire declaring that they abjured superstition and would have no more parish or priests.[65] Like Bordeaux, Mennecy decided to have a festival on both 10 and 20 Prairial using a suitable knoll at a crossroads in the village as a Mountain on which was raised the Altar of the Nation.[66] Unfortunately, for the Festival of the Supreme Being, all was not quite as well ordered as could have been wished. Any self-respecting procession needs cavalry, and in Mennecy the only two horses available, which belonged to the local butchers, Grivotte and Clouet, were duly pressed into service. All went well until after the ceremony at the Mountain when Grivotte and Clouet, who had been drinking, made a wager as to whose horse could best climb the Mountain. According to local historians there followed an ignoble incident when, after Grivotte's horse had fallen off the Mountain, Clouet's mount triumphantly attained the summit where it proceeded to profane the Altar which had just been consecrated to the Supreme Being.[67] There was a further unwelcome incident when a certain Citizen Postolle, although firmly invited on two occasions to join in the festivities, not only refused but was actually seen taking a solitary walk not a quarter league away. Postolle spent the night under guard in the local cells, while Clouet and Grivotte[68] were sent to the nearest prison in Corbeil.[69]

The walled medieval village of Belvès in the Dordogne also celebrated the *Fête*, although the only details of exactly how it celebrated are in a letter sent on 21 Prairial by the *Agent National*, Fabré, to the Committee of Public Education in Paris. The clerk recorded its receipt on 22 Messidor and sent it on to the Committee of Public Safety, who entered it in their Minute Book two days later. Fabré reports that on receipt of the decree from Paris, the church had been duly renamed and the *Fête* was held on the date specified. He goes on to say that 'I received two cases of music and patriotic hymns; but it was not possible to make use of them, due to a lack of both musical instruments and people with the talent or ability to play them.'[70] Despite the lack of music, things literally went with a bang when Fabré agreed to release some of the village's precious gunpowder at the urgent request of Baradèle, the local ironfounder who had become a manufacturer of cannon, on the grounds that 'I realised the importance of the festival and in order to inspire the required zeal allowed the foundry to sacrifice twenty pounds of gunpowder.' He concludes by assuring the Committee that the Festival of the Supreme Being had left a pleasant memory in the heart of all the citizens.

The tiny village of Theys, deep in the mountains of the Isère in the canton of Goncelin some sixteen kilometres north-east of Grenoble, is perhaps the most perfect example of how deeply the idea of the *Fête* had penetrated the national consciousness and how carefully, almost lovingly, the instructions for the *Fête* were worked out in even the smallest and most remote hamlet. The detailed instructions issued by the *Société Populaire* of Theys present a remarkable insight into the way a very small rural commune set out not just to follow Robespierre's instructions, but also to join in with his deeper intentions.[71] Everything is included, no names, accessories or movements are lacking. There are ninety-six participants individually named in the document, each has his exact role to play and everybody's part is set out clearly for them. If one adds to the named and nominated mobile participants in the procession the old person carried in his chair to represent Age, the six infants at their mothers' breasts, as well as local elected officials, there must have been somewhere near 120 souls taking an active part in the ceremonies – an amazing turnout for a small mountain village.

The examples quoted in this chapter not only confirm how widespread the celebration of the *Fête de l'Être Supreme* was throughout France; more importantly they demonstrate how far the local celebrations of the *Fête* were from being simply the slavish following of a decree handed down from a feared central government. They were the result of careful and detailed consideration by the organisers in each locality to design their celebrations so as to have the maximum impact on the particular aspirations of themselves and their fellow citizens. Certainly the fact that it was generally reported as being a perfect summer's day helped the overall feeling of joyfulness which permeates all the reports from the organisers of festivals outside Paris. How much the general hope that perhaps this really was the end of the Terror and the beginning of a new and more positive phase of the Revolution played a part is difficult to quantify, although according to contemporary reports it undoubtedly had a role to play in setting the mood for the celebrations. What is important is that any local differences of emphasis, whether by the use of banners and placards, of single as against twin-site ceremonies, or of the use of statuary and pageants, while giving a strong signal of how the Festival was enhanced by local input, are secondary when set against the national acceptance of the elevating and spiritual nature of the ultimate homage to the Supreme Being.

The overall impression of the celebration of the *Fête* throughout the nation is that it was a clear confirmation of the people's need for some sort of new, acceptably republican code of morals and ethics to fill the gap left by the removal from the official life of the nation of the previous faith-based code. The rare occasions when a municipal or area council, or more often a single authoritarian figure like Jullien in Bordeaux or Fillon in Angers, chose to ignore Robespierre's underlying ethos, actually heighten this impression, because they stand out so much from the overall picture of a nation thankfully re-embracing a proposal for a code of conduct and belief which, while within the overall ethos of Republicanism, was still firmly based on remembered moral values.

The level of organisation was naturally different between the capital and the provincial areas. In Paris, there was a very high degree of organisation and management of every aspect of the *Fête*. In addition to the obvious necessity of marshalling such a large procession, music and words had to be carefully learned and gestures practised. Everybody's exact positions on the Mountain was defined, right down to such details as when to express shouts of joy, when to smile, when to embrace the children – all were set out. From the reports of the festivities outside Paris, while everything did not always go exactly as planned and there were definitely some heated discussions at municipal council level, there seems to have been, in the main, much less formality in general movement and expression. As in all such celebrations, the very fact that it appeared more spontaneous led to a feeling of closer involvement, which must have been exactly what Robespierre was hoping for.

The conclusion must be that, while considerable ingenuity was exercised in local attempts to follow David's specifications as far as possible, for every provincial city, town, village or hamlet each individual *fête* was a one-off, unique, and with its culture arising directly from its locality. This was true not only of the pageants, banners and slogans but also of the words and music used in each locality. Outside Paris, all these elements were designed and put together by local people, poems were written by local bards and sung to tunes everybody knew, and although they may not have been as structured or as sophisticated as those of Chénier, Desorgues or Lebrun in Paris they all used language with which the majority of their fellow-citizens would be comfortable, even if they were in French rather than in the local patois. Each and every local celebration of the new official national 'religion' showed the benefit of using local input from local people and local cultural resources. Because of this the Festival of the Supreme Being, unlike its predecessors, was transmuted throughout France from the potentially arid performance of an imposed duty into a popular, joyful, participatory, truly national and at the same time truly local celebration.

Notes

1 M. Ozouf, *La Fête Révolutionnaire 1789–1799* (Paris, 1976).
2 M. Vovelle, *1793, La Révolution contre l'Église: de la Raison à l'Être Suprême* (Paris, 1988).
3 *L'Abréviateur Universel*, Issue 535 (1794), p. 2138.
4 The first major twin-site festival, the *Fête de la Réunion* in 1793, had been held only in Paris.
5 See Chapter 5, 'Financing a national festival'.
6 'Encore fallait-il que les décors prévus s'adaptent aux lieux choisis pour la fête ... les Cours et la Place de la Liberté étant loin d'être aussi vastes que le Champ de Mars parisien.' A.M. Nantes, D.2.7–8, quoted in N. Dhombes and A.-C. Déré, *Chroniques de Nantes en l'an II: pour une autre histoire de Nantes sous Carrier* (Nantes, 1993), p. 130.
7 'La raison marche à grands pas contre les trônes', 'La liberté ou la mort', 'Enfants de Mars et de Bellone'. A.M. Angers I.D.5, pp. 84–6.
8 'Nous les élevons pour la Patrie', *Plan de la fête à l'Être suprême, adopté par la commune de St-Omer, pour être exécuté le 20 prairial prochain* (St Omer, n.d.).
9 'Sous le flambeau de l'hymen nous enfanterons des héros pour la Patrie', A.M. Angers I.D.5, p. 86.
10 'Nous leur ferons oublier tous leurs maux', A. Sorel, *La Fête de l'Être Suprême à Compiègne* (Compiègne, 1872).
11 'Nous imiterons Barra et Viala', *Procès-verbal et description de la Fête de l'Être Suprême, Célébrée le 20 prairial, l'an second de la République français, une et indivisible* (Strasbourg, An II).
12 'Nous sçaurons [sic] mourir pour la Patrie', *Ordre de la fête en honneur de l'Être suprême, célébrée le décadi 20 prairial; et discours prononcés à cette occasion sur la montagne élevée au milieu de la place d'armes et au Champ-de-Mars* (Abbeville, An II).
13 'Semez dans nos cœurs la vertu et nous serons dignes de nos travaux civiques', *Commune de Nancy. Ordre de Marche de la fête à l'Être Suprême, qui sera*

célébrée dans la commune de Nancy, le 20 prairial, an2 conformément à la loi du 18 floréal dernier (Nancy, n.d.).

14 'Nous veillons pour toi', Ordre de la fête en honneur de l'Être suprême (Abbeville, An II).

15 'L'homme ment à sa conscience qui méconnoit l'existence de l'Être suprême', Plan de la Fête à l'Être Suprême; Qui sera célébrée à TOURS, le 20 Prairial, en exécution du Décret du 18 Floréal, l'an second de la République, une et indivisible (Tours, n.d.).

16 'Nous surveillons', G. Tison, La Fête de l'Être Suprême à Calais, 20 prairial, an II (Calais, 1924).

17 'Honneur et respect à la Vieillesse', Tison, La Fête de l'Être Suprême à Calais.

18 'En nous endormant au sein de l'Être suprême nous laisserons notre postérité heureuse et libre', Plan de la Fête à l'Être Suprême; Qui sera célébrée à TOURS.

19 'Le plus utile des arts doit être le plus honoré', Tison, La Fête de l'Être Suprême à Calais.

20 'Ô Nature, dans les champs fertiles et sous l'humble chaume le laboureur suit tes aimables lois et publie tes bienfaits', Plan de la Fête à l'Être Suprême; Qui sera célébrée à TOURS.

21 Pierre-Philippe-Antoine Gobet, known as Dorfeuille, was an actor, a friend of Marat and successively attached to the Girondins and Hébertist factions. He was also a friend of Fouché and of Collot d'Herbois who used him on various missions to the provinces. After the transformation of Lyon into Commune-Affranchie, Dorfeuille was made manager of the Saint-Étienne munitions factory.

22 Robespierre's objection to this hymn (see Chapter 3) had obviously not reached Commune-Affranchie, since the original version by Chénier, not the revised version by Desorgues, was sung there.

23 'La Divinité veille sur nous et ne veut que notre félicité', Fête à l'Être Suprême, Célébrée à Commune-Affranchie le 20 prairial, An 2 de la République, Bibliothèque Municipale de Lyon, Fonds Coste 1.C.350978.

24 'Être Suprême! Principe de vie et de bonheur, tes enfants se réunissent en ce jour pour t'honorer.' Fête à l'Être Suprême, Bibliothèque Municipale de Lyon, Fonds Coste 1.C.350978, Fête à l'Être Suprême, Célébrée à Commune-Affranchie le 20 prairial, An 2 de la République, Bibliothèque Municipale de Lyon, Fonds Coste 1.C.350978.

25 'la raison, le justice, la probité, la vertu et la sagesse', Fête à l'Être Suprême, Bibliothèque Municipale de Lyon, Fonds Coste 1.C.350978.

26 B. Bois, Les Fêtes révolutionnaires à Angers de l'an II à l'an VIII (Paris, 1929), pp. 2–4.

27 'la lutte contre le fanatisme et les prêtres de la Vendée n'avait pas éteint dans les âmes l'esprit religieux'. A. Mathiez, 'Robespierre et le culte de l'Être Suprême', Annales Révolutionnaires, 1910, p. 208.

28 'pour terrasser le fanatisme', A.M. Angers 1.D.5, p. 85.

29 A.M. Angers 1.D.5, p. 85.

30 'hymnes, chants, et musique analogues à la fête', A.M. Angers 1.D.5, p. 86.

31 'le reste de la journée s'est passé en douce réjouissance', A.M. Angers 1.D.5, p. 86.
32 D. Schönpflug, *Der Weg in die Terreur. Radikalisierung und Konflikte im Straßburger Jakobinerclub (1790–1795)* (Munich, 2002).
33 The three Members of the Convention for the department of the Bas-Rhin: Rühl, Coutourier and Dentzel.
34 Pierre François Monet, b. Nancy-sur-Cluses 2 June 1769. Studied at the Protestant University of Strasbourg, PhD in 1788, became Regent of the Collège Royal de Strasbourg, practised law but not particularly active in politics. In 1791 joined with his first patron Jean-Charles Laveaux in opposing the then mayor, Dietrich. After Laveaux's expulsion from the city in 1792, he became secretary of the Jacobin Society and the leader of the Francophone Jacobins in the city. In 1792, at the age of twenty-three, he secured the nomination as *procurateur-général-syndic*, replacing his new patron Bentabolke. To obtain the post of Mayor, for which the minimum legal age was twenty-five, Monet drew up and signed a certificate that he was twenty-five years and six months old. He was in fact still only twenty-four years and four months old on his appointment.
35 C. Betzinger, *Vie et mort d'Euloge Schneider, ci-devant franciscain (1756–1794)* (Strasbourg, 1997).
36 One of its most famous Alumni is Goethe.
37 These were members and descendants of the Swiss Guard regiments who had been stationed in the city since 1681.
38 D. Schönpflug, 'Le culte de la raison à Strasbourg: facteurs locaux, nationaux et régionaux', in *Les politiques de la Terreur (1793–1794), Actes du Colloque international de Rouen, Janvier 2008* (Rennes, 2008).
39 Betzinger, *Vie et mort d'Euloge Schneider*.
40 A.M. Strasbourg 1.MW.142, p. 2309.
41 A.M. Strasbourg 1.MW.142, p. 2316.
42 'en leur accordant une quantité de 50 livres de fromage des magasins de la Commune', A.M. Strasbourg 1.MW.142, p. 2409.
43 P.J. Dannbach, *Procès-Verbal et description de la Fête de l'Être Suprême, célébrée le 20 prairial, l'an second de la République française, une et indivisible* (Strasbourg, n.d.), p. 4.
44 Since this was exactly the same as for the *Fête de la Raison*, one wonders whether it had ever been dismantled.
45 After the Revolution he left Paris and became a farmer but still 'dans ses moments de loisir il consacre son talent célèbre à sa patrie'. Dannbach, *Procès-Verbal et description de la Fête de l'Être Suprême*, p. 5.
46 'cœurs sensibles et vertueux', A.M. Strasbourg 1.MW.142, pp. 2472–81.
47 See Chapter 5, 'Financing a national festival'.
48 A.M. Amiens, Archives Révolutionnaires 1.D.10.9, p. 69.
49 'Un moment de silence et de contemplation des beautés de la nature, après un hommage secret et pur dirigé vers le grand Être.' A.M. Amiens, Archives Révolutionnaires 1.I.2/2. Fêtes et Cérémonies Publiques.

50 'un bal public donné au profit des pauvres prolongea la gaîté', A.M. Amiens, Archives Révolutionnaires 1.I.2/2. Fêtes et Cérémonies Publiques.
51 'Un autel immense est élevé à la Nature', *Plan de la Fête à l'Être Suprême, qui sera célébrée à Tours* (Tours, n.d.), p. 6.
52 'Le parfum des fleurs dont l'air est embelli, monte avec la voix du Peuple, vers l'Être Suprême.' *Plan de la Fête à l'Être Suprême*, p. 6.
53 'La cérémonie fut prolongée par une scène religieuse et patriotique, dont les Artistes-Dramatistes veulent faire hommage au peuple et à l'Être Suprême.' *Plan de la Fête à l'Être Suprême*, p. 9.
54 A. Français, *Idée de la fête qui doit être célébrée à Grenoble le 20 prairial, en l'honneur de l'Être Suprême* (Grenoble, n.d.).
55 'Or, Dieu n'étant connu que par ses ouvrages, par les vertus qui émanent de lui, & qui nous y ramènent, tous les simulacres ou symboles par lesquels on voudroit le représenter ou le personnifier, seront sévèrement interdits.' Français, *Idée de la fête*, p. 1.
56 'Le peuple français reconnoît l'existence de Dieu, et l'immortalité de l'âme.' Français, *Idée de la fête*, p. 5.
57 'Tout ce que l'empire de Flore offre de plus frais et de plus gracieux ... une corbeille remplie de fleurs, d'où s'élèvent des colombes, est portée par de jeunes filles, vêtues de blanc. L'amour pudique ... est seul dans cette fête.' Français, *Idée de la fête*, p. 6.
58 Français, *Idée de la fête*, p. 7.
59 'L'orateur invoque Dieu du haut du temple, par l'attribut particulier de chaque groupe.' Français, *Idée de la fête*, p. 8.
60 *Détails de la Fête de l'Être Suprême et de l'immortalité de l'âme célébrée en la Commune de Bailleul, le 20 prairial, de la deuxième année de la République Française, une et indivisible* (Dunkerque, n.d.).
61 'La montagne sauvera la patrie. Elle écrasera le hideux fédéralisme. Elle renversera le monstre de l'athéisme et ses gagés prédicateurs. Pitt, Coburg, et leurs maîtres échoueront contre elle.' *Détails de la Fête de l'Être Suprême et de l'immortalité de l'âme célébrée en la Commune de Bailleul*.
62 Palloy claimed to be a friend of Marat and had managed to make a fortune from the destruction of the Bastille, when he got the contract to demolish it to provide the stonework for the roadbed of the new bridge across the Seine. On completion of the contract, Palloy decamped without paying his workers, and having taken refuge with the *Armée du Nord* only returned to Paris under army protection to denounce Dumouriez. He was imprisoned after Thermidor and released under the Consulate. He managed to survive a series of dubious business ventures but spent his last years in beggary trying unsuccessfully to obtain a pension first from Napoléon then from Louis XVIII. His career is described in the *Dictionnaire des hommes marquants* (London, 1800), amplified by Dauban in *Paris en 1794* (Paris, 1869), pp. 383–5.
63 'Tous les citoyens sont invités de porter leur repas et s'asseoir sans distinction, les uns contre les autres, autant que faire se pourra.' *Détail de la cérémonie qui sera observée le 20 prairial dans la commune de Sceaux l'Unité, jour du repos*

décrété par la Convention nationale, le 18 floréal, le premier jour établi comme fête républicaine consacrée à l'Être suprême et à la Nature Discours civique sur les mœurs et les vertus. Prononcé à la Fête de l'Être Suprême à la commune de Sceaux-l'Unité (Paris, n.d.).

64 Now a dormitory town for Paris, Mennecy in the Essonne was then a small farming village in the department of Seine et Marne.

65 'des habitants de Mennecy ... parurent à la barre de la Convention revêtus de chapes, et déclarèrent qu'ils avaient abjuré la superstition, qu'ils ne voulaient plus de curé', A. Aulard, Histoire politique de la révolution française: origines et développement de la démocratie et de le républiqu 1789–1804 (Paris, 1921), p. 471.

66 La Butte Montbuchet – a local landmark.

67 'il a profané l'autel qui venait d'être consacré à l'Être suprême', P. Blanchot, N. Duchon, A. Foucher and M. Vollant, Mennecy sous la Révolution, ou la révolution de Jean-Michel (La Mée sur Seine, 1989), p. 225.

68 Grivotte was already suspected of anti-revolutionary sympathies, having been a regular supplier of meat to the Garde du Corps of Louis XVI through his patron the recently guillotined local landowner, the Duc de Neufville, Officer of the Corps.

69 Blanchot et al., Mennecy sous la Révolution, p. 226.

70 'J'ay [sic] reçu deux cahiers de musique avec des hymnes patriotiques; mais il n'est pas possible d'en faire usage ici faute d'instrumens de musique et de personnes qui en ayent le talent ou l'usage.' A.N. F.17.1065.5.

71 Archives de la Bibliothèque Municipale de Lyon. Fonds Coste. 1.C.650834.

5

Financing a national festival

Prior to the celebrations of the Festival of the Supreme Being, the question of who was responsible for the finances of a festival was reasonably clear. Since all the great national festivals, from the first *Fête de la Fédération* in 1790 through to the *Fête de la Réunion* in 1793, were essentially celebrations in the capital they were financed by central government through the annual allocation of funds to the Committee of Public Education.[1] Any city which decided to emulate the capital and hold its own festival to coincide with a celebration in Paris did so voluntarily rather than because of any specific instruction from central government. This also meant that there was no obligation on central government to provide funding; any town or city which chose to follow the capital in holding a festival would therefore be wholly responsible for covering its own costs. The decree that the Festival of the Supreme Being was to be held not just in Paris but also in every commune of France immediately raised the question of whether there would be any funding from central sources, and if so, to what extent. The signs were not propitious for communes outside Paris; there was no indication at all in the wording of Robespierre's speech of 18 Floréal of any funding, nor was it referred to in the formal decree and other documents sent out to local administrations. The presumption must have been that, although the Committee of Public Education would be responsible for the expenses of the festivities in Paris, as far as the rest of the nation was concerned, unless funds were to be provided by the regional administration, each commune would be expected to accept the responsibility of arranging its own financing. How they did so, either by raising extra revenue or by recasting their budgets, was left entirely up to them.

The Committee of Public Education was responsible for a vast array of projects, only some of which were directly linked to education; since its formation in October 1791, it had become increasingly involved in the organisation and running of the national republican festivals. This function was formalised and became an official part of its responsibilities under the reorganisation of the Committee by the Convention on 13 October 1792. According to the official record in the *Procès-verbaux du Comité d'Instruction Publique de la Convention Nationale*, edited by Guillaume in 1889, the total budget allocated to the Committee for the period 1793–94 was the staggering amount of 50 million livres.[2] It must however be remembered that this almost unbelievable figure had to cover the whole of the Committee's responsibilities. These covered all aspects of education, including the provision of special schools and workshops for the handicapped, the funding of libraries, museums and tourism, plus the cost of all festivals held in the capital, as well as the salaries and pensions of all persons engaged in these activities, and the construction, maintenance and upkeep of all buildings relating to them. As is clearly demonstrated in the detailed examination of the costs of the *Fête de la Réunion* in 1793, this budget was 'made available' to the Committee, not paid into a specific account from which it could draw at will; each payment from the fund had to be justified to the central administration of the treasury who would then issue the respective *ordonnances de paiement* on the National Bank.

There is surprisingly little detailed information available on the costs of successive Revolutionary Festivals, despite the obvious fact that these were major items of expenditure firstly from the overall national budget in respect of the festivals in 1790 and 1791, then, from 1792 onwards, specifically relative to the budget of the Committee of Public Education. This chapter seeks to discover what the actual costs of the Festival of the Supreme Being were, and how they were met both in Paris and the provinces. There is ample source material available in the national archives for Paris, and in the provinces there is some information available from the departmental and municipal records. There is nevertheless a major problem in that the availability and quality of the financial records necessary to make reasonable estimates of the costs in each individual area varies greatly between the five cities used as examples in the previous chapter. In the examples used in this study, only Paris and Amiens have clear and detailed records available, while the other cities can only offer more general financial records, sometimes with some relatively minor details, but in the main without any data which can be specifically applied to the Festival. Any attempts at estimates of the true costs of the Festival are very much affected by the constraints imposed by this inconsistency in record-keeping.

The worst case is Angers, where, despite the overall records of both the preparations for, and the actual celebrations of 20 Prairial being extensive and readily available, there is an almost total lack of clear financial records, not only those specifically relating to the *Fête*, but also for general municipal financial affairs between 1791 and 1794. The financial records of Bordeaux are also incomplete due to the loss of a considerable part of the archival records of the period through a serious fire in 1862. In Strasbourg, the finances seem to have been under the direct control of the Mayor, Pierre-François Monet, who, judging by the unusual deficiencies in the otherwise well-kept municipal records of the city for the period of Summer 1794, appears to have destroyed much of the information concerning his administration on his flight from the city after Thermidor.

From 1792 onwards, once the Convention had passed a decree proclaiming the celebration of a national festival, the responsibility for its organisation and conduct would automatically fall upon the Committee of Public Education. Under the general direction of its chairman, Jacques-Louis David, it would prepare a detailed plan to be submitted to the Convention with an estimate of the funds needed, and an indication as to how these were to be provided, either from resources already attributed to the Committee or as a special item to be provided from the public purse. In the case of the Festival of the Supreme Being, there is no evidence of any approach either to the Committee of Public Safety or to the Committee of Public Education before Robespierre's speech. This may be due simply to Robespierre and his supporters in the Committee of Public Safety, particularly Saint-Just and Couthon, having little interest in financial problems. Other members of the Committee who could demonstrate some experience of financial administration, such as Carnot, Jeanbon St André, Prieur de la Marne and Prieur de la Côte d'Or, were frequently absent from Paris because of their responsibilities to the armed forces, agriculture or the munitions industry, while Robert Lindet, possibly the most able member of the Committee on financial matters, was often in opposition to Robespierre.

The challenge of funding such a large enterprise as a Revolutionary Festival can almost be seen as a microcosm of the overall financial problems with which the Jacobin administration was constantly beset. By mid-1794, the monetary problem in Revolutionary France had become acute. The control of expenditure, which should have been a function of the Convention and its Committees, was noticeable by its absence, possibly due to the fact that the Convention was still mainly composed of lawyers, the great majority of whom had had little or no exposure to, or even interest in, any form of financial or economic management strategy. In addition, they were deeply suspicious of people such as bankers or financiers who, while they might have offered the necessary knowledge and experience, were considered as automatically anti-revolutionary. By a resolution of 26 Frimaire Year II (16 December 1793), all bankers had been formally excluded from membership of the Jacobin Club.[3] This feeling that the Convention saw itself in some way as above the day-to-day financial problems of the nation was in marked contrast to the reality in the streets. Large and small businesses were being run, as ever, by their owners on solid financial lines and commercial decisions were taken based not on revolutionary zeal but on practicality. An example of this is Madame Tussaud who, when she realised that the public theatre of the Terror was rendering her waxworks show out-of-date before she had time to change her exhibits, made the decision to move to London on economic, rather than political grounds.[4]

In order to understand the cost structure of the Festival of the Supreme Being it is helpful to examine the details of the *Fête de la Réunion* in August 1793, since the design and execution of both events allow a good degree of comparison between them. The festival of August 1793 was originally scheduled to be held on the now official National Day, 14 July. To this end, in June 1793 the Committee of Public Education delegated two of its members, Lakanal and Massieu, to come up with a project for the celebration of the annual *Fête de la Fédération*. Lakanal and Massieu put forward a proposal to combine the annual national festival with a special celebration to mark the birth of the Republic and the official launch of the new Constitution. The festival would be renamed the Festival of the Unity and Indivisibility of the Republic, which also conveniently avoided any now politically unacceptable use of the words Federation or Federalism. As part of the national commitment to the new Republic and its constitution, the regional assembly of each *département* would be invited to nominate two delegates to travel to Paris to attend the festival. There they would join delegates representing the *sections* of Paris, the armed forces and the National Guard in a ceremony swearing formal allegiance to the Republic and to the new Constitution.

This proposal were debated in the Convention on 27 June 1793, but it was decided that since it would be difficult, if not impossible, to make all the necessary arrangements for a festival in July, the date of the festival would be reset as 10 August. The Convention gave the Committee of Public Education three days to present a final detailed proposal for the celebrations. It also decreed that each delegate from outside Paris would receive 6 livres journey money plus a fixed sum of 60 livres to defray the costs of their stay in Paris.[5] Three days proved an impossibly short period but a draft decree was finally presented to the Convention for its consideration on 18 July 1793, in which the Committee proposed that the new festival be called the *Fête de la Réunion* and that a special allocation of 500,000 livres be voted for preliminary expenses.⁶ The Convention passed the matter on to its finance committee, who, remembering the Committee's history of serious under-estimation of the expenses of previous festivals, felt the need for prudence, and on 20 July 1793 issued a decree setting the total budget for the new festival at a maximum of 1.2 million livres.⁷

The costs of the construction of the various pageants at the two chosen sites at the Bastille and the Champ de Mars and of the preparatory groundworks at the latter, now renamed the Champ de la Réunion, are detailed in two documents in the national archives. The first is a letter originally appointing the National Architect, Hubert, to be in charge of the works, in the margin of which he noted the amounts he had paid out and those still outstanding. The second is an extract from the minutes of the meeting of the Committee of Public Education on 17 Ventôse (7 March 1794),⁸ which details the various types of work undertaken, the amounts already paid and those still outstanding. Hubert's personal notes also confirm that the overall costs of the festival had stayed within budget at a total of 950,000 livres.⁹ This account is detailed in Table 3.

Table 3 The costs of the *Fête de la Réunion* held in August 1793

Type of work	Paid			Outstanding		
	L	s	d	L	s	d
Masons	45,265	10	0	28,592	11	9
Scaffolders	83,281	12	0	79,704	2	10
Carpenters	83,579	4	9	42,861	11	10
Ironwork	22,117	15	0	24,355	18	4
Groundworks	240,000	0	0	10,132	0	0
Painters	31,590	0	0	42,226	11	0
Decorators	14,801	16	0	0	0	0
Sculptors	32,042	0	0	8,686	0	0
Unspecified items	74,858	19	0	28,534	7	6
Paid out against receipts	36,804	4	9	200	2	0
Sundry disbursements	4,712	6	0	0	0	0
Office expenses	11,046	15	0	4,750	0	0
Totals as at 17 Ventôse (7 March 1794)	680,100	1	6	270,043	5	3
TOTAL INVOICED	950,143	6	9			
PAID TO DATE	680,100	1	6			
Outstanding	270,043	5	3			
Cash in hand	19,899	18	9			
Shortfall	250,143	6	9			

Source: A.N. AF.II.67.497.8.

As can be seen, by far the largest sum paid out was around 250,000 livres for basic groundworks and site preparation, with further considerable expenses for the wooden scaffolding and general carpentry required to construct the stages on which David would arrange his tableaux. There was also a considerable expenditure on painting and decorating and for the general metalwork needed, such as the provision of various types of fasteners, nails, screws, bolts and the like, as well as the on-site production of brackets, plates, hinges, and other items necessary for the secure fastening of the staging.

The details in the minutes show that the Committee, having received a first tranche of 700,000 livres from the Treasury, now needed to go back to them for the balance, since the final bills had still not been settled eight months after the event. Unlike the documents relating to the Festival of the Supreme Being, there are no copies of letters from contractors requesting final settlement of account, nor was a later set of accounts submitted by Hubert showing further payments. The documents in the Archives do not confirm when these outstanding accounts were finally settled, although it is likely that even if not paid in full, accommodation would have been reached at some point between March and May 1794, since it was largely the same contractors who worked on the construction of the Festival of the Supreme Being in May and June of 1794.

There is one other major item of expenditure missing from the details of these accounts, namely the expenses of the provincial and military delegates to the festival. There are two items headed 'Non-specific Expenditure' and 'Paid out against receipts' in the main account which were under the personal control of Hubert, but these have no details attached. The first of these, which totals some 75,000 livres, might just be substantial enough to cover the travel and subsistence payments for the delegates travelling to Paris from the eighty-six *départements* and from the various units of the army and the National Guard. The other sum for sundries of 36,000 livres would most probably refer to smaller payments made to individual sub-contractors. There is also a separate set of accounts from a Citizen Joly at the Hôtel de Ville in Paris detailing payments made to the various *sections* of Paris for their part in the procession, totalling 12,710 livres, paid in cash on the instruction of Hubert, again presumably included in the general non-specific expenditure.

Even before the finalisation of the accounts for the *Fête de la Réunion*, the Committee of Public Education had been required to brace itself for the rush of festivals which took place in late 1793. These began with Chaumette's *Fête de la Raison* on 10 Frimaire (30 November), followed by a Festival of the Martyrs and ending with a highly elaborate festival in honour of the retaking of Toulon by the Revolutionary armies under their new commander, Dugommier, on 27 Frimaire (17 December). The sums which the Committee of Public Education had originally earmarked from their overall budget seem already to have been exhausted, since on 11 Nivôse (31 December) the Committee of Public Safety placed a further 100,000 livres in the hands of David and of his *atelier* for the construction of 'various machines, chariots, decorations and other objects suitable for all kinds of civic and national festivals'.[10]

The documents in the national archives which relate to the costs of the Festival of the Supreme Being include letters, drafts, accounts, invoices and requests for payment, beginning with Hubert's requests on 14 Prairial (2 June 1794) to the Committee of Public Education for the release of funds for stage payments to the contractors, and stretch out to letters requesting final settlement of long-overdue accounts dated as late as 14 Pluviôse, Year IV (3 February 1796).[11] These documents formed the basis of the analysis by Guillaume in his detailed account of the finances as established by the Committee of Public Education of the amounts paid to the various contractors, artisans and artists.[12] The payment schedules set out by Guillaume show a total cost of 653,475 livres 13 sols 3 deniers (see Table 4).

The figures established from a more complete survey of the detailed files in the archives give a total cost for the Festival of 706,610 livres 13 sols 2 deniers. There are various potential areas of confusion; some accounts appear to have been duplicated, often by appearing more than once in the records of the correspondence, probably as a result of Hubert's continual badgering of the Committee for payment to his contractors. For example, Guillaume shows two payments, each for 300 livres to the sculptor, Michallon, although he only submitted one account for 300 livres, which is marked as paid by Hubert. It would appear that Guillaume drew most of his data from Hubert's major payment sequences in Prairial (June) and

Table 4 Summary of payments made by Fructidor Year II (September 1794)

Sums paid in Prairial	156,937 L 10s 0d
Sums paid in Fructidor	278,984 L 13s 0d
Sums paid for music printing	904 L 8s 0d
Balance still unpaid	216,649 L 2s 3d
TOTAL	**653,475 L 13s 3d**

Fructidor (August) of 1794, but he does not refer to payments made at later dates, as evidenced in the file at the Archives Nationales. There are other areas of confusion, since it is often difficult to establish whether a document relating to payment is simply a confirmation of expense (*ordonnement de dépenses*) issued in advance of final settlement or the actual draft (*titre de paiement*) itself. There also seems to be a difference between Guillaume's assessment of the sums still unpaid after August 1794, and those shown in the individual records studied in the national archives. It is hoped that this present analysis will help to clarify the position.

From the outset, the Committee of Public Education faced a situation in which the already acute practical problems of producing such large-scale works as were envisaged for the Festival on 20 Prairial, within the almost impossible time frame set by Robespierre in his decree, were further exacerbated by financial problems. There appears to be no record of meetings or discussions to show whether David himself had attempted a proper costing, or had asked Hubert, as the architect and engineer responsible, for an estimate of the cost of the civil works needed. In any event, since both of them would have had the accounts of the previous year's *Fête de la Réunion* before them, they may simply have assumed that the costings for the new celebration would be approximately the same.

The matter becomes further confused by the fact that it was the Committee of Public Safety, not the Committee of Public Education, which issued the first decree on funding. On 26 Floréal (15 May) this Committee issued two decrees; the first officially appointed Hubert to be in charge of the festival and specified the main source of funding as being 'funds put at the disposal of the commission'.[13] The use of the word 'commission' instead of committee is confusing, and the confusion gets worse with the second decree which specified that the first tranche of 100,000 livres was to be put at Hubert's disposal immediately, so that the work could be started. Surprisingly, the source of these funds is stated to be the Commission of Public Works – in other words the Public Works department of the city of Paris.[14] It is not clear whether the overall budget was to come from the budget of the Committee of Public Education, as referred to in their statement of 11 Nivôse (31 December) or from the city's budget for public works and, if the latter, when and how it was to provide these 100,000 livres. If the Committee of Public Safety assumed that the money would be drawn from the annual budget already voted for public works, they must have accepted that the Paris City Council would now have to drop or reschedule some other major project. One indication that this may have been their intention is a further decree, issued on the same day, confirming that the Public Works unit would only be allowed to provide labour and materials to refurbish the Théâtre National (the former Comédie Française) for a further two weeks; possibly to make the workforce available for the upcoming festival.[15] What the management committee of the Public Works department thought of this raid on their budget can only be speculated.

Technically, charging Public Works with the task of getting the management of the festival under way before a later transfer of responsibility to the Committee of Public Education is a logical delineation of responsibility, since the first jobs to be done at the Champ de la Réunion would be basic groundworks, well suited to the capabilities of the engineers and workforce of the City Council. Handing over responsibility to the Public Works department did however bring with it another problem; the first part of the festival, at the Jardin National, based around the concept of the double statue, was not so much a civil engineering as an artistic project, and was under the direct control of the craftsmen and artists in David's *atelier*. If any outside contractors were to be used, it would need to be the *atelier* which selected and instructed them, not the engineers of the Public Works department. In this sense, there would be more to gain by having the Committee of Public Education, which was already under David's leadership, responsible for this part of the overall concept.

It is difficult to assess what if any portion of the works was carried out by the Public Works department, since there is no mention of any specific payments to them in the detailed payment schedules. The logical assumption is that they would only be responsible for the preliminary groundworks, that is to say the general preparation of the site at the Champ de la Réunion, so as to make it ready for the specialist contractors to begin the erection of the Mountain. Theoretically, this area should not have needed much work, bearing in mind that the considerable sum of 250,000 livres had been spent the year before on groundwork on this site to enable the two large stages required for the theatrical pageants to be built. The Paris authorities would presumably have swallowed these extra costs as best they could within their existing budget, although there is no clear indication of whether or not they actually held the cost within the figure of 100,000 livres allocated.

Hubert was a highly competent architect and engineer and would have been under no illusions regarding the immense strain that the vast design and construction works detailed in David's instructions would put on him and his colleagues. He would have realised the need for the immediate involvement of outside contractors if he was to have any chance of getting these complex and expensive structures ready in time. He set his contractors to work immediately but before long there were financial problems. Builders and construction companies, whether large concerns or one-man bands, prefer to work under a system of 'stage payments' and although larger contractors, working for a client whom they trust, or who have a certain political or financial clout, might begin a project without an initial payment, it is common practice for a first stage payment to be made to allow for the purchase of materials so that work may begin; then, as the work progresses, the contractor will expect to be paid further sums along the way. The Paris contractors had already suffered in previous festivals from seriously late payment: some were still owed money from the previous year's festival.

By the point between late Floréal and mid-Prairial – the exact date is not clear – when the Committee of Public Education took over full responsibility for the preparations of the *Fête*, the financial situation with the contractors had become acute. By 14 Prairial (2 June) Hubert was under considerable pressure for stage payments from both the artisans and contractors working on the statues at the Jardin National and the construction companies involved with erecting the Mountain. He approached the Committee for an immediate release of funds. The Committee were in no position to accede to his demands since there were no funds voted for this particular Festival in their official budget. Hubert then approached the Committee of Public Safety directly and presented them with a list of accounts which urgently needed settling, to a total value of 272,237 livres 10 sols.[16] The Committee were sympathetic, but, having no funds of their own available for this purpose, took the easy way out by issuing a decree on 15 Prairial (3 June) in which they raided the extra two million livres which had been placed at the disposal of the Committee of Public Education two months before, reserved for 'special projects'.[17] Hubert didn't get all his bills passed, but he did get agreement for the most urgent cases to be paid on 16 Prairial (4 June), which was at least enough to keep his contractors and artisans working. Table 5 shows the payments made by Hubert to his main creditors, according to the documents referred to earlier.

Hubert still had other urgent accounts to meet and managed to get a further 34,930 livres out of the Committee on 22 Prairial (10 June). On 27 Prairial (15 June), a week after the festivities, three more stage payments totalling 33,000 livres were made to companies working at the Champ de la Réunion, so that by the end of Prairial just over a quarter of the final costs had been advanced to the contractors.[18] Payments continued to dribble out throughout 1794, stretching out to a payment to one Monclau, carpenter, for the construction of the official stand for the

Table 5 Stage payments made by Hubert to the major contractors on 16 Prairial (4 June 1794)

For work done at the Jardin National	
Bouillier, scaffolder	14,000 L 0s 0d
Laflèche, carpenter	12,000 L 0s 0d
Aubert, paper-hanger	10,000 L 0s 0d
Peyron, Mathis and Desroches, decorators	7,000 L 0s 0d
Girardin, painter	6,500 L 0s 0d
Total	**49,500 L 0s 0d**
For work done on the Mountain	
Devèze and Rallet, scaffolders	40,000 L 0s 0d
Ajour, mason	20,000 L 0s 0d
Morrisson, metalworker	10,000 L 0s 0d
Brique, Minard and Peigné, groundworkers	4,000 L 0s 0d
Inspectors and other staff	437 L 10s 0d
Total	**74,437 L 10s 0d**

Source: A.N. F.4.2090.

members of the Convention at the Jardin National, whose final bill of 417 livres 8 sols was paid in the new currency, Francs, on 12 Frimaire, Year III (2 December 1794).[19] The final major payments were the settlements of the accounts of the three main contractors at the Champ de la Réunion, who did not get their money until 16 Prairial, Year IV (4 June 1796), two years after the Festival. The very last account to be paid appears to be that of one Citizen Brunet, neither an artisan nor an artist, but a person who submitted an account for 'special services' without defining what these were, nor to whom they had been rendered. On 29 Floréal Year V (18 May 1797), almost three years after the Festival, Brunet wrote to the Minister of the Interior complaining that he had never received his promised draft.[20] His letter is marked 'paid', and Citizen Brunet's total fees of 6,600 livres for these 'special services' are included in the final figures used in this chapter.

The sums included in the dossiers of the national archives in respect of engineering and other works at the Jardin National and the Champ de la Réunion can be seen in Table 6.

If all other fringe accounts are included, the cost of staging the Festival of the Supreme Being in Paris alone finally comes in at around 710,600 livres, nearly 240,000 livres or 13 per cent less than had been spent on the *Fête de la Réunion* the year before. This difference is almost exactly

Table 6 Expenditures for the Jardin National and the Champ de la Réunion

%	Trade or profession	Livres	s	d
36%	Scaffolders	254,756	3	4
16%	Masons and marble masons	110,808	7	6
12%	Painters and paperhangers	84,889	16	3
10%	Carpenters	70,814	7	0
7.5%	Metal workers and boilermakers	52,333	6	1
7%	Artists, sculptors and artisans	48,030	19	6
4%	Groundworkers	30,837	1	9
3%	Management and support	19,392	12	4
2.5%	Miscellaneous suppliers	17,427	7	1
2%	Gardeners, florists, etc.	12,786	12	8
	GRAND TOTAL	702,076	13	6

the sum shown in the accounts for the groundworks at the Champ de la Réunion in 1793, which was of direct benefit to the Festival of the Supreme Being. If this cost element is added to the figures already quoted, the total figure for the 1794 festival would have been very close to the total expenditure for the celebrations in 1793.

It is much more difficult to establish the costs of the Festival in the provincial cities since, with the shining exception of Amiens, no clear detailed accounts are available. The general state of finances outside Paris was one of confusion and in the case of Bordeaux near bankruptcy. By mid-1794, that city did not even have the necessary funds to pay its own employees their salaries and had to apply to the Convention for an immediate subsidy.

When the city fathers in Amiens received instructions from Paris to prepare for the Festival, their first reaction was to enquire optimistically of the Departmental administration whether funds would be made available, and, if not 'the three commissioners … are authorised to meet with the *Société Populaire* and to tell them of the lack of city funds and to invite all good citizens to contribute to the expenses for the festival'.[21] The department refused to provide any monetary aid so at their meeting of 7 Prairial (26 May) the commune decided that 'all citizens will be leafleted with an invitation to contribute to the expenses of the festival of 20 Prairial by making donations to the Commissioners of the *Société Populaire*'.[22]

Most of the five districts of Amiens responded manfully, however the third district clearly felt that they were being squeezed a little too often. Their undated letter to the Council, which opens simply with the word

'Greetings' omitting the normal politeness of 'and Fraternity', is an indication of what some at least of the citizens of Amiens thought of having yet another 'voluntary' subscription thrust upon them. 'The majority of the citizens of our district came to the aid of our refugee brothers in need and contributed the sum of 1303 livres 5s. We believe that since the refugee brothers in question refused that offer, the monies should be applied to the expenses of the Festival of the Supreme Being: we believe that these remarks should be taken into consideration since it is only just that the Citizens of our district should not pay twice.'[23] The 'refugee brothers' referred to were those displaced from the area of French Flanders re-occupied by the Austrians, together with wounded French soldiers, and several hundred Flemish prisoners from the Imperial armies, all of whom had been dumped on Amiens by the provincial government. Amiens was supplied with the absolute minimum funding for their maintenance, with the result that these refugees were living in abject squalor in unsuitable locations in and around the city, some in former religious houses and some in unused penitentiary establishments.

There are three specific documents regarding the subscription income and the costings of the *Fête* in Amiens, the main one being an undated but very detailed account submitted by the city treasurer, Pierre-Louis Duclos, which shows an income of 4,771 livres 16 sols 6 deniers against a total expenditure of 3,773 livres 14s 6d, with a profit of 998 livres 2s. On 8 Messidor (26 June), the City Engineer, Rousseau, submitted revised figures which show a final total expenditure of 4,247 livres 3s 6d, and on 11 Messidor (29 June) a final set of handwritten accounts were formally signed off by the three Commissioners and the City Engineer, and submitted to the Council. These accounts show a total expenditure of 4,243 livres 3s 6d plus two unspecified sums yet to be finalised; the cost of the provision of twenty-six bottles of cider for the fiddlers (*les ménestrels*), and of two carriages to take them home. One can only presume that these musicians would have finished the day tired but happy. It should be noted that, in the original decision to fund the celebrations by public subscription, it was resolved that any monies left over after the payment of the accounts of the *Fête* were to be donated to the Poor Fund. Regrettably, there is no indication in the minutes of the Council up to the end of 1794 of any money having been transferred to this noble cause.

Although the celebrations in Amiens were extensive, the total cost was relatively low compared to some other cities, principally due to them having discounted those aspects of David's instructions which struck the members of the City Council as either too difficult or too expensive. Amiens is a clear example of how a provincial city could hold a large and, by normal standards, ornate festival, while carefully controlling the total expenditure. Other provincial cities, such as Nantes, Nancy and Blois all had festivities very similar to those of Amiens with large and highly organised processions in accordance with David's instructions. The difference in final cost in every case would have been a simple question as to whether or not such large structures as David had specified for Paris were considered either appropriate or feasible by the municipality concerned.

There are almost no references anywhere in the records available at either the Municipal Archives of Angers, or the Departmental Archives of Maine-et-Loire, either of the total amount spent on the festival in Angers, or how such funds were provided and from what source. One problem is that, although the records of the Council meetings of Angers for the period covering the *Fête* are extensive and available, the financial records are not. It must be accepted that Angers was still, to some extent, on a war footing, and while this may not be the only, or even the true cause, what is evident is that the general financial record-keeping of the city of Angers left much to be desired. This lack of information does not only refer to the *Fête* but is also true of other financial matters, such as payments to employees, general costs, etc., which one would expect to find in the municipal registers. This state of affairs was obviously ongoing: the Administrators of Maine-et-Loire complained in a letter sent to all communes in the *département*, including Angers, on 19 Fructidor, Year III (5 September 1795) that they still did not have any accounts at all for 1791, 1792 or 1793.[24] In fact, by 1794, the finances of the entire *département* were in a parlous state, largely due to shortfalls in the collection of taxes. The situation in Angers itself was particularly serious, as evidenced by a *Bordereau* of April 1795, referring to the finances of the city for the years 1793–94 which shows a shortfall of nearly 60 per cent of the projected income over the two years (see Table 7).

When the municipal council of Angers was officially informed of the decree of 19 Floréal by the *Agent National* Fillon, at its meeting on

Table 7 Shortfall in real against estimated income for the city of Angers, 1793–94

	Land taxes (Livres)		Property taxes (Livres)	
	1793	1794	1793	1794
Sums due as per the Rolls	979,460	734,596	310,655	146,995
Sums actually received	498,140	99,572	231,033	72,351
Shortfall	481,320	635,024	79,622	74,644

4 Prairial, although arrangements were put in hand both for the change of inscription on the façade of the cathedral and for the celebrations of 20 Prairial, there is no record of any discussions or decisions regarding budgets or costs regarding the festival in the municipal registers of Angers for the period. With no record of any special funding being voted or a subscription fund being set up, the presumption must be that the whole charge was incorporated in the general municipal budget, but without any concrete information the costs of the festival in Angers can only be the subject of speculation. The actual mechanics of the occasion, as described in Chapter 4, show that, as in Amiens, no special structures were built, and the memorial pillar intended as a permanent commemoration of the event in the Mail was never erected. The fact that the major speeches and ceremonial were held inside the newly christened Temple of the Supreme Being would also have kept the costs down. It would not be unreasonable to assume, therefore, that the costs would be slightly in excess of those noted for Amiens, probably somewhere between 5,000 and 7,000 livres.

Since a considerable part of the Municipal Archives of the city of Bordeaux for the Revolutionary period suffered very serious damage in a fire in 1862, many of the original registers of meetings of the City Council for the period from early Floréal to Messidor and from late Messidor to Fructidor (May to September 1794)[25] only exist as damaged remnants. Other documents, although still officially present in the archives, have more recently suffered severe water damage and it is possible that documentation on the finances of the Festival is in those records which are no longer available for consultation.

By the end of 1793, because of the almost complete lack of control in the municipal treasurer's department, the financial situation in Bordeaux was giving rise to serious anxiety. In April 1794 a new municipal treasurer, Grignon, was appointed, and on 23 Floréal (12 May) he wrote to the Municipal Council stating that he could not issue a formal report on the state of the finances, as there were documents missing, misfiled or not entered, a situation which he strongly hinted to have been due to the deliberate actions of his predecessor. Because of this, he did not expect to be in a position to report on the 1793 accounts until much later in the year and in the interim he persuaded the Council to pass an immediate ordinance tightening up procedures in the Financial Office so he could at least stop any further malfeasance.[26] He finally submitted his preliminary report a month later in July. It must have made very disturbing reading, since the Council published an account of it in the *Journal du Club National de Bordeaux*, on 28 Messidor (16 July 1794) in which they blamed the deficiencies on the deliberate actions of those previously involved in the control of the city finances.[27]

Grignon wrote again to the Council on 5 Thermidor (23 July) stating that there were still vital documents missing and when he finally presented the accounts on 7 Thermidor (25 July), they showed a situation similar to that in Angers and other cities, where the anticipated municipal income had fallen disastrously because of the complete collapse of the system of land and property taxes on which the city finances were based. In Bordeaux, the actual income had fallen from over 10 million livres in 1793 to 3 million livres by mid-1794. Things were so bad that, on 6 Fructidor (23 August), Grignon advised the Council to contact Jullien, the *Représentant en Mission*, and seek his urgent help in approaching Paris for an immediate injection of funds, as the city was now effectively bankrupt.

As can be imagined, the accounts of the Festival were a minor item compared to the seriousness of the overall situation, but the set of accounts prepared by Grignon for submission to Paris does show an item for 'unspecified expenses, roughly estimated at 233,400 livres'.[28] This is a very significant sum for unspecified matters and might well have included the accounts for the Festival. There is only one account in the documents which is clearly for the Festival, a payment to a contractor, Baty, for 2,000 livres for wooden scaffolding, presumably for the Mountain at the Champ de Mars.[29] Assuming this is a normal stage payment, it may be presumed that the contractor's total account would be at least double that figure. On the basis of the charges seen in other areas, an expenditure of this size on the Mountain and the fact that the celebrations in Bordeaux were not huge since, of all the structures specified by David, only the Mountain was built, it would seem reasonable to assume that the overall costs would be higher than those in Angers, probably around the 15,000 livres mark. On 24 Nivôse (17 January 1795) Bordeaux was bailed out with an injection of 300,000 livres from central government to cover urgent salary payments.[30]

In Lyons, the chief expense of the public works department of the city during early 1794 was for the continuation of the demolition of those parts of the old walls which had suffered major damage during the siege, and for the reconstruction of buildings in these areas. There are many mentions of different sums being voted to the city engineer's department in the records, but there is no clear indication whether such sums were solely for this work or whether part was used for the preparations for the Festival on 20 Prairial. It is reasonable to assume that the same work gangs would be used for the civil works for the Festival as were employed in the ongoing major reconstruction works. For example, when the council meeting of 9 Prairial (28 May) had heard and approved the official *Plan pour la fête* submitted by the *Agent National*,[31] this was immediately followed by a request from Dulot, the city engineer, for an extra 250,000 livres 'to make payments to workers employed in demolition'. As has been seen in the discussion of the festival in Lyons in Chapter 5, Dulot had to build a considerable structure on the Place Égalité, including a double statue as in Paris.

From the council registers it would seem that no special sums were voted for the Festival, just as no special sums had been voted for earlier celebrations, so it must be assumed that it was the practice in Lyons to englobe all such celebrations within the overall municipal budget. There are equally no specific details of accounts paid, with one exception: the cost of the musicians. On 23 Prairial (11 June 1794), the Council agreed to pay a special levy of 1,434 livres 10s to the city musical director, Richter, for the musical costs of the Festival.[32] At least the great statue of Hercules wielding his club, flanked by the figure of Liberty and Equality in place of the altar in the Cathedral, which had already been installed for the *Fête de la Raison*, would not have been charged to this *fête*. The main charge would be the very considerable structure at the Place Égalité. This can be conveniently compared to the works at the Jardin National in Paris, which would assume a sum of between 150,000 and 200,000 livres as a reasonable assessment of the cost of this element of the Festival. However, since, unlike Paris, there was only one centre of celebration, the total further cost, allowing for the procession, bunting, signboards, bouquets and general expenses can reasonably be assumed to be around 50,000 livres, giving an overall maximum estimated figure of 250,000 livres. Compared to what can be assessed of the expenditure of other major cities such as Bordeaux and Strasbourg, this is a very considerable sum, even bearing in mind the political imperative under which the council of the newly named *Commune-Affranchie* might feel it incumbent on them to demonstrate solidarity with Robespierre and the central Jacobin government.

The documentation of the costs and funding of the Festival in Strasbourg is also very patchy and while there are tantalising references in the official records of the meetings of the City Council to discussions of finances and decisions being taken, these lack sufficient detail to enable cross-referencing with other documents. The city accounts for the period are also muddied by other factors, some directly relating to the behaviour of the Mayor, Monet. Firstly, like Jullien in Bordeaux, he decided to hold another large civic festival on 12 Prairial, just eight days before the due date of the Festival of the Supreme Being, so a large proportion of the cost of decorating the streets and the cathedral would have been taken up by the budget of that festival. In addition, in Strasbourg the main parts of the celebrations were held not in the open air but inside the cathedral, now surmounted by a huge Phrygian bonnet, within which there was already a small Mountain carrying an altar of the Nation.

There are no detailed accounts for either festival in the municipal registers, according to which the Mayor and the City Engineer were deputed on 6 Prairial (25 May 1794) to 'make all the necessary arrangements' for both celebrations.[33] The only specific accounts found for the Festival of the Supreme Being, which total 18,002 livres 10s, show only relatively minor sums for construction work. The largest item is 3,000 livres for printing, followed by 2,992 livres for Burger, described as a tinsmith, for 'Republican decorations in the temple' and 1,484 livres to Froidevaux, a carpenter, presumably for construction work carried out within the Temple. It is noticeable that the second largest single account is for 2,383 livres paid to the Police 'for the maintenance of public order'. There is also an item shown as 'general expenses' for 1,377 livres.

There must have been other expenses, but if these were entirely the province of the Mayor and the City Engineer, it is not surprising that the records are faulty, since Monet left Strasbourg hurriedly shortly after the news of Robespierre's fall in Thermidor reached the city, and it is reasonable to assume that he deliberately destroyed documents relating to his time as mayor. On the assumption that any other costs were incorporated into the Mayor's personal budget, and having regard to the re-use of the decorations from the festival held on 12 Prairial, it is reasonable to assume a total cost of between 40,000 and 50,000 livres, placing the costs in Strasbourg nearer those of Bordeaux than those of Lyons.

The really difficult question is: what was the real cost of the *Fête* in terms of monetary values, and how can we convert these almost mythic figures into meaningful sums? By mid-1794 the monetary problem in Revolutionary France had become acute, with a severe shortage of real coinage, *monnaie de metal*. Government promissory notes and the new Assignats were totally unacceptable to foreign suppliers of foodstuffs, ores, metals, and other essential raw materials, who would only accept payment on shipment and in hard coinage, so any 'real' money had to be reserved for the payments of these items.[34] Theoretically this was not a problem as far as the Festival was concerned; any funds provided by a government agency or municipality would be in 'internal' money to be used to pay suppliers of goods and services within the country only, and these would inevitably be made available in promissory notes, Drafts or Mandates or, if cash was requested, payment would be in Assignats.

The problem is how to establish a real value for these figures. The original idea of printing Assignats to solve the financial problems of successive Revolutionary governments proved to be even more dangerous and impractical than Dupont de Nemours had warned it would be. Despite this it became the settled policy of successive administrations. In February 1793 the Convention was persuaded to print a further 800 million livres worth of Assignats with face values ranging from 10 sols up to 400 livres, and with a reserve power to print more, up to a total value of 3,100 million livres if necessary.

One possible method would be to compare the costs of the *Fête* with produce and service prices as fixed by the Maximum. The original Maximum set in September 1793 was intended to fix the prices of thirty-eight nominated products and of daily wages nationally, based on values to be fixed by each district, of which there were between three and nine in each *département*. This meant that each district in each *département* was effectively able to nominate the levels of the Maximum in its own area to suit its own local commerce, which naturally led to considerable differences across the country. For example, a *département* in the North, like the Somme, would keep the price of potatoes and hard fruit such as apples low and the price of imported produce from the South like citrus fruit, maize or olive oil high, while the reverse would be the case in a *département* in Provence. In November 1793 the Convention modified the law to set up the Second General Maximum which was to be based on the 1790 prices from each *département* for nominated products, plus a fixed increase of one-third. This complete list, the General Table of the Maximum, was presented to the Convention on 4 Ventôse Year II (22 February 1794) and sent out to all districts[35] with instructions as to how to calculate the 'right' selling price for all articles.[36] It never worked properly and the law was finally abrogated in Frimaire, Year III (November 1794).

If this comparison is to be viable, it is important to get as reasonably accurate an evaluation as possible. It is difficult to use standard prices for general produce, because of the wide differences between areas, but some idea can be gained by comparing the price of such basics as beef, pork and *vin ordinaire* in Paris and four of the five cities discussed in this chapter (see Table 8).

The figures for Angers are unavailable, as the Maine-et-Loire was one of those *départements* which never submitted a detailed Maximum listing.

A more accurate method might be to look at the rates of pay for skilled workers, particularly in those trades concerned with the construction and decoration of the festival sites. Although these figures are not available for the provincial areas, there are documents in the national archives

Table 8 Official commodity prices established by the Law of Maximum 4 Ventôse Year II (22 February 1794)

City	Beef	Pork	Vin ordinaire
	Price per pound weight		Price per pin[a]
Amiens	19s 0d	14s 9d	14s 0d[b]
Bordeaux	13s 5d	13s 2d	6s 0d[c]
Commune-Affranchie	10s 8d	10s 8d	7s 10d[d]
Paris	15s 4d	10s11d	9s 3d[e]
Strasbourg	12s 8d	12s 0d	4s 0d[f]

[a] Pinte de Paris as common measure.
[b] A.N. F.12.1544.47. Département de la Somme.
[c] A.N. F.12.1544.2. Département de la Gironde.
[d] A.N. F.12.1544.36. Département du Rhône.
[e] A.N. F.12.1544.30. Commune de Paris.
[f] A.N. F.12.1544.36. Département du Bas-Rhin.

which give not only the official daily rates of pay for labourers and tradesmen in Paris, as set out as part of the Declaration of the Maximum by the City Council, but, more importantly, show the real rates actually paid to these workers. From this source it can be seen that a skilled scaffolder or carpenter got a premium of 58 per cent over the official rate, a journeyman mason 45 per cent and a blacksmith or tinsmith 25 per cent.[37] This not only gives the true rates paid, it also confirms the severe shortage of skilled workers in the Paris area. Therefore, evaluating the costs of the Festival in Paris based on a common mean instead of the 'official' figures, using the 'real' figure of 6 livres per day of eight hours for a skilled journeyman mason as the basis, means that the total cost of the festival, estimated at 706,610 livres, is equivalent to nearly 118,000 man/days of skilled labour. The comparative rates of pay between specialist tradesmen (journeymen) in Paris and London, using comparative statistics from Hunt,[38] Bowley[39] and Gilboy,[40] gives us the day rates shown in Table 9.

Using this analysis, if the costs of the Festival in Paris can be estimated at some 118,000 man/days of a journeyman mason, the equivalent figure, using the London wage rates for the same period, indicates that the comparative cost of the Festival in Paris expressed in sterling comes out at just under £15,000 – a large but not incredible sum. These day-rates for building trades operatives in Paris also show that as a direct comparison of wage rates the purchasing power of a livre in Paris was equivalent to no more than 8–10 pence in London.

Table 9 Comparative rates of pay between specialist tradesmen (journeymen) in Paris and London

	Paris	London
Mason	6 L 0s 0d	£0 2s 6d
Carpenter	5 L 0s 0d	£0 3s 6d
Smith	6 L 10s 0d	£0 4s 0d

The comparison of contemporary equivalent costs is borne out by the comparative values of the livre as a tradable currency. By August 1793, the trading value of the French currency had fallen to rock-bottom. In early 1784, after Turgot's reforms, Bills of Exchange, based on the Écu of 3 livres which was the standard denomination of exchange, had been trading in London at around 30 pence sterling per Écu.[41] By 1793 the Écu was trading at 8¼ pence,[42] which would give the sterling equivalent as £10,885. These figures are much more in keeping with reality than would be the use of the official value of the livre as set out by the Convention. The decision of the Convention on 17 Vendémiaire (8 October 1793) to close the French frontiers to English trade and Robespierre's intervention the next day to seize all English assets in France effectively left France with the free Swiss exchange in Basel as the sole possible trading place for French paper money. The decree of the Committee of Public Safety of 21 Pluviôse (9 February 1794)[43] that the trading value of the Écu would be officially set at the 1784 rate of 30 pence sterling bore no relation to reality. By Prairial, the notional free market rate for French Bills of Exchange – if anyone could be found to trade in them – was still around 8 pence sterling per Écu. Using the 30 pence rate, the sterling costs of the Festival in Paris come out at the totally improbable sum of around £29,200, against around £10,600 at the 8 pence rate. The fact that by Prairial Year II there was effectively no-one trading in French currency or Bills of Exchange, even on the Basel market, makes this comparison impractical as a method of estimating real costs.

Each of the suggested methods of estimating the real cost of the Festival in Paris has its own problems but the comparison with day wages seems to be the method which has the most practical use, since it is specific to the area under consideration and, more importantly, the documents available give the true rates at which tradesmen working in Paris at the time of the *Fête* were being paid, rather than the misleading official Maximum figures.

In conclusion, this chapter has attempted to evaluate the costs of the Festival in specified areas, which showed a wide range of costs varying from over 700,000 livres in Paris to an estimated average of 5,000 livres for provincial cities such as Amiens. The difference between the costs in Paris and in the various provincial centres was always to be expected, since the spectacle in Paris was inevitably going to outstrip anything the provinces either could or would offer. The costs of the Festival in the provinces, as evidenced by the five cities which have been examined, underline the considerable differences in the type and scale of festival between cities which were demonstrated in Chapter 4. Those areas like Lyons, which felt it necessary to demonstrate their attachment to central government, put on an expensive and costly show. In the middle were the more reasonable administrations of a cautious nature who, with careful budgeting, had a great day for relatively little outlay; some, as was the case in Bordeaux, did the best they could within severe financial constraints. Of the examples cited, only Amiens managed to hold an effective Festival without reaching into the municipal budget, though wider research may well turn up other towns which took the same prudent approach.

It is unreasonable to even attempt to evaluate, still less accurately estimate, the total costs nationally; the spread is so wide that any attempt to strike a mean can only be speculative. Still, assuming Strasbourg and Bordeaux as the norms for the bigger cities and Amiens as a reasonable template for the smaller cities and larger towns, such as Tours, Grenoble and others discussed in the previous chapter, it is possible to make a rough assessment of the average costs of the Festival throughout France. Disregarding the cost of over 700,000 livres in Paris, which was always going to be a special case, and the other abnormally high cost in Lyons of some 250,000–300,000 livres, it may be assumed that the probable average figures for the major cities would fall somewhere between 20,000 and 30,000 livres, while for the minor cities and large towns it would be of the order of 5,000–8,000 livres. How much, or rather how little, a village might have spent is impossible to estimate.

Notes

1 For more details of the various responsibilities of the Comité de l'Instruction Publique see B. Baczko, *Une éducation pour la démocratie: textes et projets de l'époque révolutionnaire* (Paris, 2000).
2 C.I.P., Vol. 2, p. 77.
3 Robespierre, *Œuvres*, Vol. 10, p. 259.
4 See P. Pilbeam, *Madame Tussaud and the History of Waxworks* (London, 2002).
5 C.I.P., Vol. 2, p. 77.
6 C.I.P., Vol. 2, p. 79.
7 A.P., Vol. 17, p. 27.

8 *Comptes pour la Fête de la Réunion*, C.I.P Registre de Délibérations 17 Ventôse, An II / Fête de la Réunion – Résumé de Comptes.
9 Hubert's own notes in the margin of the letter appointing him give a total of 949,943 livres 14s 7d.
10 'diverses machines, chars, décorations et autres objets propres à toute sorte de fête civique et nationale'. A.N. AF.II.67.497.3.
11 A.N. F.4.2090. Fêtes Nationales.
12 C.I.P., Vol. 4, pp. 591–3.
13 'Le citoyen Hubert dirigera l'exécution de cette fête et la dépense sera portée et payée sur les fonds mis à la disposition de la commission comme toutes les autres dépenses publiques dont elle est chargée.' A.N. AF.II.67.497.8.
14 'Le Comité de salut public arrête que la Commission de Travaux publics fera remettre au Citoyen Hubert la somme de Cent Mille Livres pour commencer à faire exécuter les chars, bannières, et tous les instrumens [sic] nécessaires aux fêtes nationales qui seront disposés dans un magasin que le Citoyen Hubert indiquera. Cette somme sera prise sur les fonds mis à la disposition de ladite Commission et le Citoyen Hubert lui rendra compte de son emploi.' A.N. AF.II.67.497.9.
15 'Le Comité de salut public arrête que le Citoyen Hubert chargé de la direction des travaux du Théâtre National, Rue de la Loi, pourra mettre en réquisition pour deux décades seulement les ouvriers et les matériaux nécessaires à la conclusion de ces travaux.' A.N. AF.II.67.493.48.
16 A.N. F.4.2090.
17 These included Grégoire's national linguistic census and Lakanal's educational projects.
18 A.N. F.4.2090.
19 As the exchange rate from Livres to Francs had been fixed including the devaluation of the Assignat, he lost over 20 per cent on the deal.
20 A.N. F.4.2090.
21 A.M. Amiens, Archives Révolutionnaires 1.D.10.9, pp. 65–6.
22 A.M. Amiens, Archives Révolutionnaires 1.D.10.9, pp. 65–6.
23 'la majeure partie des Citoyens de notre arrondissement sont venus au secours de nos frères indigents réfugiés et y ont contribué pour la somme de 1303# 5s. Nous croyons que, les réfugiés ayant généreusement refusé ces secours, ils pourraient être appliqués aux frais de la Fête à l'Être Suprême: nous estimons que notre observation doit être d'autant mieux prise en considération qu'il est de toute justice que les Citoyens de notre arrondissement ne payassent pas deux contributions.' A.M. Amiens, Archives Révolutionnaires. 1.I.2/2.
24 A.D. Maine-et-Loire 1.L.522.
25 A.M. Bordeaux D.108, 109, 111, 112.
26 A.M. Bordeaux L.5.18.
27 *Journal du Club National de Bordeaux*, Issue 5, pp. 1–2.
28 A.M. Bordeaux L.5.30.
29 A.M. Bordeaux L.5.32.
30 A.M. Bordeaux L.6.13.

31 A.M. Lyon 1295.WP.12, p. 156.
32 A.M. Lyon 1217.WP.7, p. 52.
33 A.M. Strasbourg 1.MW.142, p. 2309.
34 By 1794 the grain suppliers, especially the Moroccan and Algerian shippers, were refusing to accept payment other than by cash in hard coin in sacks on the dockside, before the grain ships left their home port.
35 There are two copies in the Archives Nationales. AD.XI.75 and AD.XVIII.C.315.
36 This was to be the import or production cost of 1790, plus 33 per cent, with the addition of transport costs and wholesale and retail profit margins of 15 per cent.
37 A.N. AE.II.3063, AD.XI.75.99 and F.12.1544.31.
38 E.H. Hunt, 'Industrialization and regional inequality – wages in Britain 1760–1914', *Journal of Economic History*, 66 (1986): 935–66.
39 A.L. Bowley, *Wages in the United Kingdom in the 19th Century* (Cambridge, 1900), sections 11 & 12 'Wages in the Building Trades'.
40 E.W. Gilboy, *Wages in 18th Century England* (Cambridge, 1934).
41 J. Bouchary, *Le marché des changes à Paris à la fin du 18ième siècle (1778–1800)* (Paris, 1938), pp. 161–2. All transactions were in nominal Écus, standardised as 1 Écu = 3 Livres.
42 Bouchary, *Le marché des changes*, pp. 161–2.
43 *Recueil des Actes du Comité de Salut Public*, Aulard et al., eds (Paris, 1895), Vol. 2, p. 5.

6

Contemporary comments on the Festival

Any attempt to evaluate the genuine reaction of the people of France to the celebrations of 20 Prairial must rely on an evaluation of the evidence provided by contemporary reports and commentaries, for which there are varying sources. Some of these are official versions of the proceedings at an individual local festival, normally submitted by the local administration, while others are more personal accounts, written by people who were present at the celebrations of the Festival, either in Paris or in the provinces. These documents are vital in any attempt to gain a real understanding of what really happened throughout France during the celebrations of 20 Prairial. More importantly, they are the only real indication of the effect the *Fête* had on the nation as a whole.

The majority of those who published some form of personal history or *mémoire* of the Revolution claim to have been present at the main event in Paris. Most of them, like Mercier and Baudot, concentrate on the political aspects of the event; we have Baudot to thank for the most detailed account of the imprecations hurled at Robespierre during the procession.[1] Some of the more interesting memorials are from observers who comment not only on the political, but also on the social and cultural dimension. These personal recollections of the *Fête*, whether written immediately after the event, or as part of more reflective *mémoires* published many years later, are of considerable value in trying to assess the true response of the nation to Robespierre's unexpected proposition, since they also often demonstrate the differences between the way that the political classes and the general public approached the celebrations of 20 Prairial.

There is always the problem of what credence to give to accounts published by political figures writing after the events of Thermidor. One of the major problems with the accounts of eyewitnesses, even those which were accepted and widely used by later nineteenth century historians such as Michelet or Quinet as evidential data, is that they all had specific political fish to fry, and one must be constantly aware of the problems inherent in their political and personal bias. Some of the more determined atheists among the revolutionaries understandably found the basic idea of a cult dedicated to a 'Supreme Being' rather than the more 'republican' idea of Reason very difficult to accept. Nevertheless others, like Maréchal, conceded the need for the renewal of a national morality system, and, in that context, accepted the idea of the Supreme Being as being both revolutionary and republican. For many of the political classes, the close association of the Festival with its prime mover, Robespierre, was also linked to their fears that he would use the occasion to make his bid for absolute personal power and declare himself dictator. This certainly affected the views of such figures as Vilate and Lecointre, whose accounts of the *Fête*, written after Thermidor, were designed less as an evaluation of the events of 20 Prairial than as an opportunity to vilify Robespierre and whiten their own roles.

Whether the authors of these commentaries approach the matter from a political or a non-political basis, the detail they offer has to be treated with considerable caution. Even if their claim to have been present at the event itself is accepted, it is the accuracy, or more precisely the integrity, of their recollection which may be questionable. To help us get an acceptable overview of the effect of events in Paris, there are various accounts which merit consideration. Some are from political figures like Joachim Vilate, Sylvain Maréchal and Boissy d'Anglas, but by far the most reliable direct record of the proceedings in Paris is that written by two individuals from the Guillaume Tell area in Paris, Citizens Bontemps and Barry, who give a detailed account of the festival from the point of view of two people who were themselves actually marching in the procession. As a counterweight to the accounts of those involved as official participants, we have the commentaries of Ruault, Nodier and Fiévée, all of whom claim to have been non-participatory spectators.

This body of evidence can conveniently be divided into three categories. The first consists of reports from official bodies from communes all over France, such as a municipal council, an organising committee or a local *Société Populaire*. These were intended both for publication and distribution in their local area, but also importantly for dispatch to Paris, as an official confirmation that the orders set out in the decree of

19 Floréal had been followed. These reports set out how the Festival was celebrated in a particular area, with specific details of the processions, the speeches, and the hymns and prayers offered in honour of the Supreme Being. Despite being couched in the stiff formalised language commonly used for official reports, such documents do offer some guidance to the reaction of local people.

The second category covers reports in both the Parisian and provincial press. In most cases, the Parisian press contented themselves with reprinting a version of the official handouts similar to those they had already published in the days preceding the Festival. Comments of a more general or critical nature are extremely rare. A few of the provincial press published reports on the Festival in their own area, but the majority published extensive commentary on the events in Paris; again it is extremely difficult to find any critical comment on either the local celebrations or those reported from Paris. The final, and more interesting category, is the recorded memories of individuals who were present at the Festival, usually in Paris; regrettably there are very few commentaries available from people who were present at one of the celebrations outside the capital.

What is immediately striking is that there are two aspects of the celebration of the Festival throughout France which are common to all contemporary accounts, whether official or unofficial. The first is that the weather was perfect for the great occasion; every account reports on this aspect of the great day, usually tying it in with the happy idea that the Supreme Being was smiling down on a France preparing to honour Him as the Creator of Nature and protector of the Republic. The second is the clear impression that the general ambiance both in Paris and the provinces was one of joy and spontaneity. Even those contemporary commentators who had no love for Robespierre, and who saw the Festival purely as part of his drive to become dictator of France, agree with the general comments that this was the overriding feeling in the celebrations both in Paris and in the provinces. This seems also to be true both for those members of the public chosen to take an active part in the celebrations and for the great mass of the population as well.

It is also clear that there was a widespread expectation that the Festival would be the signal for some great announcement which would mark the end of the first stage of the Revolution, and the transition to the Republic of Virtue. Several commentators specifically refer to this feeling of euphoria, heightened in Paris by the temporary dismantling and removal of the guillotine from the Place de la Révolution. As Michelet put it, 'Everyone thought this was final.'[2] This general expectation of a happy transition to more ordered and quieter times was not only true of Paris; an examination of the reports on the Festival coming in to the Convention and its committees from every part of France demonstrates the same general feeling of hope. All these reports, from the great cities down to the smallest hamlets, stress that throughout France the people were not only following instructions from the Convention when they were asked to smile during the celebrations, they were doing so spontaneously and joyfully.

Curiously, there is actually no official report of the proceedings in Paris. The members returned to the Convention building after the Festival on 20 Prairial, but soon dispersed; although this was officially a meeting of the Convention, it was not one which could pass any laws or resolutions, since the public galleries were closed. The Convention met again as usual on the next day, 21 Prairial (9 June), under the presidency of Robespierre. The first to speak was one of Robespierre's supporters, Eugène Gossuin,[3] who proposed that a full report on the previous day's Festival be inserted into the minutes and printed and distributed nationally as though the Festival itself were an official meeting of the Convention. 'I ask today that the report on yesterday's sitting, for it was a sitting, and one of the most impressive that the Convention has held, be sent to all *départements*, districts, municipalities, *Sociétés Populaires* and to the army, and that this report include the details of the Festival, the speeches by the President and the most important events which took place in this majestic ceremony.'[4] According to the minutes, this was agreed, but before any action could be taken there were other, less positive comments. One of Robespierre's opponents, Pierre Pocholle,[5] while agreeing that a report should be printed, took serious exception to the signboards at the Champ de la Réunion, 'as for the slogans on the various faces of the mountain of liberty, many colleagues have noticed with me that they are not suitable for the subject and they could give a false idea of the Supreme Being, one other than that which we should have. I insist that all slogans relating to the Festival of the Eternal be submitted to examination by the Committee of Public Education before their incorporation in the official report.'[6]

Pocholle was supported by several more of Robespierre's opponents, notably Thirion[7] and Ruamps.[8] The formal report was laid aside, and neither incorporated in the minutes, nor printed and distributed nationally as originally voted by the Convention. The result is that the only official mention in the parliamentary records is the text of Robespierre's three speeches, two at the Jardin National and one at the Champ de la Réunion. However, according to the *Gazette Nationale*, Vaud, the spokesman for the *Commission des dépêches*, commented later in the same session on the continuous arrival of congratulatory letters dispatched from the provinces before the Festival: 'It is a spectacle worthy of universal notice and of permanent remembrance, to see a family of twenty-five million brothers greeting the break of day to lift their souls and their voices towards the Father of Nature.'[9]

The nearest thing to an official report was that published in the *Gazette Nationale* (dated 22 Prairial but not actually printed until the issue of 25 Prairial) which begins with the words 'Of all the festivals celebrated since the beginning of the Revolution none took place with more harmony, brotherly love and solidarity than that of the last tenth-day.'[10] After detailing the events of 20 Prairial, but omitting the speeches made by Robespierre since they were already included in the minutes of the Convention for the sitting of 21 Prairial, the report ended with the words 'The beauty of the day, the purity of the decorations, the open happiness of the people, the solidarity of feelings expressed by every attitude, every movement, every discourse of the citizens, finally the friendliness and good order which marked every aspect of the ceremonies created the most beautiful festival, whose memory will last for ever in the records of the Revolution.'[11] This report confirms the general tenor of reports from the Parisian press, all of which mentioned the general feeling of joyousness and cordiality which prevailed everywhere throughout the celebrations.

The press response to the festival in the capital was, as would have been expected, immediate and positive. However, any such response must, like those from official sources in the provinces, be regarded with some caution, since, by the spring of 1794, press censorship, although officially non-existent, was effectively absolute.[12] Most of the Parisian periodicals were strictly partisan and *L'Auditeur National*, *Le Républicain Français*, *L'Abbréviateur Universel* and *Les Annales Patriotiques et Littéraires* all gave basic accounts of the proceedings at the Festival, but without detailed comment. The *Journal de la Montagne* added to its general description of the ceremonies a specific comment on the joyful nature of the public participation, concluding with a vision of 'a city in which the whole population openly proclaimed the existence of the Divinity, the immortality of the Soul and death to tyrants'.[13] This is the first official reference to the total lack of any form of unruly behaviour either by the public or by the participants. It is perhaps striking that there was a universal assertion that the whole day passed without incident. In its report on 25 Prairial (13 June), *L'Abréviateur Universel* commented favourably on the fact that the whole day passed in the utmost civic amity, without the forces of order having to be called in, remarking that 'good order and harmony prevailed without there being any need to involve the armed forces'.[14] *Les Annales Patriotiques et Littéraires*, in their issue of 22 Prairial (10 June), stated that, although they did not intend to comment on the actual proceedings, since this had been set out in previous issues, they would comment on the behaviour of the participants: 'The lovely day and the immense crowd of all the inhabitants of this vast city, met together to render homage to the Author of Nature, gave this celebration an air of majesty in complete contrast to the pettiness and absurdity of previous celebrations ... the procession took nearly four hours to cross the new bridge, and the festival did not suffer from any unpleasantness.'[15]

It is notable that this newspaper felt the need to emphasise the peaceable nature of the events of 20 Prairial and to contrast this with previous festivals, particularly as it was the same newspaper which had commented unfavourably on the unruly behaviour of the participants in Chaumette's disastrous *Fête de la Raison* in November 1793, and expressed its disgust that the proceedings in Notre-Dame had culminated in scenes of public drunkenness and lechery. The most complete comment is that in *Le Messager du Soir*, 'the whole population of Paris assembled on the celebration sites, the mixture of every age and sex became one family joined by the same feelings. A pure joy lit up every face, and everyone appeared to be appreciative both of the spectacle they themselves formed and of the great cause in which they were joined.'[16] This comment is even more interesting if two other factors are taken into consideration. Firstly, that this periodical was the one which may be considered the most objective – or rather the least partisan – and therefore more likely to have a readership based less on factional lines than other periodicals, and secondly, the fact that *Le Messager du Soir* printed an edition specially '*pour colporteurs*' which meant that it would have had a wide distribution outside the capital and any comment in this particular journal would have been widely read outside Paris.[17]

In examining the formal reports on the Festival in the provinces and thereby attempting to estimate the real impact of the Festival of the Supreme Being in the nation as a whole, the historian is faced with one of the standard problems of evaluation of this type of document: how much is merely the florid rhetoric of political correctness, and how much is a real attempt to transmit the true feelings of the participants? Every commune ordered a formal report to be prepared on their own celebrations, which was then printed and distributed locally, as well as being sent to the authorities in Paris. These reports give details of what happened and when it happened, facts important in themselves and which have provided the basis for an earlier chapter. While they do not offer any officially sanctioned indication of the genuine reaction of the citizens concerned, such phrases as 'there was general happiness: that of a great family united by the feeling of filial piety' from Amiens;[18] or 'gentle brotherly love filled all hearts'[19] which occurs in the official report from Lyon, strongly indicate how the joyous nature of the occasion slid into even these otherwise formal reports. In the case of Angers, where the municipal council specifically addressed their official report to the Representatives of the Mountain, rather than to the Convention, they assured them that 'all the inhabitants of Angers ... and the surrounding areas, vied for the honour of marching ... in propriety and solemnity to honour the Author of Nature'.[20]

The obvious problem is how much of this admittedly often overblown language can be assumed to be the municipal councillors or members of the local *Société Populaire* telling Paris what they thought it wanted to hear, and how far can it be accepted as a true reflection of the feelings of both participants and spectators? One of the indicators is in the examination of the phraseology of many of these reports which includes the use of words such as family feeling, joy, friendly embraces, smiles; words not commonly used in reports of previous festivals. The conclusion must be that beneath the formal stilted language there was a real and genuine core of joy running through the nation.

It is more difficult to obtain a broad vision of the reports and commentaries in the provincial press, whether this is due to the nature of the newspapers involved or simply because of the paucity of copies in local archives. In Angers the local press, *Les Affiches d'Angers*, followed the Paris papers when it commented in its issue of 22 Prairial (10 June) that 'Solidarity, friendship and everything needed for perfect happiness was imprinted on all hearts ... this wonderful day was accompanied by the greatest joy and orderliness.'[21] Two days later the same paper reported Gossuin's motion to insert the official report in the proceedings of the Convention and also Pocholle's critical remarks regarding the slogans at the Champ de la Réunion.[22] In Bordeaux, regrettably, the records of the local newspaper, the *Journal de Bordeaux et du département du Bec d'Ambès* are very incomplete and the only available copies for the period covering the Festival of the Supreme Being are those for 22 and 28 Prairial (10 and 16 June), neither of which has a report on the Festival, either in Bordeaux or Paris. A similar situation prevails in Lyon, where the archival records are incomplete with no direct commentary available from the local press.

In Strasbourg the only daily newspaper printed at the time was *Der Weltbote*, published exclusively in German. In his issue of 27 Prairial,

Butenschön, the proprietor, prints translations of Robespierre's speeches at the Jardin National and Chénier's poetry, and in his commentary he waxes lyrical, lamenting the fact that he himself was not enough of a poet to do them justice, 'Benevolent God, why hast Thou not made me a poet so that I could reproduce adequately the anthems of Thy great feast in my native tongue!'[23] Later in the same article, he cannot restrain himself from begging his fellow citizens to learn French so that they might understand the speeches of this 'noble soul' and be able to appreciate the poet's 'godlike images' in the original.[24] Even accepting Butenschön's flights of rhetoric, it is noticeable that he is equally comfortable with the word 'God' as with 'Supreme Being' in his commentaries. Butenschön also published a monthly cultural magazine called *Argos* but this carried no specific commentary on the actual events.

To set the personal reports on the Festival in Paris in chronological order, the nearest report to the event itself is undoubtedly that made by Bontemps and Barry to their fellow citizens in the *section* of Guillaume Tell, written immediately after their participation in the event.[25] Next would be Ruault's letter to his brother dated 2 Messidor[26] and Boissy d'Anglas' *Essai sur les fêtes nationales*,[27] published on 12 Messidor, all in Year II. These are followed by Maréchal[28] and Vilate[29] both of whom published their commentaries in Year III, then by Nodier's *Souvenirs, épisodes et portraits* in 1831,[30] Mercier in 1862,[31] Baudot in 1893[32] and finally Fiévée's testimony, reprinted by Lescure in his *Journées Révolutionnaires de 1789 –1799*, published in 1895.[33]

The clearest and most precise report on the Festival in Paris is the *Précis de la fête célébrée à Paris le 20 prairial*, written by Bontemps and Barry, and printed as part of a document detailing speeches made at various tenth-day meetings in the *section* of Guillaume Tell, one of the smaller and more densely populated areas of Paris, now the Quartier du Mail in the 2° Arrondissement. The very detailed description indicates that its authors must have been among the members of their *section* marching in the procession and present at the ceremonies at both sites. There is further confirmation of this, when they say of the departure of the procession from the Jardin National that 'We left for the Champ de la Réunion in proper order.'[34] Although the bulk of the *Précis* is factual, concerned with details of the ceremonies and the procession, there are two references to the joyful feelings of the participants, one at the Jardin National when 'the garden resounded with cries of joy', and at the end of the ceremonies at the Champ de la Réunion when 'all the citizens joined together in mutual embrace and ended this great day raising to the skies the national slogan: *Vive la République française*'.[35]

If one accepts the letters of Nicolas Ruault as genuine, he must also be accepted as an accurate commentator. By 1794, Ruault had been retired for some years, and does not seem to have been involved in either the political or the artistic side of the Festival. As an interested but not engaged participant, his account seems generally reliable, although he seems more interested in Lecointre's failed assassination bid than in the actual events of the Festival. In his letter to his brother dated 2 Messidor (20 June 1794) he writes

> Nowadays I take no part in what is going on, despite the sublime Festival of the Supreme Being, decreed and presided over by Maximilien Robespierre. It is said that that madman, Lecointre of Versailles, had taken it into his head to sacrifice for God and the Nation the great president on the altar raised to the Nation at the Champ de Mars; that would have been the best thing he could ever do both for Robespierre and for humanity ... However it seems that this Lecointre was not granted the grace necessary. Robespierre returned after the procession just as he went, covered with applause from his own party and secret curses from those who hate the human blood which he is causing to flow more than ever since the law he brought in on 21 Prairial.[36]

It is worthy of note that, despite his obvious dislike of Robespierre, Ruault still refers to the *Fête* as *sublime*, a word which a man of letters such as himself would not have used lightly.

As a Member of the Convention, Boissy d'Anglas[37] would have taken part in the ceremonies both at the Jardin National and at the Champ de la Réunion as well as marching in the procession. He published his *Essai sur les fêtes nationales* on 12 Messidor (30 June 1794) in the form of an address to the Convention on the general problem of national festivals, which he saw as becoming so numerous as to risk getting out of control.[38] It is difficult to establish exactly what his motives were in offering his essay at this time. Obviously there was some self-seeking motivation; he appears to be manoeuvring for a nomination to the Committee of Public Education, using the idea of a commentary on public festivals as a good stalking horse. He accepts the role of festivals in that they make instruction real, give movement and life to the sacred principles of morality[39] and are a precious method for perfecting civic education.[40] He was very impressed by the Festival in general: 'I dare believe that it would be impossible to think of this unforgettable festival without emotion, just as it was impossible to take part without feeling.'[41] He was particularly impressed by the quality of both the poetry and the music, which he compares favourably to that of the *Fête de la Raison*.

On the nature of the worship he writes 'The soul was elevated and softened by the sounds of martial and touching music, by the singing of hymns, by the influence of poetry and the arts ... I compared this solemn worship with the demeaning and often shameful practices to which superstition has brought man, and I bless the wisdom of those who have restored to truth and to mankind that holy state they should never have lost.'[42] He did however take serious exception to what he calls an allegorical dumb-show of burning the statue of Atheism to reveal the figure of Wisdom, which he felt diminished the solemn nature of the occasion. In common with the majority of commentators, Boissy d'Anglas was struck by the fact that the involvement of the public did not lead to scenes of excess, but that, on the contrary, dignity, decorum and decency were the overriding impressions.

Even some militant atheists, such as Sylvain Maréchal, embraced the idea of a Cult of a Supreme Being with marked enthusiasm, considering it to be a profoundly Republican ideal. His pamphlet is carefully targeted at the areas outside Paris: he does not give a detailed report on the events in the capital, concentrating his remarks on the lessons to be drawn from the fact that it was the fruits of the countryside which made the display of arts and crafts so impressive. He also draws specific attention to the nobility of sentiment displayed on the signboards around the Mountain at the Champ de la Réunion, which he lists in detail.[43] He finishes with a peroration, calling upon his readers to imbue themselves with these sentiments, and to place on their own Tree of Liberty the slogan from the Tree of Liberty under whose branches the Mountain and the Convention placed themselves at the Festival: 'Take care of me always, and your children will harvest my produce and bless you from beneath my branches.'[44]

At the time of the *Fête*, Joachim Vilate was a member of the Revolutionary Tribunal, with an official residence in what had been the Pavillon de Flore, in the Tuileries, now the Jardin National. Vilate had been a figure of some importance in the events of 10 August 1792, under the *nom de plume* of Sempronius Gracchus, and became a member of the Revolutionary Tribunal in 1793. In 1794 he was publicly attacked in the Convention by Robespierre and Legendre, accused of being a spy for Pitt, and vilified by Barère as 'the national executioner'. Despite these anti-Robespierre credentials, he was imprisoned after Thermidor. While in prison he wrote two anti-Robespierre pamphlets, the main one being his *Causes secrètes de la Révolution*, and the second a pamphlet on the Catherine Théot affair and what he claimed to have been Robespierre's involvement with the prophetess, *Les Mystères de la Mère de Dieu dévoilés*.[45] Despite his attempts to regain favour, he remained in prison until he was tried and executed with other members of the Tribunal in May 1795.[46] While he does not comment directly on the events of the Festival itself, Vilate does confirm the fine weather and the general atmosphere of joy. He was the first commentator to mention that after the long period of drab dressing, the ladies of Paris chose the occasion of the Festival to appear again in their full pre-revolutionary finery. He also comments in detail on Robespierre's mental state when they met in the Jardin National after the procession:

> Going through the Hall of Liberty I met Robespierre, dressed as a Representative of the People and clutching a mixed posy of flowers and corn; for the first time his face was transformed with joy. He had not had lunch. With my heart full of the noble feelings engendered by this great day I invited him to my lodging, he immediately accepted. He was amazed to see the great mass of people which filled the Tuilerie gardens, all of whose faces radiated hope and happiness. The elegance of the dress of the ladies added to the beauty of the day. It was clear that this was the festival of Nature. Robespierre ate very little. He looked often at the glorious spectacle. He seemed intoxicated with enthusiasm. 'Look, here is the most interesting aspect of the people. The universe is assembled here. O Nature, how glorious and sweet is your power. How the tyrants must quail at the idea of this Festival.' That was all he said ... Maximilien stayed until half past midday.[47]

The timing is seriously suspect since the ceremonies were due to begin in the Jardin National at 9 a.m., and we know that, from the report in *Les Annales Patriotiques et Littéraires* the procession took four hours to cross the bridge, after which there were the songs, speeches, and act of worship at the Mountain. It is most unlikely that Robespierre and the others would have been back at the Convention buildings before late afternoon.

The historian Charles Nodier would have been fourteen when he was taken to the festival in Paris. In his recollections of the event, published in 1831, he prefaces his description by saying that although he regrets being old enough to remember the event, he thanks God that he was young enough to have enjoyed it without it being coloured by the memories of that terrible period.[48] He presents an altogether more rosy vision of the events of 20 Prairial, drawing a picture of the people seeing in the combination of the magnificence of the occasion and in the glorious weather a sure proof of reconciliation between God and France. According to his memory, greenery and bunting filled every street, all the boats on the Seine were covered in flags, and the site of the guillotine had disappeared under a mass of bunting and flowers. In his memory it was this last effect which added to the widespread expectation that a general amnesty would be proclaimed and Nodier suggests that if Robespierre had dared take this final step and declared an amnesty, the national response would have been such that all the difficulties he faced would have been smoothed over.[49]

He concludes with the most moving descriptions of what it was like to be in the crowd on the day of the *Fête*: 'People who had never met came together, people embraced people they did not know; the public street banquets brought together rich and poor, aristocrat and Jacobin, and in all this enormous mass there was no fuss, no arguments, no incidents.'[50] Once again we see the emphasis on the good conduct of the population and the total lack of any untoward behaviour. During his lifetime, Nodier was attacked by Royalists and Republicans alike as being too favourably disposed towards Robespierre since he was, in contrast to his contemporaries, and despite his personal detestation of the politics of the Terror, prepared to state publicly his opinion that Robespierre was always motivated by the highest moral intentions.[51]

The comments by Joseph Fiévée are particularly interesting. From the text in his *Mémoires*, edited by Lescure and published in 1875, it would seem that Fiévée was himself present at the *Fête*, which might be considered a little surprising since he was, at the time, living a semi-clandestine existence as a pro-monarchy, pro-church practising homosexual.[52] Fiévée also mentions the assumption that, with the disappearance of the scaffold, an amnesty was imminent, and, like Vilate, he reflects both the glorious weather and the fact that the ladies of Paris society were back in their pre-revolutionary plumage. His comments reinforce the general view of the overriding impressions of joyfulness, neighbourliness and good behaviour. 'Robespierre's creation of the Festival of the Supreme Being was a total success. It was believed to be the prelude to a general amnesty, since on that day the executioner was absent. The weather was beautiful. The crowds were so large that it seemed that Paris had risen from the dead, rejuvenated, busy and sparkling; the ladies dared once more to appear with their old finery and every face shone with friendliness.'[53]

Regrettably there are very few direct commentaries available on the events of 20 Prairial outside Paris, other than those figuring in the reports of local organisers. There are however two interesting notes on the Festival made by foreigners who were either present at the event or in France soon afterwards. The first is a letter from an Irishman, Archibald Hamilton Rowan[54] sent from Orléans in June 1794.

> On our arrival in Orleans, the decree acknowledging God and the immortality of the soul, which had just passed the Convention, was about to be promulgated by a great fête. All the public functionaries, of every sort, civil and military, were assembled in the chief church, which was then opened

to the public. About halfway up the very handsome steeple of the church, a large board was placed on which the words *Le peuple français reconnoit l'Être Suprême et l'immortalité de l'Âme* was blazoned in large gold letters with a screen before it. At a signal, the screen fell, amidst the firing of cannon and musketry, and bands of music playing, while the multitude responded '*Vive Robespierre*' who was supposed to be the framer of the decree.[55]

The second is an undated letter from Major Tench of the Royal Marines,[56] probably written when he was held as a prisoner-of-war in Quimper in 1795: 'A building which would have excited my curiosity ... I arrived too late to see – a Temple of Reason built for the exercise of the new religion of France.'[57]

These different commentaries advance our understanding of the way the people of France viewed the events of 20 Prairial, and how the arrangements of the various festivals all over France contributed to make Robespierre's vision of the whole nation coming together in a joyous act of homage to the Supreme Being, Creator of Nature and Protector of France a reality. All the accounts discussed in this chapter lead inescapably to the conclusion that, on the day of the *Fête*, the overriding feeling was one of unity in the present and hope for the future. Despite the fact that no-one, least of all Robespierre himself, had given any indication of a major shift of policy, there seems to have been in Paris and several provincial cities, an expectation that this day would see something momentous, perhaps a general amnesty, perhaps even the end of the Terror.

During the period when the preparations for the greatest festival the Revolution would ever see were advancing joyfully all over France, and even on the day of the Festival itself, conspirators in Paris were busy setting about creating a faction strong enough to bring down the man they feared was about to proclaim himself dictator. It is easy to see how Barère and Billaud-Varennes in the Committee of Public Safety and their co-conspirators, Vadier and Amar in the Committee of General Security, felt that they were now completely excluded from any real process of government. They were openly bitter about the fact that their opinions no longer counted and that on all matters of real importance to the Republic were seen as being under the personal control of Robespierre and Saint-Just. Robespierre had always had active opponents in the Convention. Not only active de-Christianisers such as Fouché and Lequinio, but other radicals such as Merlin de Thionville, Lecointre de Versailles and Bourdon de l'Oise had openly opposed him before in both the Convention and the Jacobin Club. Yet this group of opponents hardly seemed to be joined together by a unified political agenda. In many cases, their opposition can be more properly put down to personal grievances.

As Thompson points out, it was the misfortune of Robespierre's outlook and temper that he could never discriminate between personal and political grievances, so that his personal foes were driven into political opposition, and his political opponents into personal hatred, which effectively doubled the number of his enemies.[58]

As the effect of the Festival continued to reverberate throughout France, letters congratulating the Convention on its wisdom and expressing solidarity with Robespierre's idea of a Supreme Being watching over France, continued to flow to Paris and into the records of the Committee of Public Education all through that summer. Sadly, the hope that the Festival would mark a clear watershed between the politics of the Terror and the hoped-for preparation for the coming of the Republic of Virtue was to be suddenly and brutally killed off just two days after the Festival.

Notes

1 L.-S. Mercier, *Paris pendant la Révolution, ou Le Nouveau Paris (1789–1798)* (Paris, 1862) and M.-A. Baudot, *Notes Historiques sur la Convention, le Directoire, l'Empire et l'exil des votants* (Paris, 1893), p. 5.
2 'On crut que c'était pour toujours', J. Michelet, *Histoire de la Révolution Française*, Vol. 19, originally published 1847–52, P. Villaneix, ed. (Paris, 1974), p. 868.
3 Eugène Constant Gossuin (1758–1827), elected member of the Assembly then of the Convention for the Nord, was a supporter of the Mountain and of Robespierre personally. As *Représentant en Mission* to the Army of the North he was instrumental in the discovery of the treachery of Doumouriez. Sent by the *Comité de salut public* to investigate treason in the Département of the Bouches du Rhône, he was absent from Paris during Thermidor. He was later a member of the Cinq-Cents and active in the conspiracy of 18 Brumaire. Napoléon rewarded him with the post of *Commissaire des Eaux et Fôrets*.
4 'Je demande aujourd'hui que le procès-verbal de la séance d'hier, car c'était une séance, et des plus belles que la Convention ait tenues, soit envoyé aux départements, aux districts, aux municipalités, aux sociétés populaires et aux armées, que le procès-verbal renferme les détails de la fête, les différents discours prononcés par le Président, et les évènements les plus remarquables qui ont eu lieu dans cette cérémonie auguste.' A.P., Vol. 9, p. 440.
5 Pierre-Pomponne Pocholle (1764–1831). Député for the Seine-Inférieur. De-Christianiser. Best known as the destroyer of the tomb of Agnès Sorel at Loches in 1793. Allied with Thirion and Ruamps, a supporter of Hébert and considered an Indulgent. Appointed *Représentant en Mission* with Chalier to Lyon in 1793. Later member of the Cinq-Cents. When France obtained the Ionian Islands by the treaty of Campo-Formio in 1797, Napoléon sent him as *Commissaire* to Corfu in the newly acquired 'Département d'Ithaque'.

6 'Les inscriptions placées sur les différentes faces du rocher de la liberté, plusieurs de mes collègues en ont remarqué avec moi, qui ne sont pas dignes du sujet, et qui seraient propres à donner, de l'Être Suprême, une idée contraire à celle que nous devons en avoir. Je demande que toutes les inscriptions, relative à la fête de l'Eternel, soient renvoyées, à l'examen du comité d'instruction publique, avant d'être insérées au procès-verbal.' A.P., Vol. 9, p. 440.

7 Didier Thirion (1763–1815). Député for the Moselle. Montagnard but later leading Thermidorean conspirator. Avid de-Christianiser, when as *Représentant en Mission* in 1793 he exhumed and publicly burned the hearts of Henri IV and Marie de Médicis at La Flèche.

8 Pierre-Charles Ruamps (1750–1808). Député for the Charente Inférieur. Anti-Robespierre Montagnard, he opposed the Loi du 22 Prairial, threatening to commit suicide publicly if it passed: 'Si ce décret passe je me brule la cervelle.' Arrested in March 1795, imprisoned in Besançon then released under the amnesty of 4 Brumaire An IV (26 October 1795), when he retired to his native Charente. Arrested on a charge of treachery in 1808, he was sentenced to be deported to Cayenne but died (some say committed suicide) before the sentence could be carried out.

9 'C'est un spectacle digne de regards à l'univers et du souvenir des siècles, de voir une famille de vingt-cinq millions de frères devancer ensemble la naissance du jour pour élever son âme et sa voix vers le Père de la nature.' *Gazette Nationale*, 25 Prairial An II (13 June 1794), pp. 688–9.

10 'De toutes les fêtes célébrées depuis le commencement de la Révolution aucune n'a été exécutée avec plus d'harmonie, de fraternité et d'ensemble que celle du décadi dernier.' *Gazette Nationale*, 25 Prairial An II (13 June 1794), pp. 688–9.

11 'La beauté du jour, la fraîcheur des décorations, la franche gaîté du peuple, l'unanimité des sentiments exprimés par toutes les attitudes tous les mouvements tous les discours des citoyens, enfin la cordialité et l'ordre qui ont régné dans tout le cours de la cérémonie en ont fait la plus belle fête dont le souvenir puisse être perpétué dans les fastes de la révolution.' *Gazette Nationale*, 25 Prairial An II (13 June 1794), pp. 688–9.

12 See C. Bellanger, J. Godechot, P. Guiral and F. Terrou, eds, *Histoire générale de la presse française* (Paris, 1969), p. 515.

13 'une ville où le people tout entier, proclament hautement l'existence de la divinité, l'immortalité de l'âme et la mort des tyrans', *Journal de la Montagne*, Vol. III, No. 44.

14 'le bon ordre & l'harmonie a régné sans qu'on ait été obligé d'employer les secours de la force armée', *L'Abbréviateur Universel*, Issue 528, p. 2110.

15 'Un beau jour, et la foule immense de tous les habitants d'une vaste cité, réunis pour rendre hommage à l'auteur de la nature, donnoient à cette fête un caractère de majesté qui contrastoit singulièrement avec la mesquinerie et le ridicule de nos anciennes processions … Le cortège a été près de quatre heures à défiler sur le nouveau pont, et la fête n'a été troublée par aucun accident fâcheux.' *Les Annales Patriotiques et Littéraires*, Issue 525, p. 2313.

16 'toute la population de Paris ... ne formaient qu'une même famille réunie par les mêmes sentiments. Une joie pure animait toutes les physionomies et tous semblaient se féliciter du spectacle qu'ils se donnaient mutuellement et du grand objet pour lequel ils se trouvaient assemblés.' *Le Messager du Soir*, Issue 660, 21 Prairial An II (9 June 1794).
17 See L.-E. Hatin, *Bibliographie Historique et Critique de la Presse Périodique Française* (Paris, 1868), p. 233.
18 'la satisfaction étoit générale: c'étoit celle d'une grande famille réunie par les sentiments de la piété filiale', A.M. Amiens 1.D.10.9, p. 82.
19 'la douce fraternité embrasait tous les cœurs', A.M. Lyon 1.C.651107, p. 5.
20 'Tous les habitants d'Angers ... et des environs paraissaient se disputer l'honneur de marcher avec le plus de décence et de gravité pour aller rendre hommage à l'auteur de la nature', A.M. Angers 1.D.5, p. 88.
21 'L'union, l'amitié et tout ce qui annonce un bonheur parfait était imprimé dans tous les cœurs ... La plus grande joie et la plus grande tranquillité ont accompagné et terminé cette belle journée.' *Les Affiches d'Angers*, Issue 82, p. 435.
22 *Les Affiches d'Angers*, Issue 82, p. 441.
23 'Gütiger Gott, warum hast Du mich nicht zum Dichter gemacht, dass ich die Hochgesänge Deines grossen Festes in meiner Muttersprache nachlallen könnte!' Strasbourg, *Der Weltbote*, No. 79, p. 307.
24 'Lernet französisch Bürger, ich bitte Euch um Gotteswillen, damit Ihr verstehet was diese edle Seele sprach. Welches göttliche Gemälde gibt der Repräsentant Chénier in seinem Hochgesang zur Ehre des Höchsten!' *Der Weltbote*, No. 79, p. 307.
25 'Précis de la fête célébrée à Paris le 20 prairial, l'an 2 de la République française, une et indivisible, rédigé par les citoyens BONTEMPS et BARRY', in *Discours prononcés les jours de décadi dans la section de Guillaume Tell* (Paris, An II).
26 N. Ruault, *Gazette d'un Parisien sous la Révolution: Lettres à son frère.1783–1796*, A. Vassal and C. Rimbaud, eds (Paris, 1976).
27 F.A. Boissy d'Anglas, *Essai sur les fêtes nationales, adressé à la Convention Nationale; par Boissy d'Anglas Représentant du Peuple, Député pour le Département de l'Ardèche* (Paris, An II).
28 S. Maréchal, *Tableau historique des événements révolutionnaires, depuis la fondation de la République jusqu'à présent, rédigé principalement pour les campagnes* (Paris, An III).
29 J. Vilate, *Causes secrètes de la révolution du 9 au 10 thermidor; par Vilate, ex-juré au tribunal Révolutionnaire de Paris, détenu à La Force* (Paris, An III).
30 C. Nodier, *Souvenirs, épisodes et portraits pour servir à l'histoire de la Révolution et de l'Empire* (Paris, 1831).
31 Mercier, *Paris pendant la Révolution*.
32 Baudot, *Notes Historiques*.
33 'Mémoires de Fiévée', in M. de Lescure, *Bibliothèque des Mémoires relatifs à l'histoire de France pendant le 18° siècle*, Vol. XXIX (Paris, 1875).

34 '*On* est parti pour le Champ de la Réunion dans le plus bel ordre.' Bontemps and Barry, *Discours prononcés*, p. 9 (author's emphasis).
35 'tous les citoyens et citoyennes, confondant leurs sentiments dans un embrassement mutuel, ont terminé ce beau jour en élevant vers le ciel ce cri de la patrie: *Vive la République française*', Bontemps and Barry, *Discours prononcés*, p. 8.
36 'Je ne prends plus guère de part à tout ce qui se pratique aujourd'hui, malgré la sublime Fête de l'Être Suprême décrétée et présidée par Maximilien Robespierre. On dit que ce fou de Lecointre de Versailles aurait conçu le dessein d'immoler à Dieu et à la Patrie ce grand président, le jour de la fête au Champ de Mars, sur l'autel dressé à cette patrie: c'était ce qu'il pourrait faire de mieux en sa vie et pour Robespierre et pour l'humanité. ... Mais il paraît que la grâce efficace a manqué à ce Lecointre. Robespierre est revenu de la procession comme il y était allé, couvert d'applaudissements par les gens de son parti et des exécrations secrètes de ceux qui ont horreur du sang humain qu'il fait verser plus abondamment que jamais depuis la loi qu'il a fait rendre le 21 prairial.' (Ruault, *Gazette*, p. 351)
37 François Antoine, Comte de Boissy d'Anglas (1756–1826). Député for the Ardèche. Leading Protestant moderate and member of the Plain, voted for banishment in the trial of Louis XVI, after Thermidor became leader of the moderate faction, elected to the Comité de salut public in November 1794. President of the Cinq-Cents at the murder of Féraud in May 1795, he retired after Brumaire. Later made his peace with Napoléon who made him a Comte de l'Empire in 1808. Supported the Restoration of Louis XVIII who made him a Peer of France in 1815. Member of the Consistory of the French Reformed Church 1815–26.
38 Robespierre, in his speech of 18 Floréal, proposed thirty-five *fêtes* in addition to that of the *Être suprême*.
39 'mettent l'enseignement en action, donnent du mouvement et de la vie aux préceptes sacrés de la morale', Boissy d'Anglas, *Essai sur les fêtes*, p. 14.
40 'un moyen précieux de perfectionnement', Boissy d'Anglas, *Essai sur les fêtes*, p. 26.
41 'Il sera impossible, j'ose le croire, de se rappeler sans attendrissement cette fête à jamais célébrée, comme il était impossible d'y assister sans émotion.' Boissy d'Anglas, *Essai sur les fêtes*, p. 68.
42 'L'âme était élevée et attendrie par les sons d'une musique énergique et touchante, par le chant des hymnes, par l'influence de la poésie et des arts ... je comparais ce culte auguste à toutes les pratiques puériles, et souvent affreuses, que la superstition avait enseignées aux hommes, et je bénissais la sagesse de ceux qui avaient restitué à la raison et à l'humanité l'empire sacré qu'elles n'auraient jamais dû perdre.' Boissy d'Anglas, *Essai sur les fêtes*, p. 67.
43 Maréchal, *Tableau historique*. He is the only commentator to list all the signboards at the Champ de la Réunion.

44 'Soyez toujours assez généreux pour me conserver; vos enfans cueilleront mes fruits, et vous béniront sous mon ombrage.' Maréchal, *Tableau historique*, p. 137.
45 J. Vilate, *Les Mystères de la Mère de Dieu dévoilés* (Paris, n.d.).
46 After Thermidor all the members of the Revolutionary Tribunal, led by the Chief Prosecutor, Fouquier-Tinville, were arrested. They were tried in 1795. Vilate, along with Fouquier-Tinville and fourteen others, was sentenced to death and guillotined on 18 Floréal Year III (7 May 1795).
47 'En passant dans la salle de la Liberté, je rencontrai Robespierre, revêtu de costume de représentant du peuple, tenant à la main un bouquet mélangé d'épis et de fleurs; la joie brillait pour la première fois sur sa figure. Il n'avait pas déjeuné. Le cœur plein de sentiment qu'inspirait cette superbe journée, je l'engage à monter à mon logement; il accepte sans hésiter. Il fut étonné du concours immense qui couvrait le jardin des Tuileries; l'espérance et la gaieté rayonnaient sur tous les visages. Les femmes ajoutaient à l'embellissement par les parures les plus élégantes. On sentait qu'on célébrait la fête de la nature. Robespierre mangeait peu. Ses regards se portaient souvent sur ce magnifique spectacle. On le voyait plongé dans l'ivresse de l'enthousiasme. '*Voilà la plus intéressante portion de l'humanité. L'univers est ici rassemblé. O Nature, que ta puissance est sublime et délicieuse! Comme les tyrans doivent pâlir à l'idée de cette fête.*' Ce fut là toute sa conversation! ... Maximilien resta jusqu'à midi et demi.' (Vilate, *Causes secrètes de la Révolution*, pp. 233–4)
48 C. Nodier, *Souvenirs de la Révolution et de l'Empire* (Paris, 1850), p. 288.
49 C. Nodier, 'Eloquence Révolutionnaire, La Montagne', in *Souvenirs de la Révolution et de l'Empire*, Vol. I (Paris, 1857), p. 288.
50 'On se rapprochait sans se connoître, on s'embrassoit sans se nommer; les banquets publics servis dans les rues réunissoient le riche au pauvre, l'aristocrate au jacobin, et cette cohue énorme fut sans confusion, sans dispute, sans accident.' Nodier, 'Eloquence Révolutionnaire', p. 288.
51 Nodier, 'Recueil de pièces trouvées chez Robespierre l'aîné', in *Souvenirs de la Révolution et de l'Empire*, Introduction.
52 Joseph Fiévée was a remarkable character for his period. Openly homosexual and originally highly supportive of the disestablishment of the Church, he became increasingly monarchist and a member of the royalist counter-revolutionary group led by the Abbé de Montesquiou. He corresponded secretly with Louis XVIII and in 1798 published under an assumed name *La Dot de Suzette*, a fierce satire on the morals of the Directoire which had enormous success. At Brumaire he supported Napoléon, who later sent him on a diplomatic mission to Britain, accompanied by his partner Théodore Leclercq who acted as his official hostess, as he did in Nevers when Fiévée was *Prefet* there. After the Restoration he co-published *Le Conservateur* with Chateaubriand. Despite his extreme right-wing views, his imprisonment in 1818 made him a popular martyr to press freedom. He published his correspondence with Napoléon in 1836. For a detailed biography see J. Tulard, *Joseph Fiévée, conseiller secret de Napoléon* (Paris, 1985).

53 'Robespierre inventa la Fête de l'Être Suprême: elle réussit complètement ... On pouvait la considérer comme le prélude d'une amnistie; car le jour de sa célébration le bourreau se reposa. Il faisait un temps admirable. La foule était si considérable que Paris semblait sortir des tombeaux, mais rajeuni, actif et brillant; les femmes osèrent reparaître dans leur ancienne élégance; et sur toutes les figures éclatait un sentiment de cordialité.' *Mémoires de Fiévée*, in Lescure, *Bibliothèque des Mémoires*, p. 161.

54 Archibald Hamilton Rowan was imprisoned in Dublin in 1794 as a member of the United Irishmen. He escaped to France but on arrival in Brest was imprisoned as an English spy. He was released by Prieur de la Marne and allowed to continue his journey to Paris. After Thermidor he found little interest in aiding revolution in Ireland and in 1795 went to America.

55 W.H. Drummond, *Autobiography of A. H. Rowan, Esq. With additions and illustrations by W. H. Drummond* (Dublin, 1840).

56 Watkin Tench was Major of Marines on HMS *Alexander* which surrendered to the French during the battle off Ushant on 1 June 1794 (13 Prairial, Year II). He was imprisoned in Quimper during 1794 and 1795.

57 Watkin Tench, *Letters Written in France to a Friend in London: Between the Month of November 1794 and the Month of May 1795* (London, 1796).

58 See J.M. Thompson, *Robespierre* (New York, 1968), Vol 2, pp. 234-5.

7

After the Festival

Letters of congratulation and support on the Festival continued to flow into Paris until well after the actual celebrations of 20 Prairial. After the overwhelmingly positive reception which the Festival had received throughout France, there seemed to be a clear expectation that the period after the 20 Prairial would see at least some form of mitigation of the Terror, if not a general amnesty. The only question was when and how these expectations would be fulfilled. On the day after the Festival the Convention voted to have the speeches Robespierre had made on 20 Prairial incorporated in the minutes while further speeches were made praising the atmosphere of brotherly love and national reconciliation which the celebrations had engendered. Yet there was no movement from either Robespierre himself or his inner circle; no proposals were being made for any form of follow-up either in Paris or in the provinces.

If Robespierre really believed that Republican France was ready to emerge from the darkness of the early Revolution into the light of a new national morality, surely this would have been the moment to impose this principle. The evidence clearly indicates that there was a remarkable atmosphere of fraternal joy, the entire nation seemed to be joined in the idea of worship of the Supreme Being. Equally there were clear indications of a positive expectation that the Festival would presage the final end to the Terror and the dawn of the long hoped-for Republic of Virtue. Had Robespierre chosen to utilise the massive assurances of solidarity from the provinces in response to his speech of 18 Floréal, there was undoubted potential for the establishment of an unassailable political and moral power base. The overwhelmingly positive reaction to the *Fête* could have placed in his hands the two control elements necessary to ensure the success of his ideal state: the necessary moral authority on which to base the Republic of Virtue, and the political power to impose it.

These expectations had also been fed by the secondary proposal in Robespierre's speech of 18 Floréal; the establishment of a series of smaller civic festivals to be celebrated continuously throughout the year. These were not specifically Deist in nature, there was no suggestion of any role for organised religion, so it would be assumed that the more moderate members of the Convention, who shared Robespierre's distaste for atheism, would support them. Had they been followed through, these minor festivals, by acting as a direct link to the ethos of the celebrations of 20 Prairial, might well have helped ensure the continued promotion of the civic and moral issues at the heart of the speech of 18 Floréal. The proposed succession of civic celebrations would also have presented an obstacle to the torpedoing of Robespierre's project by the de-Christianisers and atheists. They would have found it difficult to castigate as 'fanaticism' events dedicated to such all-embracing virtues as motherhood, filial piety or old age.

What happened two days after the Festival must have been as much of a surprise to the bulk of the population as had been the proclamation of the Festival itself. On the morning of the 22 Prairial, Vaud reported to the Convention on the correspondence so far received and made a speech in praise of the brotherly love shown at the Festival. The same afternoon, Couthon, on behalf of the Committee of Public Safety, went to the podium to introduce the infamous *Loi du 22 Prairial*. This law, which ushered in the bloodiest period of the Terror, was the complete opposite of what had been expected. The general atmosphere of hope had been further strengthened by the dismantling of the guillotine on the Place de la Révolution in the days before the Festival. On the very next day, 23 Prairial, the machine was re-erected on a site at the end of the Faubourg Saint-Antoine, near the remains of the Bastille and in the forty-eight hours which followed the executioners posted a record total of ninety-seven executions.

The effect was immediate in Paris, but, given the chaotic nature of communication between the capital and the provinces, the news both of the new law and of the re-erection of the guillotine would not have reached the majority of provincial cities for at least another three to five days. Although there is no direct record of the celebrations continuing outside Paris, it is reasonable to assume that the general level of euphoria would have continued in many areas, while everyone was waiting for further good news from the capital. There is unfortunately no written evidence of the feelings which the arrival of the next set of dispatches from

Paris created. The feelings of deception, especially in those areas where the expectations were most pronounced, can only be imagined.

During the period when Robespierre was preparing his attempt to re-introduce a system of national morality his enemies, headed by Vadier of the Committee of General Security and aided by Barère and Billaud-Varennes in the Committee of Public Safety, were actively plotting his downfall. They needed to present some serious accusation of treachery to the Revolution, so they sought to implicate Robespierre in the activities of one of the extreme prophetic sects, led by the prophetess Catherine Théot, supported by an old ally of Robespierre, the ex-Carthusian Dom Gerle. Théot claimed that she had been told in a vision that she would shortly be given power to rule the world with the Chosen One at her side. She never named the Chosen One but popular rumour, carefully nurtured by his opponents, suggested that it was to be Robespierre. On 27 Prairial (15 June 1794), a week after the Festival of the Supreme Being, a report entitled 'Actions of the false prophetess Catherine Theos [*sic*]' and written by Barère, was presented to the Convention by Vadier. The Convention voted to have Théot and Gerle sent to the Revolutionary Tribunal on a charge of treason. Although Robespierre firmly denied any involvement with the Théot sect, on 8 Messidor (26 June 1794) he personally instructed the Chief Prosecutor, Fouquier-Tinville, in the name of the Committee of Public Safety, that the case against her was to be dropped. According to the Deputy for the Sarthe, René Levasseur, it was this which caused a furious row on 10 Messidor between Robespierre and some other members of the Committee of Public Safety. Levasseur, who was present at the meeting, reported that Robespierre stormed out shouting 'Save the nation without me!' to which Lindet replied 'The nation is not only one man!'[1]

From 11 Messidor onwards, Robespierre took no further part in the deliberations of the Committee, and effectively disappeared from public life until his final disastrous speech to the Convention on 8 Thermidor. It has been suggested by commentators as disparate as Bouchez and Roux, and Mary Young, that the reason why Robespierre stormed out of the Committee of Public Safety and out of public life was because of the failure, as he saw it, of his attempt to integrate his new republican morality into the mainstream of the Revolution. While there is some merit in this argument, it seems unlikely that that could have been the only, or even the main cause of his absence for the entire thirty-day period up to his final appearance before the Convention. Whether Robespierre's disappearance from public life was in any way linked with his feeling that his colleagues in the Committee were not wholeheartedly embracing his new national morality system, or whether it was due to a combination of other matters, including ill-health, must remain a mystery. It is certainly true that Robespierre had had recurrent health problems ever since his arrival in Paris in 1789. He was subject to frequent and sudden debilitating attacks of fever and, according to Nabonne, by the beginning of Prairial Year II (June 1794), he also suffered from a general ulceration of both legs – a condition severe enough to have made him doubt whether he would be able to take the lead, or indeed any part at all, in the procession on 20 Prairial.[2] His sister Charlotte confirms in her memoirs that he was very unwell, but does not indicate specifically either what he was suffering from or how serious it was.[3]

The period from the Festival until Robespierre's execution on 10 Thermidor has been the subject of deep and penetrative analysis by all of Robespierre's biographers. Every one of them has been faced with the problem of trying to understand and explain not only his abandonment of his own proposal for a new republican morality, but also his withdrawal from public life between 10 Messidor and his return to the Convention for his last speech on 8 Thermidor. It is possible that the unexpected intensity of the vocal attacks which he had to take on board during the procession in Paris from such opponents as Lecointre, Bourdon de l'Oise and Merlin de Thionville so shook his belief in both himself and his goal as to raise the fear that his power base was no longer strong enough for him to impose his personal vision on the nation. Even if he was not yet convinced of the strength of the alliance against him led by Vadier and the Committee of Public Safety allied to Barère and Billaud-Varenne, his personal papers indicate that he suspected it. This, despite his control of the majority of the *sans-culottes* in Paris and the overwhelmingly positive response of the mass of the people, might also have had a negative effect in his analysis of the situation. There is also the strong possibility that, despite his repeated references to his being '*of the people*', and seeing himself as their champion in the fight to establish 'virtue' as the national guiding principle, he had now so far removed himself from any comprehension of their real needs and aspirations, as to be, in the end, incapable of seeing what was on offer. Quite apart from his problems with the permanent political struggle within the Convention, he seems to have been so caught up in his own dark thoughts during Messidor and early Thermidor, so enmeshed in his personal problems that he could no longer comprehend that there might be available to him this new and largely unforeseen national support base, which, had he used it wisely, could have changed the political climate to his advantage.

Robespierre's month-long disappearance from public life served not only to heighten the feeling that he was part of some conspiracy to transform the Republic, it also allowed those already conspiring against him free rein to talk to other members of the Convention more openly about their project; what had been a hole-and-corner business now became public. This could now be presented even to members of the Convention as legitimate opposition to a system in which major policy decisions were being made by an unseen cabal, who could be neither questioned nor called to account, since Robespierre no longer attended either the Convention or the Committee. On the other hand, there seemed to have been no diminution either of his continued control of the Jacobin Clubs or of his support by the *sans-culottes* of Paris, through his chief supporter in the capital, Payan. None of his potential opponents dared yet show their hand against a power base which, as was demonstrated during the events of Thermidor, could have put thousands of armed militants on the streets in support of Robespierre, if any move were made openly against him.

Robespierre's disappearance from both the Committee and the Convention finally killed any chance that the general worship of the Supreme Being would be followed throughout France. In his last disastrous speech to the Convention on 8 Thermidor, Robespierre again reverted to the themes of morality, virtue, death and the afterlife. There is a problem as to precisely what he did say in that speech, since the version originally reprinted after the seizure of his papers was not in accordance with either the original text or with some of the crossings out and rewrites in his own hand, all of which add considerably to the difficulty of establishing exactly what his mindset was when preparing his speech for the Convention. Instead of offering a clear vision of what he believed needed to be done to save the Republic, he made a series of attacks on specific opponents, particularly those who had accused him of seeking to become dictator. He mentioned the Supreme Being again, reminding his hearers that when they agreed to the decree of 18 Floréal the very idea of a moral basis for the revolution was attacked by all of France's enemies, stressing again the importance of accepting the idea of life after death, and reminding his hearers of how, on 20 Prairial, the entire nation had come together.

The desire for some form of state morality or state support of religion brought into the open by Robespierre's festival did not disappear after Thermidor; it merely sank back below the surface. The problem of the national desire for some form of organised religion with the concomitant risk of a Catholic backlash remained a matter of concern to successive governments. The idea of neutralising any potential danger by attempting to channel the public desire for some form of acceptable state-sponsored religion into a path more suitable to the needs and aspirations of the government seemed, as Bianchi commented, to confirm the national need: 'It shows the persistence of the idea of a Revolutionary (state?) religion aimed at a largely unknown population to oppose Catholicism, or at least to fill the gap caused by its temporary removal.'[4]

Six weeks after Thermidor, the Second Sans-culottides day (18 September 1794) saw the publication of the decree formally separating Church and State. Cambon, using as an excuse the need to make cuts to the national budget, seized the opportunity to remove all funding from the Constitutional Church. Nationally, despite some re-emergence of de-Christianisation, there was increasing discontent among those who still practised the Catholic faith and who continued to press for the re-opening of churches. On 3 Ventôse Year III (21 February 1795) Boissy d'Anglas presented a report which led to the Convention permitting the practice of religion 'in any building which the priests and the people could procure for that purpose', providing that the priests were prepared to take the original oath of 14 August 1792. In the same year Grégoire succeeded in re-establishing the Constitutional church.

In an attempt to settle the problem, Merlin de Thionville proposed in 1796 that the Directory, headed by La Réveillière-Lépeaux, should actively support Theophilanthropy, a new Deist belief system put forward in a work published by a Paris printer, Chemin Despontès.[5] This new movement combined many of the ideas of the Cult of the Supreme Being, especially in its emphasis on the importance of internationalism and family harmony, while maintaining an unimpeachable political position in its opposition to any resurgence of Catholicism. This movement became the recipient of large amounts of government funding, and by the end of 1797 had taken control of some fifteen parishes in Paris. When Napoleon left for Italy in 1797, La Réveillière-Lépeaux ordered him to use the opportunity to 'crush the priestly power of Rome, enemy of Liberty' in the name of Theophilanthropy.[6] Official approval and funding notwithstanding, the awkward mixture of Deism, populist Rousseauvian philosophy and patriotism which this new movement peddled offered no real response to the religious aspirations of the mass of the nation so that it had almost completely disappeared by the end of 1798.

Neither the use of the name Supreme Being nor the underlying moral concept were to disappear completely with the fall of Robespierre. Even though the semi-religious element disappeared, the name itself did not vanish after Thermidor and it is noticeable that nobody, not even the most committed atheist, put forward a proposal, either in the Thermidorean Convention or later during the Directory, to change the names of the Temples of the Supreme Being either back to Temples of Reason or to their original religious names. The inscription *Temple de l'Être Suprême* remained in place for many years, often staying on the fascia of churches not only after the re-instatement of the Catholic faith with the Concordat of 1801, but even on some churches after the Restoration. Until 1799 many festivals outside Paris continued to be held either under the auspices of the Supreme Being or at least in the building carrying that name. The Festival of the Foundation of the Republic was celebrated on 10 Vendémiaire Year III (2 October 1794) in Foix, as it was in the majority of provincial towns and cities throughout France 'at the Temple of the Supreme Being'.[7] The municipal registers of Strasbourg refer to a procession two years later 'to the Temple of the Supreme Being'[8] and every municipal archive offers examples of the name of the Supreme Being continuing to figure in official celebrations, at least until the Concordat of 1801, and in some smaller towns even later. The words '*Le peuple français reconnaît l'existence de l'Être suprême et l'immortalité de l'âme*' can still be seen on an external wall of the Cathedral of Clermont-Ferrand and above one of the porches of the church of Saint-Sulpice in Paris.[9]

The problem of establishing an acceptable national morality continued to bedevil successive Revolutionary administrations. It was finally settled after Napoleon Bonaparte seized power on 18 Brumaire Year VIII (9 November 1799). Bonaparte was clearly aware of the necessity of ensuring the support of those still practising the Christian faith in France. Once in power he began to allow non-alienated churches to reopen, and granted amnesties to some deported non-juror priests. Although personally indifferent to religion, he clearly understood the political necessity of a strong united church in France, one which would be both a force for order and social harmony and a pillar of his own administration. It is a measure of Bonaparte's political acumen that he was aware not only of the dangers still inherent in the religious situation, but also appreciated the enormous political advantage to be gained from solving this apparently intractable national problem. By the Concordat of 1801 Bonaparte succeeded where Robespierre had failed in re-establishing the Catholic Church as the state church, even incorporating many of the original reforms of 1789, such as the supervision by the state both of all appointments of the higher clergy and the responsibility for the salaries of the lower clergy. With the success of his negotiations with Rome, Bonaparte not only legitimised the national desire for a state-approved morality based on religious ethics, he also ensured its continued control by the temporal power.

Notes

1 'Sauvez la patrie sans moi!' 'La patrie n'est pas un homme!' For a detailed description of the event see G. Walter, *Maximilien de Robespierre* (Paris, 1961), pp. 449–53.
2 B. Nabonne, *La Vie Privée de Robespierre* (Paris, 1938), p. 222.
3 A. Laponneraye, ed., *Mémoires de Charlotte Robespierre sur ses deux frères; précédés d'une introduction par Laponneraye et suivis de pièces justificatives* (Paris, 1835).
4 'Elle prouve la permanence de l'idéal d'une religion (d'état?) révolutionnaire s'adressant à un peuple largement mythique pour combattre le catholicisme ou tout au moins combler le vide causé par sa disparition provisoire.' S. Bianchi, 'Théophilantropie', in *Dictionnaire historique de la Révolution française*, A. Soboul, ed. (Paris, 1989), p. 1030.
5 J.-B. Chemin-Dupontès, *Manuel des théophilanthropophiles ou adorateurs de Dieu et amis des hommes* (Paris, An III).
6 'anéantir la puissance sacerdotale de Rome, ennemi de la Liberté', A Mathiez, *La Théophilanthropie et le culte décadaire* (Paris, 1904).
7 L. Blazy, *Les fêtes nationales à Foix sous la Révolution* (Foix, 1911), pp. 8–9.
8 A.M. Strasbourg 1.MW.146.
9 As this book is being written the church is undergoing extensive refurbishment. It must be hoped that the inscription will survive the building and redecoration work.

Conclusion

If, as has already been argued, the Cult of the Supreme Being offered such evident and immediate potential political force to Robespierre, it becomes all the more difficult to understand why the whole ethos of the Supreme Being could disappear so completely and so quickly. With the events of 20 Prairial, Robespierre seemed to have performed the almost impossible feat of uniting the nation in a brilliant combination of revolutionary zeal allied to the underlying hunger for an acceptable belief system. Without betraying the Revolution in any way, without any suggestion of re-installing the old church, he had touched the wellspring of goodwill of the majority of the nation; he had reached out to the desire in much of the nation for something to fill what Pascal called 'the infinite gulf' in the national consciousness.[1] It seems from the evidence of many of the contemporary reports that there was a genuine expectation that the fact of the guillotine's disappearance from the Place de la Révolution would mark the end of the Terror and the birth of the Republic of Virtue. There is also the evidence of the level of national support which was so obvious in the reports coming into Paris; evidence which, had Robespierre been aware of its import, might have led him to take very different decisions in the immediate period after the Festival. It may be that this was another example of the atmosphere of plot and counter-plot, another facet of the climate of conspiracy which imbued the later Jacobin administration and which deliberately kept these documents from him. On the other hand, as has been suggested in a previous chapter, it might simply have been due to the inefficiency of the secretary of the Committee of Public Education, Arbogast and his staff.

The question remains: what, in fact, were these crowds celebrating? Certainly some of them would have been hoping that this celebration, held as it was on the day of the feast of Pentecost in the old calendar, was a sign that some form of religious freedom was returning. Others, while accepting that the removal of Atheism as an official facet of public life was a good thing, could essentially see no difference between a Goddess of Reason and a Supreme Being, since neither was real, neither was part of national life, neither had any impact on the everyday life of the masses. The 'consoling idea' of immortality had its positive aspects, but was that all that was on offer? No-one seemed to be seriously working towards filling the God-shaped hole in most people's lives, and this new moral system, unlike a real religion, seemed to be totally lacking in the essential ingredients necessary for its successful continuation. Unlike the old church there was no rulebook, no uplifting or edifying stories to be heard, no martyrs and saints to look up to, even the martyrs of the Revolution seemed to be missing. There were no pastors or community leaders, and no spokesmen were visiting the *sections* to imbue them with the necessary fervour to make the converts any new cult needs if it is to survive. Equally, unlike a 'proper' religion, none of the chosen slogans at the two sites offered either the long-term prospect of salvation or the short-term prospect of charitable assistance, two vital elements of any religion for which the old middle classes and the new poor respectively might have been hoping. From the evidence of some of the speeches given in the provinces, it would seem that some speakers at the celebrations were having problems with using the specific terms Robespierre proposed and found it difficult to move easily from the concept of Reason as the moral driver of the Republic, which they had been proposing only a few months, earlier, to this new semi-religious concept. There are several examples, including speeches in Lyons and Strasbourg, where the word Reason is used alongside, if not in place of, the new concept words of Supreme Being and Immortality.

However, there can be no doubt as to the success of the day as far as the organisation and the *Fête* itself were concerned. Every contemporary commentator, even such vilifiers of Robespierre as Vilate and Ruault, was full of praise for the celebrations themselves and seem to have generally approved of the idea of honouring the Supreme Being. As far as can be gathered, throughout the nation the people seem to have thoroughly enjoyed themselves, both in the formal events of the day and later in their more informal local celebrations. It would seem that Robespierre, despite the public attacks on him during the procession in Paris by his opponents in the Convention, could rejoice in the spectacle of the population of France apparently wholeheartedly accepting the idea of joining together joyfully to honour the Supreme Being. At that level, it is clear that the day had been a great success, everyone had enjoyed themselves and the idea of the Supreme Being, as a potential national belief system, was up and running. Yet it is one thing to have a great festival which, for a brief span, apparently unites the whole of the nation in joyful celebration, and quite another to lay the groundwork for something which, if successful, would become an intrinsic part of national life from then on.

It might have been expected that, following the success of 20 Prairial, all these questions would be rapidly and efficiently addressed, to ensure that the new belief system would be incorporated into the life of the nation as quickly and as deeply as possible. This simply did not happen, and the vilifying comments of Robespierre's more extreme political opponents, despite their assertion that they were not attacking the idea of the Supreme Being as such, led inescapably to it being seen merely as being the vehicle for the self-aggrandisement of its chief advocate.

The surprise is that having successfully established the idea of the Festival with the apparent approbation of the nation, Robespierre took no further action to build on what he had created, and the question of why he did not do so has fascinated historians ever since. It would have seemed obvious that some sort of organisation would be put into train to ensure that the national public expressions of gratitude to and adoration of the Author of Nature and the Protector of the Nation would continue and grow, and do so to the greater profit of the Jacobin cause. Despite vague hints in the speech of 18 Floréal, no practical steps were taken by either Robespierre or his supporters. There was not even a minimal formation at national or local level of the organisation which the new belief system would need. No effort seems to have been made to involve the national network of *Sociétés Populaires*, which would surely have been the ideal local level organisers, and who, given their general loyalty to Robespierre personally, would probably have been happy to be so empowered.

Did the unexpected intensity of the vocal attacks which Robespierre had had to take on board during the procession temporarily shake his belief in both himself and his goal, did it consider him to fear that his power base was no longer strong enough for him to impose his personal vision on the nation? Robespierre's health was also a factor; ever since his arrival in Paris in 1789 he had been subject to sudden excruciating headaches, debilitating attacks of fever, and more recently unexplained swellings of his legs. It may be that all this, combined with his personal problems, created a climate in which he could not appreciate the true situation and the level of support which he seemed to have created nationally. He seems to have been so caught up in his own dark thoughts and his personal problems especially during Messidor and early Thermidor, that he could no longer comprehend that there might be available to him this new potential national support base, which, had he used it wisely, could have changed the political climate to his considerable advantage.

The problem of the final evaluation of the influence of the *Fête* must remain inextricably bound up with the fate of its founder and dominant figure, Maximilien Robespierre. It is each individual historian's responsibility to decide, on the evidence we have, how far he can personally be charged with not seizing the opportunity which the national outpouring of feeling for the *Fête* offered. Could he, in one great visionary declaration, have simultaneously offered a general amnesty, proclaimed the birth of the Republic of Virtue, and obviated the potential problem caused by the smouldering embers of the old religion? Had he chosen this option, he might well have succeeded, considering the level of popular support demonstrated during the *Fête*, if not in establishing his ideal state, at least in establishing one in which the underlying morality which was still present in the conscience of the majority of the French people would have fused with their acceptance of the aims of the Revolution.

There are two aspects of the events of 20 Prairial which stand out above everything else. The first is that it was a day of national joy – every commentator on the *Fête* agrees on this point. Even the weather was perfect. The second is that the entire nation came together in an act of truly national rejoicing. Most importantly it was a day when not only did the whole nation enjoy itself nationally, it equally did so locally. The Festival was celebrated in almost every city, town, village and hamlet throughout France: the emphasis was totally on local participation; local officials organised the celebrations; speeches were made by local orators; local poets had their work declaimed by local actors, or arranged by local musicians to be sung by local choirs. The processions were made up of local people who were applauded by their neighbours. In the formal ceremonies, the Creator of the Universe seemed to be smiling down on his favoured nation as old men led forward the youths who swore to march under his banners and the mothers held their babies aloft for his blessing. It was a day in which the whole nation did the same thing at the same time and, remarkably for France in 1794, in the same language. There were, of course, local references in individual ceremonies, but they were all centred on the national theme; there is no evidence of any attempts at regionalism, either in the language or in the nature of the ceremonies.

All the available evidence strongly supports the contention that the Festival of the Supreme Being on 20 Prairial, Year II was not, as so many historians have previously maintained, a sterile event, whose only significance was to mark the apogee of Robespierre's drive for total power before the descent towards Thermidor. The question remains, was the Festival, as Ozouf claims, 'The last revolutionary festival worthy of any attention'[2] or was it, on the contrary, as Vovelle asserted, mere 'Smoke and mirrors'?[3] Buchez and Roux had already suggested in 1838 that 'The acclamation of Robespierre's statement of belief from one end of the Republic to the other, whose unanimity was confirmed daily by the correspondence received, showed to all that this statement of belief could be a basis of great strength',[4] and more recent examination of archival evidence has led to the wheel coming almost full circle in the evaluation of the importance of Robespierre's vision of a new and specifically Republican morality.

Even allowing for the prevailing climate of heroic rhetoric and over-elaborate prose, what cannot be ignored in the accounts of the events of 20 Prairial Year II is that it was considered by those who took part in it as a day of genuine national solidarity. From the records, not just the main cities but the vast majority of France came together in an act of devotion, honouring as much the new Nation as the Supreme Being. Throughout France the day ended with people enjoying themselves in their own communities; sometimes with formal banquets as in Bordeaux, sometimes with dancing in the public squares, as in Amiens and Angers, or with *repas civiques* and street parties as in Strasbourg, Lyon and in the Paris *sections*. Many of these revellers hoped and believed that this would be the moment when France would finally emerge from the darkness of the early Revolution into the light of a new national morality, maybe even into the dawn of the Republic of Virtue. This national euphoria may have only lasted one day, but for many of those participating that day was Easter, Pentecost and the *Fête-Dieu* all rolled into one. In short it was, as so many reports called it, 'A day never to be forgotten.'[5]

Notes

1 'ce gouffre infini qui ne peut être rempli que par un objet infini et immuable, c'est-à-dire Dieu même', Pascal, Pensées III.ii.V, *Œuvres complètes*, Bossuet, ed. (Paris, 1779).
2 'La dernière fête révolutionnaire digne de quelque attention', M. Ozouf, *La Fête Révolutionnaire 1789–1799* (Paris, 1976), p. 191.
3 'Mystique et illusion', M. Vovelle, *Les Images de la Révolution française* (Paris, 1988).

4 'L'acclamation qui avait salué, d'un bout de la République à l'autre, la profession de foi de Robespierre, et dont l'unanimité était attestée chaque jour par la correspondance, découvrait à tous les yeux qu'il y avait dans cette profession de foi la base d'un grand pouvoir.' P.-J.-B. and P.-C. Roux, *Histoire parlementaire de la Révolution française: ou Journal des assemblées nationales depuis 1780 jusqu'en 1815* (Paris, 1838), Vol. 33, Preface, pp. ix–x.
5 'Un jour à jamais memorable.'

Bibliography

Official sources

Archives Parlementaires de 1787 à 1860. Recueil complet des Débats législatifs et politiques des Chambres Françaises, fondé par MM. Madival et Laurent, continué par l'Institut d'Histoire de la Révolution française, Université de Paris I (Paris, 1972)
Procès-verbaux du Comité d'Instruction Publique de la Convention Nationale, Guillaume, M.J., ed. (Paris, 1889)
Recueils des Actes du Comité de Salut Public, Aulard *et al.*, eds (Paris, 1895)
Réimpression de l'ancien Moniteur: seule histoire authentique et inaltérée de la révolution française depuis la réunion des États-généraux jusqu'au Consulat (mai 1789–novembre 1799) (Paris, 1858)

Archival sources

ARCHIVES NATIONALES, PARIS

AE.II.3063	Tarif du Maximum des salaires, gages, main-d'œuvres, journées de travail, dans l'étendue de la Commune de Paris
AF.II.17	Minutes des procès-verbaux des séances du Comité d'Instruction publique, An II
	AF.II.17.117 Minutes du procès-verbal de la séance du 19 Floréal, An II
AF.II.22	Minutes d'actes et matériaux des procès-verbaux. Août 1792 – Germinal An II
AF.II.60	Arrêtés du Comité de salut public. Mai 1793 – Prairial An II
	AF.II.60.438 Arrêtés du 1 floréal au 29 prairial
AF.II.66	Arrêtés du Comité de salut public – An II
	AF.II.66.484 Arrêté ordonnant l'impression du rapport de Robespierre sur le culte de l'Être suprême

BIBLIOGRAPHY

AF.II.67   Comité de salut public: Instruction publique; Écoles nationales; Institut national de musique; Théâtres; Musées; Musée d'histoire Naturelle; Fêtes nationales; Inventions

    AF.II.67.493.3   Arrêté ajournant la représentation de la pièce «Paméla»

    AF.II.67.497.8   Arrêté relatif à l'exécution du décret sur la fête nationale du 20 prairial

AF.II.80   Commission de Travaux publics

    AF.II.80.590   Travaux publics – matériel – Brumaire/Prairial An II

    AF.II.80.590.45   Arrêté concernant les embélissements à faire dans le Palais national et son jardin, sur le plan d'Hubert

AF*.II.47   Registres originaux des arrêtés du Comité de salut public 25 septembre 1793–6 germinal, An II

    AF* II.47.67   Arrêté du Comité de salut public le 4 frimaire, An II

F.4.2090   Comptes et Comptabilité – Fêtes Nationales

    Manchette 4 – Fêtes Nationales de l'Être suprême, des Victoires, de J.J. Rousseau, Marat, Barra, Viala, Pompe funèbre de Ferraud

    F.4.2090.4   Fête nationale de l'Être suprême

F.12.1544   Maximum – Tables dressées en exécution des décrets du 8 vendémiaire, du 11 brumaire et du 6 ventôse, et classées par ordre de départements

    F.12.1544.2   Département de la Gironde/du Bec d'Ambès

    F.12.1544.30-31   Ville de Paris

    F.12.1544.36   Départements du Rhin (Bas et Haut), du Rhône et de la Loire

    F.12.1544.47   Département de la Somme

F.17.1065   Comité de salut public – correspondance

    F.17.1065.5   Listes de députation des artistes de l'Institut national de musique pour enseigner aux citoyens, dans les sections, le chant des hymnes adoptés pour la Fête de l'Être suprême

    F.17.1065.5   Célébration de la fête du 20 prairial à Melun et à Belvès (Dordogne)

MUNICIPAL ARCHIVES

Archives Municipales – Amiens

1.D.10.9   Archives Révolutionnaires Registre de Délibérations du Conseil Général de la Municipalité d'Amiens

1.I.2/2   Archives Révolutionnaires – Fêtes et Cérémonies Publiques – Fête de l'Être suprême – Prairial An II

H – C. 3793/42 – Marche de la Fête Civique et Républicaine qui aura lieu le 30 Brumaire de l'an second de la République
H – C. 3793/48 – Discours prononcé au nom du Conseil Général de la Commune d'Amiens, le 20 prairial jour de la Fête de l'Être Suprême Discours prononcé par le Président de la Société Populaire d'Amiens le 20 prairial

Archives Municipales – Angers
Registre de délibérations de la Municipalité d'Angers, An II Vol. 5 1.D.1.5

Archives Municipales – Bordeaux – Fonds Révolutionnaires
Registres de délibérations du Conseil Général de la Municipalité de Bordeaus, An II

D.108, D.109, D.110, D.111, D.127, D.144
I.16   Ordre de la Marche pour la Fête de l'Unité
I.18   Inventaire sommaire Vol. 4
I.18.64   Lettre de Jullien, Agent du Comité de salut public, aux officiers municipaux
L.5.18   Département des finances
L.5.30–32 Département des finances – Compte-rendu au peuple par l'administration
L.6   Inventaire sommaire – Finances
L.6.5   Mémoire sur la situation des finances de la Commune de Bordeaux, sur les charges qu'elle a à supporter et sur les secours qui lui sont nécessaires pour les acquitter
L.6.13   Rapport sur les dettes les plus insistantes
P.10.2   Plan de la Fête du 20 Prairial

Archives Municipales – Lyon
Registres de délibérations du Conseil Général de Commune – Affranchie, An II

WP.002 – Finances
310 WP.7
1295 WP.12
1406 WP – Finances

Archives de la Bibliothèque Municipale de Lyon – Fonds Coste
1. C.111698
1. C 350978 – Fête à l'Être Suprême, Célébrée à Commune-
Afranchie le 20 prairial An II de la République
1. C 651107 – Medaillon frappé pour la Fête de l'Être Suprême
1. C 650834 – Antoine Sabatier, *La Fête de l'Être suprême à Theys (Isère)*, Extrait du *Bulletin Historique et archéologique, LE VIEUX PAPIER*, Tome 16 – Fascicule No. 110, Décembre 1924 (Lille, 1924)

Archives Municipales – Strasbourg
Registres de délibérations du Conseil Municipal de la Ville de Strasbourg, An II
1.MW.60

1.MW.93
1.MW.139
1.MW.142
83.MW.19
183.MW.34

DEPARTMENTAL ARCHIVES

Archives Départementales de Maine-et-Loire
1.L.30 – Registre de Délibérations An II
1.L.411 – Angers
1.L.522 – Finances – Angers

Archives Départementales du Nord
L-1254/1 – Plan de la Fête de l'Être Suprême à Lille
L-1254/3 – Détails de la fête de l'Être Suprême et de l'immortalité de l'âme, célébrée en la Commune de Bailleul
L-7088-183 – Procès-verbal du conseil de la Commune de Douai du 3 prairial, An II. Plan de la Fête qui sera célébrée le 20 prairial

Archives Départementales du Pas de Calais – Collection LAROCHE
B1339/17 – Registre des délibérations du conseil-général de la commune d'Arras

Archives de la Police – Paris
AA.159 – Registres An II
AA.159.247/248 – Section des Invalides

Newspapers

PARIS – BIBLIOTHÈQUE NATIONALE DE FRANCE

PARIS – BIBLIOTHÈQUE HISTORIQUE DE LA VILLE DE PARIS

L'Abréviateur universel
L'Auditeur nationale
Les Annales Patriotiques et Littéraires
Le Bulletin Républicain, ou Papier Nouvelle de tous les Pays et de tous les jours
La Chronique de Paris
Le Courrier de la Convention et de la Guerre
Le Courrier Républicain
La Feuille Villageoise
Le Journal des Débats et des Décrets
Journal de la Montagne
Le Journal du Matin
Le Journal du Soir
Le Messager du Soir
Le Républicain Français

Angers – Bibliothèque Municipale, Toussaint
Les Affiches d'Angers ou Moniteur du Département de Maine et Loire

Bordeaux – Bibliothèque Municipale, Méridec
Bulletin et Affiches de Bordeaux et du Département du Bec d'Ambès
Journal du Club National de Bordeaux, Rédigé par deux de ses Membres

Strasbourg – Bibliothèque nationale de France – Strasbourg
Der Weltbote, allgemeine Zeitung für jedermann
Straßburgische Zeitung und mit derselben vereinigt Der Weltbote
Argos, oder der Mann mit hundert Augen

Pamphlets, leaflets and reprints

BIBLIOTHÈQUE NATIONALE DE FRANCE, PARIS

Série LB40

LB40-920   *Rapport fait par Édouard Poncet à la société populaire et régénérée de Brest, au nom de son comité d'instruction publique, le 25 prairial, l'an II de la république française … contenant les détails de la fête célébrée dans cette commune en l'honneur de l'Être suprême* (Brest, n.d.)

LB40-2714   *Antoine Français, Idée de la fête qui doit être célébrée à Grenoble le 20 prairial, en l'honneur de l'Être Suprême, présentée à la Société populaire de Grenoble, au nom de son Comité d'instruction publique; & adoptée par elle, ainsi que par les Commissaires de la Commune* (Grenoble, 1794)

LB40-3029   *Projet de la fête à l'Être Suprême, proposé par le comité d'instruction de la Société des Jacobins de Toulouse, pour avoir lieu Décadi prochain, 20 prairial, conformément au Décret de la Convention nationale* (Toulouse, n.d.)

Série LB41

LB41-1103   *Véritable détail de la cérémonie qui doit être célébrée Décadi 20 prairial, l'indication des places que doivent occuper la Convention Nationale, les Sections de Paris, la Cavalerie, la Musique, les Vieillards, les Mères de familles, les filles et les adolescens: avec l'ordre, la marche et les noms des rues par lesquelles passera ce cortège. Suivie de l'hymne qui doit être chanté par le peuple, au Champ de la Réunion, en l'honneur de l'Être suprême. Par J.M. Deschamps de la Section du Contrat Social, rue J.J. Rousseau, No. 4* (Paris, n.d.)

LB41-1104   *Plan de la Fête à l'Être Suprême, qui sera célébrée à TOURS, le 20 Prairial, en exécution du Décret du 18 floréal, l'an second de la République, une et indivisible* (Tours, n.d.)

LB41-1105   *Plan méthodique d'exécution pour la fête à l'Être suprême, qui aura lieu le 20 prairial, l'an deuxième de la république, dans la commune de Versailles* (Versailles, n.d.)

LB41-1107   *Ordre de la fête en honneur de l'Être suprême, célébrée le décadi 20 prairial; et discours prononcés à cette occasion sur la montagne élevée au milieu de la place d'armes et au Champ de Mars* (Abbeville, An II)

LB41-1110   *Couplets chantés, au nom de la jeunesse, le jour de la fête de l'Être suprême, 20 prairial, 2e année de la république une et indivisible par de jeunes élèves de la pension du citoyen Audet. Discours prononcé par le citoyen Beuzelin, Agent National de la Commune de Caen le décadi 20 prairial, l'an II de la république une et indivisible, pour la fête de l'Éternel. Vœux à l'Éternel, prononcés par une jeune fille. Discours prononcé par le citoyen Le Carpentier, membre de la Société Populaire de Caen, le décadi 20 prairial, l'an deuxième de la république une et indivisible, pour la fête de l'Éternel. Prière à l'Éternel, prononcée par le maire de Caen. Hymne à l'Éternel* (Caen, n.d.)

LB41-1112   'Fête à L'Être Suprême célébrée à Commune-Affranchie (ci-devant Lyon) en 1794'. Reprint in 1838 by Imprimerie de L. Boitel, Lyon, of the original report printed by Destafanis in Prairial, An II. *Société Populaire des Jacobins de Commune-Affranchie, Amis de Chalier et de Galliard. FÊTE À L'ÊTRE SUPRÊME, Célébrée à COMMUNE-AFFRANCHIE le 20 prairial an 2 de la République* (Commune-Affranchie, n.d.)

LB41-1127   François-Antoine Boissy d'Anglas, *Essai sur les fêtes nationales, adressé à la Convention Nationale; par Boissy d'Anglas Représentant du Peuple, député par le département de l'Ardèche* (Paris, An II)

LB41-1150   *Causes secrètes de la Révolution du 9 au 10 Thermidor, par Vilate, ex Juré au Tribunal Révolutionnaire de Paris, détenu à la Force. A Paris, l'an III de la République* (n.p., n.d.)

LB41-3234   *Instruction pour l'ordre à observer le jour de la Fête de la Réunion au 10 août l'an 2 de la République française* (Paris, n.d.)

LB41-3888   *Proclamation du Conseil Général de la Commune d'Angers, relative à la Fête consacrée à l'Être Suprême, qui doit être célébrée le 20 Prairial* (Angers, n.d.)

LB41-3889   *Fête à l'Être suprême et à la Nature Le Conseil général de la commune d'Orléans à ses concitoyens, le 15 prairial, an 2* (Orléans, n.d.)

LB41-3890   *Plan allégorique d'Un Jardin de la Révolution française et des vertus républicaines par le Citoyen Verhelst envoyé au Comité de salut public, le 15 prairial de l'an deuxième* (Paris, n.d.)

LB41-3893   *Ordre et Marche de la fête à l'Être suprême, qui aura lieu décadi prochain, 20 prairial, conformément au décret de la Convention nationale* (n.p., n.d.)

LB41-3895   *Détails exacts des cérémonies et de l'ordre à observer dans la fête de l'Être suprême* (n.p., n.d.)

LB41-3896   *Détails exacts de l'embellissement des Jardins publics et de la Convention Nationale, et autres lieux, pour le 20 prairial, jour de la Fête en honneur de l'Éternel Suivi du superbe Monument qui va être*

	élevé sur le Pont Neuf, représentant le Peuple Français terrassant le fanatisme, le royalisme et le fédéralisme Extrait du registre des arrêtés du Comité de Salut Public, du 25 Floréal, de l'an deuxième de le République française, une et indivisible (Paris, An II)
LB41-3897	Liberté, Egalité ... Le peuple français reconnaît l'existence de l'Être suprême et l'immortalité de l'âme (Douai, n.d.)
LB41-3898	Commune de Nancy. Ordre de Marche de la fête à l'Être Suprême, qui sera célébrée dans la commune de Nancy, le 20 prairial, an 2 conformément à la loi du 18 floréal dernier (Nancy, n.d.)
LB41-3899	Manière de célébrer dans les campagnes la fête à l'Être suprême, qui doit avoir lieu le 20 prairial l'an 2 de la République française ... par C. Thiébaut (Nancy, n.d.)
LB41-3900	Plan de la fête à l'Être suprême, adopté par la commune de St-Omer, pour être exécuté le 20 prairial prochain (Saint-Omer, n.d.)
LB41-3903	Fête à l'Être suprême et à la Nature, célébrée à Chaumont, chef-lieu du département de la Haute-Marne, décadi 20 prairial (Chaumont, n.d.)
LB41-3905	Discours prononcé dans la fête célébrée en l'honneur de l'Être Suprême, par la commune de Marseille, le 20 prairial par le Représentant du Peuple, Maignet (Marseille, An II)
LB41-3914	Département de Seine-et-Marne. Recueil contenant 1° Rapport du Comité de salut public, du 18 floréal, sur les fêtes nationales, suivi du décret du même jour: 2° Discours de Maximilien Robespierre, prononcé à la fête de l'Etre suprême ... 3° Hymnes des citoyens Marie-Joseph Chénier, ... Liégeard fils, ... et Guéniot, ... 4° Invocation à l'Être suprême, par Maure ... suivi du Procès-verbal de la commune d'Auxerre, séance du 21 Prairial; 5°Catéchisme républicain, par le C. Lachabeaussière 6° Détail de la fête à l'Etre suprême, célébrée à Melun le 20 Prairial; 7° instruction des administrations de Seine-et-Marne, aux administrés de son ressort (Melun, An II)
LB41-5470	Précis de la Fête à l'Être Suprême, célébrée à Troyes, le 20 Prairial, deuxième année républicaine. Imprimé par ordre du Conseil-Général de la Commune (Troyes, n.d.)
LB41-5703	Détails de la fête de l'Être Suprême et de l'immortalité de l'âme, célébrée en la Commune de Bailleul, le 20 prairial, de la deuxième année de la République Française, une et indivisible (Dunkerque, n.d.) reproduced in Colloque sur L'Être suprême, Arras, Centre culturel Noirot, 1989 (Arras, 1991)

Série LC

LC2-207	L'Auditeur National, Journal de Législation, de Politique et de Littérature
LC2-412	Journal du Soir, de politique et de littérature
LC2-809	Discours prononcés les jours de décadi dans la section de Guillaume Tell (Paris, An II)

Série LD

LD 188-2   *Manuel des théoanthropophiles ou adorateurs de Dieu et amis des hommes, contenant l'exposition de leurs dogmes, de leur morale et de leurs pratiques religieuses, avec une instruction sur l'organisation et la célébration du culte, rédigé par C*** (Chemin-Dupontès)* (Paris, An III)

Série LE

LE38-978   *Convention Nationale. Opinion de Merlin (de Thionville), sur les fêtes nationales, prononcée dans la séance du 9 vendémiaire an III de la République* (Paris, An III)

LE38-1129   *Convention Nationale. Organisation et tableau des fêtes décadaires. Par J.-F. Barailon, représentant du peuple, député par le département de la Creuse. Imprimée par ordre de la Convention nationale* (Paris, An III)

LE38-2140   *Convention Nationale, Instruction Particulière pour les commissaires chargés des détails de la fête à l'Être Suprême, qui doit être célébrée le 20 prairial, conformément au décret de la Convention Nationale du 18 Floréal, l'an deuxième de la République française, une et indivisible. Imprimée par ordre de la Convention Nationale* (Paris, n.d.)

Bibliothèque Historique de la Ville de Paris

10 073(98)   *Convention Nationale. Adresse de la municipalité de Paris à la Convention Nationale dans la séance du 27 floréal de l'an second* (Paris, n.d.)

12 272(6)   *Plan de la Fête à l'Être Suprême qui sera célébrée à Nantes* (Nantes, n.d.)

28 094   *Plan de la Fête à l'Être Suprême qui sera célébrée à Tours* (Tours, n.d.)

104 142(22)   *Détail de la cérémonie qui sera observée le 20 prairial dans la commune de Sceaux-l'Unité, jour du repos décrété par la Convention nationale, le 18 floréal, le premier jour établi comme fête républicaine consacrée à l'Être Suprême et à la Nature. Discours civique sur les mœurs et les vertus. Prononcé à la Fête de l'Être Suprême à la commune de Sceaux-l'Unité* (Paris, n.d.)

611 705(6)   *La Fête de l'Être Suprême: scènes patriotiques, mêlées de chants, texte – 23 pages, pantomimes et danses, du Citoyen Cuvelier ... Musique d'Orthon Vandenbrook à Paris: Théâtre de la Cité Variétés, le 20 prairial de l'an 2* (Paris, n.d.)

957434   *A l'Être Suprême, Société des Amis de la Liberté et de l'égalité, Metz* (Metz, n.d.)

958317   *Discours prononcé par le Président du District de Vienne, le 20 prairial de l'an 2, à la Fête de l'Être Suprême* (Vienne, n.d.)

959995   *Discours sur l'existence de l'Être Suprême et de l'immortalité de l'âme prononcé dans le Temple de l'Éternel à Orléans, le 20 prairial par le Citoyen Aignan, Agent national près du district d'Orléans* (Orléans, n.d.)

961311 *Vive la République française, une et indivisible. Liberté, égalité, fraternité ou la mort. Discours prononcé par Michault, Citoyen français, à Vaugirard. Le jour de la fête de l'Être Suprême, l'An deuxième de la République. Dont l'impression a été arrêtée par la Commune* (Vaugirard, n.d.)

Books

Agulhon, Maurice, *Marianne au combat: L'imagerie et la symbolique Républicaine de 1789 à 1880* (Paris, 1979).
—— 'Faut-il avoir peur de 1789?' *Histoire Vagabonde*, 2 (1988): 244–61.
Andress, David, *The Terror: Civil War in the French Revolution* (London, 2003).
—— ed. *Experiencing the French Revolution* (Oxford, 2013).
Aulard, Alphonse, *Histoire politique de la révolution française: origines et développement de la démocratie et de la république 1789–1804*, 5th ed., 2nd reprint (Paris, 1921).
—— 'Aux apologistes de Robespierre', *La Justice*, 28 September 1885.
—— *Le culte de la Raison et le culte de l'Être Suprême* (Paris, 1892).
—— ed., *Recueil des Actes du Comité de Salut Public* (Paris, 1895).
Baczko, Bronislaw, *Une éducation pour la démocratie: textes et projets de l'époque révolutionnaire* (Paris, 2000).
Baker, Keith Michael, *Inventing the French Revolution: Essays on French Political Culture in the Eighteenth Century* (Cambridge, 1990).
Baudot, Marc-Antoine, *Notes Historiques sur la Convention, le Directoire, l'Empire et l'exil des votants* (Paris, 1893).
Bellanger, Claude, Jacques Godechot, Pierre Guiral and Fernand Terrou, eds, *Histoire générale de la presse française* (Paris, 1969).
Bessand-Massenet, Pierre, *Robespierre: L'homme et l'idée* (Paris, 2001).
Betzinger, Claud, *Vie et mort d'Euloge Schneider, ci-devant franciscain (1756–1794)* (Strasbourg, 1997).
Bianchi, Serge, *La Révolution culturelle de l'an II: Élites et peuple* (Paris, 1982).
—— 'Théophilantropie', in *Dictionnaire historique de la Révolution française*, Albert Soboul, ed. (Paris, 1989).
Blanchot, P., N. Duchon, A. Foucher and M. Vollant, *Mennecy sous la Révolution, ou la révolution de Jean-Michel* (La Mée sur Seine, 1989).
Blazy, L'Abbé Louis, *Les fêtes nationales à Foix sous la Révolution* (Foix, 1911).
Bois, Benjamin, *Les Fêtes révolutionnaires à Angers de l'an II à l'an VIII* (Paris, 1929).
Boissy d'Anglas, F.A., *Essai sur les fêtes nationales, adressé à la Convention Nationale; par Boissy d'Anglas Représentant du Peuple, Député pour le Département de l'Ardèche* (Paris, An II).
Bouchary, Jean, *Le marché des changes à Paris à la fin du 18ième siècle (1778–1800)* (Paris, 1938).
Bouloiseau, Marc, G. Lefebvre, Albert Soboul, Gustave Laurent *et al.*, eds, *Œuvres complètes de Maximilien Robespierre* (Paris, 2000–11).
Bowley, A.L., *Wages in the United Kingdom in the 19th Century* (Cambridge, 1900).

Bredin, Jean-Louis, *Sieyès: La clé de la Révolution française* (Paris, 1988).
Brookner, Anita, *Jacques-Louis David* (London, 1980).
Brooks, Peter, *The Melodramatic Imagination* (New Haven, 1976).
Brunel, Françoise, *Thermidor: La chute de Robespierre* (Bruxelles, 1989).
Brunot, Ferdinand, *Le Français en France et hors de France au XVIII siècle* (Paris, 1967).
Buch, Esteban, *La neuvième de Beethoven* (Paris, 1999).
Buchez, Philippe-Joseph-Benjamin and Pierre-Célestin Roux, *Histoire parlementaire de la Révolution française: ou Journal des assemblées nationales depuis 1780 jusqu'en 1815* (Paris, 1838).
Calonne, Albéric de, *Histoire de la Ville d'Amiens* (Amiens, 1899).
Campbell, Peter R., Thomas E. Kaiser and Marisa Linton, eds, *Conspiracy in the French Revolution* (Manchester, 2007).
Campion, M.A., *Les Fêtes nationales à Caen sous la révolution* (Caen, 1877).
Carlyle, Thomas, *The French Revolution; A History* (London, 1837).
Chartier, Roger, *Les origines culturelles de la Révolution française* (Paris, 1990).
Chemin-Dupontès, Jean-Baptiste, *Manuel des théophilanthropophiles ou adorateurs de Dieu et amis des hommes* (Paris, An III).
Clarke, Joseph, *Commemmorating the Dead in Revolutionary France* (Cambridge, 2007).
Cobb, Richard, *The Police and the People: French Popular Protest, 1789–1820* (Oxford, 1970).
—— *Reactions to the French Revolution* (Oxford, 1972).
—— *Paris and its Provinces, 1782–1802* (Oxford, 1975).
Cobban, Alfred, *The Social Interpretation of the French Revolution* (Cambridge, 1964).
—— *Aspects of the French Revolution* (St Albans, 1973).
Dalisson, Rémi, *Célébrer la nation; Les fêtes nationales en France de 1789 à nos jours* (Paris, 2009).
Dannbach, Philipp Jacob, *Procès-Verbal et description de la Fête de l'Être Suprême, célébrée le 20 prairial, l'an second de la République française, une et indivisible* (Strasbourg, n.d.).
Dauban, Charles-Aimé, *Paris en 1794* (Paris, 1869).
Dean, Rodney, *L'Église constitutionnelle, Napoléon et le Concordat de 1801* (Paris, 2004).
—— *L'abbé Grégoire et l'Église constitutionnelle après la Terreur 1794–1797* (Paris, 2008).
—— *L'Assemblé constituante et la réforme ecclésiastique 1790* (Paris, 2014).
Desan, Suzanne, *Reclaiming the Sacred: Lay Religion and Popular Politics in Revolutionary France* (Ithaca, 1990).
Deschamp, *Véritable Détail de la cérémonie qui doit être célébrée décadi 20 prairial ... Suivi de l'hymne en honneur de l'Être suprême* (Paris, n.d.).
Dhombes, Nicole and Anne-Claire Déré, *Chroniques de Nantes en l'an II: pour une autre histoire de Nantes sous Carrier* (Nantes, 1993).

Drummond, W.H., *Autobiography of A. H. Rowan, Esq. With additions and illustrations by W. H. Drummond* (Dublin, 1840).
Dowd, David Lloyd, *Pageant Master of the Republic: Jacques-Louis David and the French Revolution* (Lincoln, 1949) reprinted (New York, 1969).
Doyle, William, *The Oxford History of the French Revolution* (Oxford, 1989).
Dupont, Anne-Marie and Armand Cosson, *Les Fêtes Révolutionnaires dans le Gard* (Nîmes, 1994).
Duprun, Jean, 'Les "noms divins" dans deux discours de Robespierre', *Annales historiques de la Révolution française*, 44 (1972): 172–6.
Erhard, Jean and Paul Viallaneix, eds, *Les Fêtes de la Révolution: Colloque de Clermont-Ferrand, juin 1974* (Paris, 1977).
Ferro, Alfred, *Histoire et Dictionnaire de Paris* (Paris, 1996).
Fiévée, Joseph, 'Mémoires', in *Bibliothèque des Mémoires relatifs à l'histoire de France pendant le 18º siècle*, Vol. XXIX, M. de Lescure (Paris, 1875).
Forrest, Alan, *Paris, the Provinces and the French Revolution* (London, 2004).
Furet, François, *Penser la Révolution française* (Paris, 1978).
Furet, François, Mona Ozouf et al., *Dictionnaire Critique de La Révolution française* (originally published in 1988), revised paperback edition in five volumes *Événements: Acteurs: Institutions et Créations: Idées: Interprètes et Historiens* (Paris, 1992–2007).
Furet, François and Denis Richer, *La Révolution française* (Paris, 1978).
Gagnebin, Bernard and Marcel Raymond, eds, *Jean-Jacques Rousseau, Œuvres Complètes* (Paris, 1964).
Gaxotte, Pierre, *La Révolution française* (Paris, 1947).
Gilboy, E.W., *Wages in 18th Century England* (Cambridge, 1934).
de la Gorce, Pierre, *Histoire religieuse*, Vol. 3 (Paris, 1909).
Gueniffey, Patrick, *La politique de la terreur. Essai sur la violence révolutionnaire 1789–1794* (Paris, 2000).
Guérin, D., *La lutte des classes sous la 1ère République, 1793–1797* (Paris, 1968).
Guillemin, Henri, *Robespierre. Politique et mystique* (Paris, 1987).
Hamel, Ernest, *Histoire de Robespierre, d'après des papiers de famille, les sources originelle et des documents entièrement inédits* (Paris, 1865).
Hampson, Norman, *The Life and Opinions of Maximilien Robespierre* (London, 1974).
Hardman, John, *Robespierre* (Longman, 1999).
Hatin, Louis-Eugène, *Bibliographie Historique et Critique de la Presse Périodique Française* (Paris, 1868).
Haydon, Colin and William Doyle, eds, *Robespierre* (Cambridge, 1999).
Hazareesingh, Sudhir, *The Saint-Napoleon: Celebrations of Sovereignty in Nineteenth-Century France* (Oxford, 2005).
—— 'Preface', in *Célébrer la nation: Les fêtes nationales en France de 1789 à nos jours*, Rémi Dalisson (Paris, 2009).
Hédouin, Pierre, Mosaïque, *Peintres-Musiciens-Littérateurs-Artistes Dramatiques: à partir du 15e siècle jusqu'à nos jours* (Paris, 1856).

Herpin, E., 'Les Fêtes à Saint-Malo pendant la Révolution', in *Annales de la Société d'histoire et d'archéologie de l'arrondissement de Saint-Malo, Année 1908*, J. Haize, ed. (Saint-Servan, 1909), pp. 187–207.
Huet, Marie-Hélène, *Rehearsing the Revolution: The Staging of Marat's Death* (Berkeley, 1982).
—— *Mourning Glory: The Will of the French Revolution* (Philadelphia, 1997).
Hunt, E.H., 'Industrialization and regional inequality – wages in Britain 1760–1914', *Journal of Economic History*, 66 (1986): 935–66.
Hunt, Lynn, *Politics, Culture and Class in the French Revolution* (London, 1994).
Ihl, Olivier, *La fête républicaine* (Paris, 1996).
Jaurès, Jean, *Histoire socialiste de la Révolution française*, Albert Soboul, ed. (Paris, 1972).
Labica, Georges, *Robespierre: Une politique de la philosophie* (Paris, 1990).
Laponneraye, Albert, ed., *Mémoires de Charlotte Robespierre sur ses deux frères; précédés d'une introduction par Laponneraye et suivis de pièces justificatives* (Paris, 1835).
Lecointre, Laurent, *Conjuration formée dès le 5 préréal (sic) par neuf représentants du peuple contre Maximilien Robespierre, pour l'immoler en plein Sénat. Par L. Lecointre, député de Versailles, Seine-et-Oise* (Paris, An II).
Lefebvre, Georges, *La Grande Peur* (Paris, 1932).
—— *La Révolution française*, 2nd ed. (Paris, 1957).
—— *Études sur la Révolution française*, 2nd ed. (Paris, 1963).
Lehning, James R., *The Melodramatic Thread: Spectacle and Political Culture in Modern France* (Bloomington, 2007).
de Lescure, M., *Bibliothèque des Mémoires relatifs à l'histoire de France pendant le 18º siècle, Vol. XXIX* (Paris, 1875).
Linton, Marisa, 'Robespierre's political principles', in *Robespierre*, Colin Haydon and William Doyle, eds (Cambridge, 1999).
—— 'Fatal friendships: the politics of Jacobin friendship', *French Historical Studies*, 31(1) (2008): 51–76.
—— *Choosing Terror: Virtue, Friendship, and Authenticity in the French Revolution* (Oxford, 2013).
Lods, Armand, *Le Culte de la Raison et de l'Être Suprême en Alsace et à Montbaillard* (Besançon, n.d.).
Maréchal, Sylvain, *Tableau historique des événements révolutionnaires, depuis la fondation de la République jusqu'à présent, rédigé principalement pour les campagnes* (Paris, An III).
Martin, Jean-Clément, *Violence et révolution. Essai sur la naissance d'un mythe national* (Paris, 2006).
Maslan, Susan, *Revolutionary Acts: Theatre, Democracy, and the French Revolution* (Baltimore, 2005).
Mason, Laura, *Singing the French Revolution, Popular Culture and Politics 1787–1799* (New York, 1996).
Mathiez, Albert, *La Théophilanthropie et le culte décadaire* (Paris, 1904).

—— 'Robespierre et le culte de l'Être Suprême', *Annales Révolutionnaires*, 1910.
—— *Les Origines des cultes révolutionnaires* (Paris, 1904) reprinted (Geneva, 1977).
McPhee, Peter, *Robespierre: A Revolutionary Life* (Yale, 2012).
Mercier, Louis-Sébastien, *Paris pendant la Révolution, ou Le Nouveau Paris (1789–1798)* (Paris, 1862).
Michelet, Jules, *Histoire de France, Vol. VI, La Révolution*, originally published 1847–52, Pierre Villaneix, ed. (Paris, 1974).
Michon, G., *Correspondance de Maximilien et Augustin Robespierre* (Paris, 1928).
Mignet, F.A., *Histoire de la Révolution française depuis 1789 jusqu'en 1814* (Paris, 1827).
Monnier, R., 'L'Image de Paris de 1784 à 1794: Paris, capitale de la Révolution', in *Les Images de la Révolution française*, M. Vovelle, ed. (Paris, 1989).
Nabonne, Bernard, *La Vie Privée de Robespierre* (Paris, 1938).
Neuvéglise, Leblond de, *La vie et les crimes de Robespierre* (Augsburg, 1795).
Nodier, Charles, *Souvenirs, épisodes et portraits pour servir à l'histoire de la Révolution et de l'Empire* (Paris, 1831).
—— *Souvenirs de la Révolution et de l'Empire* (Paris, 1850).
—— 'Eloquence Révolutionnaire, La Montagne', in *Souvenirs de la Révolution et de l'Empire, Vol. I* (Paris, 1857).
—— 'Recueil de pièces trouvées chez Robespierre l'aîné', in *Souvenirs de la Révolution et de l'Empire, Introduction* (Paris, 1857).
Ozouf, Mona, *La Fête Révolutionnaire 1789–1799* (Paris, 1976).
—— 'Le renouvellement de l'imaginaire collectif', in *Les Fêtes de la Révolution: Colloque de Clermont-Ferrand, juin 1974*, Jean Erhard and Pierre Viallaneix, eds (Paris, 1977).
Palmer, R.R., *The Year of the Terror: Twelve who Ruled France 1793–1794* (Oxford, 1989).
Parker, Noel, *Portrayals of Revolution: Images, Debates and Patterns of Thought in the French Revolution* (Hemel Hempstead, 1990).
Pascal, Blaise, *Pensées III.ii.V, Œuvres complètes*, Charles Bossut, ed. (La Haye, 1779).
—— *Les Provinciales, Pensées et opuscules divers*, Gérard Ferreyrolles and Philippe Sellier, eds (Paris, 1999).
Pierre, Constant, *Bernard Sarrette* (Paris, 1895).
—— *Les Hymnes et Chansons de la Révolution* (Paris, 1904).
Pilbeam, Pamela M., *Madame Tussaud and the History of Waxworks* (London, 2002).
Plongeron, Bernard, *Conscience religieuse en Révolution* (Paris, 1969).
Pujol, J. ed., *Documents sur la Révolution à Bordeaux, publiés pour le Bicentenaire de la Révolution française* (Bordeaux, 1989).
Renard, *Collection générale des tableaux de dépréciation du papier-monnaie: publiés dans chaque département en exécution de la loi du 5 messidor, An 5* (Paris, 1825).
Robert, Frédéric, *La Marseillaise* (Paris, 1989).

Robespierre, Maximilien, *Œuvres complètes de Maximilien Robespierre*, Marc Bouloiseau et al., eds (Paris, 2000).
Ruault, Nicolas, *Gazette d'un Parisien sous la Révolution: Lettres à son frère 1783–1796*, Anne Vassal and Christine Rimbaud, eds (Paris, 1976).
Rudé, George, *The Crowd in the French Revolution* (Oxford, 1959).
Sabatier, Robert, *La Poésie du dix-huitième siècle*, Vol. 4 of *Histoire de la Poésie française* (Paris, 1975).
Schönpflug, Daniel, *Der Weg in die Terreur. Radikalisierung und Konflikte im Straßburger Jakobinerclub (1790–1795)* (Munich, 2002).
—— 'Le culte de la raison à Strasbourg: facteurs locaux, nationaux et régionaux', in *Les politiques de la Terreur (1793–1794)*, Actes du Colloque international de Rouen, Janvier 2008 (Rennes, 2008).
Smyth, Jonathan, 'Public experience of the Revolution: the national reaction to the proclamation of the *Fête de l'Être suprême*', in *Experiencing the French Revolution*, David Andress, ed. (Oxford, 2013).
Soboul, Albert, *Sentiments religieux et cultes populaires pendant la Révolution* (Paris, 1957).
—— *La Révolution française* (Paris, 1984).
Sorel, Alexandre, *La Fête de l'Être Suprême à Compiègne* (Compiègne, 1872).
Staël, Germaine de, 'Considérations sur les principaux événements de la Révolution française', in *Œuvres complètes de Madame la baronne de Staël*, Auguste de Staël, ed. (Paris, 1820).
Starobinski, Jean, *Jean-Jacques Rousseau: La Transparence et l'Obstacle, suivis de sept essais sur Rousseau* (Paris, 1972).
—— *1789: Les Emblèmes de la Révolution* (Paris, 1979).
Tackett, Timothy, *Religion, Revolution and Regional Culture in Eighteenth-century France: The Ecclesiastical Oath of 1791* (Princeton, 1986).
Tallett, Frank, 'Robespierre and religion', in *Robespierre*, Colin Haydon and William Doyle, eds (Cambridge, 1999).
Tench, Watkin, *Letters Written in France to a Friend in London: Between the Month of November 1794 and the Month of May 1795* (London, 1796).
Thompson, J.M., *The French Revolution* (London, 1951).
—— *Robespierre* (London, 1968).
Tison, G., 'La Fête de l'Être Suprême à Calais, 20 prairial, an II', in *Société historique du Calaisis. Bulletin Septembre–Octobre 1924* (Calais, 1924).
Tocqueville, Alexis de, *L'Ancien Régime et la Révolution* (Paris, 1988).
Tulard, Jean, *Joseph Fiévée, conseiller secret de Napoléon* (Paris, 1985).
Van Kley, Dale, *The Religious Origins of the French Revolution: From Calvin to the Civil Constitution, 1560–1791* (New Haven, 1996).
Vilate, Joachim, *Les Mystères de la Mère de Dieu dévoilés* (Paris, n.d.).
—— *Causes secrètes de la révolution du 9 au 10 thermidor; par Vilate, ex-juré au tribunal Révolutionnaire de Paris, détenu à La Force* (Paris, An III).
Vovelle, Michel, *Religion et Révolution, la déchristianisation de l'an II* (Paris, 1976).

—— 'Sociologie et Idéologie', in *Les Fêtes de la Révolution: Colloque de Clermont-Ferrand, juin 1974*, Jean Erhard and Pierre Viallaneix, eds (Paris, 1977).

—— *1793, La Révolution contre l'Église: de la Raison à l'Être Suprême* (Paris, 1988).

—— *Les Images de la Révolution française* (Paris, 1988).

Wahnich, Sophie, *La liberté ou la mort: Essai sur la Terreur et le terrorisme* (Paris, 2003).

—— *La Révolution française: Un évènement de la raison sociale* (Paris, 2012).

Walter, Gérard, *Maximilien de Robespierre* (Paris, 1961).

Whitworth, John, 'L'envoi des adresses à la Convention en réponse au décret du 18 floréal: une étude des archives parlementaires', *Annales historiques de la Révolution française*, 298 (1994): 201–68.

Young, Mary, *Augustin: The Younger Robespierre* (London, 2011).

Zimmerman, F., 'Bernard Sarrette, fondateur du Conservatoire', *France musicale*, 21 November 1841.

Index

Notes: In some indirect references, 'Festival of the Supreme Being' has been abbreviated to 'FoSB' to save space. References including a lower case 'n' such as '143n37' refer to endnotes, in this case note 37 on page 143.

Abbeville 83
L'Abréviateur universel, 42, 131
Affiches d'Angers, Les 133
Amar, Jean-Baptiste 139
Amiens 4, 6, 36, 80, 82, 84, 90–1, 104, 114–17, 124, 133, 158
Amis de la Patrie, *section* des 53
Amis du Peuple 83
Ancien Régime 17, 21–2, 66
Angelot, Citizen (Metz) 43
Angers 6, 34, 36, 80–2, 84, 87–8, 91, 97, 104, 116–18, 121, 133, 158
Annales Patriotiques et Littéraires 131–2, 137
Arbogast, Louis-François 43
Arcis, *section* des 53
Army of the North 140n3
Army of the Rhine 88, 90
Assignats, system of 120–1
atheism 19–20, 22, 26, 44, 79, 90, 128
 covering the whole nation 22, 26
 double statue of 51, 56–8, 64–6, 80–1, 85, 92, 119
 rejection of 20, 155

Aubert (tapisseur) 58
L'Auditeur National, 131
Aulard, Alphonse 2–4, 95

Bailleul 80, 82, 83, 93–4
Baradèle (ironfounder, Belvès) 96
Barère, Bertrand 19, 136, 139, 148–9
Barras, Paul 70
Barry, Citizen (FoSB eyewitness) 66, 70, 128, 134
Bastille 25, 51, 68, 101n62, 107, 147
Baty (contractor, Bordeaux) 118
Baudot, Marc-Antoine 69, 127, 134
belief system, need for 21, 128, 146, 150–2, 156
Belvès (Dordogne) 36, 95
Berger (Mayor of Angers) 87
Bernard (pastor) 15–16
Bernard (papermaker) 58
Bianchi, Serge 151
Bibliothèque nationale 65
Bicentenary celebrations, violence in 8n10

Billaud-Varennes, Jacques-Nicolas 139, 148–9
Blois 116
Boissy d'Anglas, François Antoine, Comte de 128, 134–6, 143n37, 151
Bonaparte, Napoléon 101n62, 144n52, 151–2
Bonne Nouvelle, *section* of 42
Bontemps, Citizen (FoSB eyewitness) 66, 70, 128, 134
Bordeaux 36, 80–2, 84, 91, 97, 105, 114, 117–18, 133, 158
Bourdon de l'Oise, Leonard 59, 71, 139, 149
Bourgogne, Rue de 68
Bowley, A.L. 122
Brissot, Jacques-Pierre 13
Brunet, Citizen 113
Bruny (composer) 67
Buchez, P.-J.-B 3, 5, 148, 158
  see also Roux, P.-C.
Burger (tinsmith, Strasbourg) 120
Butenschön (editor, *Der Weltbote*) 38, 134

Calais 43, 82–3
Cambon 14, 151
Carnot, Lazare 41, 105
Carrousel, Place du *see* Réunion, Place de la
Catholic Church 24, 151
  discontent in 151
  disestablishment of 11
  general catechism of 19
  re-establishment of 151–2
centralisation of power 51
Chabot (priest) 16
Chalier, Marie-Joseph 85
Champ de la Réunion (Champ de Mars, Paris) 51, 53, 55–9, 63, 66–70, 107, 111–14, 130, 133, 135–6
  cost of groundworks at 114
Champ de Mars (Bordeaux) 82, 118
Champ de Mars (Champ de la Montagne) (Lyons) 85

Chaumette, Pierre-Gaspard 2, 11, 13–14, 25, 32, 35, 42, 55, 89, 108, 132
Chénier, Marie-André 25, 64
Chénier, Marie-Joseph 18, 25, 50, 64–5, 70, 85, 98, 134
Chevalier (painter) 59, 61
churches renamed Temples of Reason 13, 36, 89, 139, 152
churches renamed Temples of the Supreme Being 82, 87–93, 117, 152
Clermont-Ferrand, Cathedral of 152
Clouet (butcher, Mennecy) 95
Collenot d'Angremont 76n41
Collot d'Herbois, Jean-Marie 56, 85
Comédie Française 111
Commission des dépêches 130
Committee of General Security (Comité de Sûreté Générale) 19, 139, 148
Committee of Public Education (Comité d'Instruction public) 5, 25, 35–8, 42, 43, 53, 56, 61, 72, 95, 103–12, 135, 154
  budgeting for Festivals 106–9
  lack of financial knowledge 105–6
  reorganisation of 104
Committee of Public Safety (Comité de salut public) 5, 13, 17–19, 23, 38, 53, 56, 61, 64, 87, 95, 105–6, 109–10, 112, 123, 139, 140n3, 147–9
  setting trading values 123
Commune-Affranchie *see* Lyons
Compiègne 83
Concordat of 1801 152
Convention, The 13–14, 16, 17, 20, 23, 35, 40, 62, 105, 146
  acute financial problems 105–6, 120–3
  agreeing to festival of the Supreme Being 23
  as a mass of intrigue 20
  dress at FoSB 62
  objecting to guillotine 68
  setting Maximum prices 121

INDEX

Courtois, Edmé Bonaventure 70
Couthon, Georges Auguste 17–18, 40, 105, 147

Danton, Georges-Jacques 11, 14, 17, 44, 56
  execution of 17
David, Jacques-Louis 18, 25–6, 31–2, 65, 105, 108–11
  building the Mountain 55, 57, 58
  detailed instructions for FoSB 32, 49–52, 84, 89, 97, 115–16, 118
  de-Christianisation, process of 6, 13–14, 18–19, 21, 24–5, 33–4, 39, 42, 79, 84, 88, 91, 139, 147, 151
Declaration of the Rights of Man 15, 23, 34, 93
Deism, forms of 3, 13, 34, 85, 147
Demachy, Pierre-Antoine 61
Demosthenes 12
Denis the Areopagite 62, 74n24
Deschamp (composer) 67
Desmoulins, Camille 11
Desorgues, Théodore 64–5, 98
Despontès, Chemin 151
Dietrich, Philippe Frédéric 88, 100n34
Directory, The 151
Dominique, Rue 68, 72
Dorfeuille (actor) *see* Gobet
Douai, commune of 44
Duclos, Pierre-Louis 115
Dugommier, Jacques François 109
Duhem, Pierre Joseph 69
Dulot (city engineer, Lyons) 119
Dumouriez, Charles-François 140n3
Dupont de Nemours, Pierre Samuel 121
Duprun, Jean 62
Dupuy, Jean-Baptiste 85

l'Ecole Militaire, Avenue de 67

Fabré, René (Agent National) 95–6
Faubourg Saint-Antoine 147

Festival of the Foundation of the Republic 152
Festival of the Martyrs 109
Festival of the Supreme Being (Fête de l'Être Suprême)
  announced by Robespierre 22–6
  David's instructions for 32, 49–52
  Decree for 34, 38, 39, 87
  eyewitness accounts of 37
  feelings of joy at 72, 73, 96–8, 129–31, 157–8
  financial problems of 112
  good behaviour at 132
  huge cost of 113, 123
  local variations to 40–5, 87–91
  national participation in 3, 6, 31–4, 50, 157
  proclamation of 10, 34
  provincial aspects of 5, 78–98
  reaction to 1–2, 31–45, 146
  role of marshals in 53
  route of procession 54, 57, 67–8
  slogans at 66, 71, 82–3, 93–4, 97, 130, 133
  unique nature of 33
  viewed as an oddity 3
Fête de la Federation 25, 33, 93, 106
Fête de la Raison 13–14, 32, 52, 85, 89–90, 108, 119, 132, 135
Fête de la Réunion 25, 31, 33, 51–2, 58, 93, 104, 106, 108, 110, 113
  chaotic nature of 52
  costs of 104, 108, 110, 113
Fête-Dieu 26
Fiévée, Joseph 2, 128, 134, 138, 144n52
Fillieux (deputy Agent National, Lyons) 85
Fillon (Agent National, Angers) 84, 87, 97, 116
Flanders, refugees from 4, 115
Fleurus, Battle of 94
Foix 152
Fouché, Joseph 42, 79, 85, 99n21, 139
Fouquier-Tinville, Antoine Quentin 144n46, 148
Français, Antoine 92–3

178 INDEX

Fréron, Louis-Marie-Stanislas 70
Froidevaux (carpenter, Strasbourg) 120
Fromageat, Citizen 53
Furet, François 19

Garnier de l'Aube, Antoine-Marie-Charles 70
Gazette Nationale 66, 130–1
Gerle, Dom Christophe Antoine 148
Gien (Loiret) 36
Gilboy, E.W. 122
Gobet, Pierre-Philippe-Antoine (actor, known as Dorfeuille) 85, 99n21
Gossec, François Joseph 25, 50, 64–5
Gossuin, Eugène 130, 133, 140n3
Grégoire, Henri l'Abbé 43, 151
Grenoble 80, 92–3, 124
Grève, Place de 67, 76n41
Grignon (treasurer, Bordeaux) 117–18
Grivotte (butcher, Mennecy) 95, 102n68
Guérin, Daniel 4
Guffroy, Armand-Benôit-Joseph 70
Guillaume, M.J. 71, 104, 109–10
Guillaume Tell, *section* of 66, 128, 134
guillotine 67–8, 76n41, 102n68, 129, 137, 144n46, 147, 154
Guyardin, Louis 88

Hamel, Ernest 2
Hébert, Jacques-René 11, 14, 26, 140n5
Hédouin, Pierre 64–5
Henri IV, King 141n7
Hercules, statues of 55, 59, 70, 93, 119
Hideous Atheism, statue of 51, 56–8, 64–6, 80–1, 85, 92, 119
Hubert (city architect, Paris) 25, 49–50, 53, 56, 61, 65, 67, 107–12
  financial problems with Festivals 112
Hunt, E.H. 122

Indulgents, The 69, 140n5
Institut national de la musique 65
Invalides, Esplanade des 68
Invalides, Hôtel des 72
Isère River 93, 96

Jacobin Club of Paris 69, 79, 139
  excluding bankers 106
  reaction to Festival 41
  Robespierre's speeches to 12–15, 42, 69
Jacobin Clubs 32–4, 39, 88, 150
Jacobin Society 33, 41, 53, 100n34
Jacquemart (papermaker) 58
Jardin National (Tuileries) 51, 53, 56, 58, 66–8, 111–13, 134–7
Joly, Citizen 108
Journal de Bordeaux 133
Journal de la Montagne 131
Journal du Club National de Bordeaux 117
Julien, Citizen (Paris) 53
Jullien, Marc-Antoine 36, 81, 84, 97, 118–19

Lakanal, Joseph 106
Lamarie (City Architect, Nantes) 82
Laveaux, Jean-Charles 100n34
Lebas, Philippe 88
Lebrun, Pierre-Henri 98
Leclercq, Théodore 144n52
Lecointre de Versailles, Laurent 59, 69–70, 128, 135, 139, 149
Legendre, Louis 136
Lequinio, Jean-Marie 139
Lescure, M. de 134, 138
Levasseur, Réne 148
Liberty, statues of 67, 119
Lille 36
Lindet, Robert 105, 148
Locke, John 12, 19
Loi du 22 Prairial 41, 141n8, 147
Lombards, *section* des 53
Louis XV, King 67

Louis XVI, King 67–8, 76n41,
  102n68, 143n37
  execution of 67, 76n41
Louis XVI, Pont *see* Révolution,
  Pont de la
Louis XVIII, King 143n37, 144n52
Louis-le-Grand, College of 12
Lutheran Protestants 89
Lyons (Commune-Affranchie) 6,
  80–1, 84–5, 118–20, 124, 133,
  155, 158
  bombardment of 85
  medallions from 85–6

Maine-et-Loire 116, 121
Mainoni (Agent National,
  Strasbourg) 84, 89
Maison-Commune, *section* de la 53
Marat, *section* of 42
Maréchal, Sylvain 2, 26, 71, 128, 134, 136
Marseillaise, La 70, 92
Massa (sculptor) 58
Massieu, Jean-Baptiste 106
Mathiez, Albert 2, 4, 34, 87
Maubilliarcq, Pigault 43
Maximum (pricing system) 121–3
Mayenne 43
Méhul, Étienne-Nicolas 25, 50
Mennecy 95, 102n64
Mercier, Louis-Sebastian 127, 134
Merlin de Thionville,
  Antoine-Christophe 59, 71, 139,
  149, 151
Messager du Soir, le 132
Metz 43
Michallon, Claude (sculptor) 109
Michelet, Jules 62, 71, 128–9
Milhaud, Jean-Baptiste 88
Momoro, Antoine-François 14
Monclau (carpenter) 112
Monet, Pierre-François 84, 88–90,
  100n34, 105, 119–20
Moniteur, Le 41
Mont-Marat, Commune de 42

Montaut (opponent of
  Robespierre) 69
Montesquieu 12, 16, 19
Morrisson (merchant, Paris) 58
Morrisson (serrurier) 59
Mutius-Scaevola, *section* of 42

Nabonne, Bernard 149
Nancy 43, 83, 116
Nantes 82, 91, 116
Neufville, Duc de 102n68
Neuvéglise, Leblond de *see* Proyart,
  Abbé
Nevers 42, 79
Nodier, Charles 128, 134, 137–8
Notre Dame de Paris 13, 26, 52, 55, 132

Orleans 34, 80, 138
Ozouf, Mona 3–6, 79, 158

Palloy the Patriot 94, 101n62
Paris
  Church of Saint-Sulpice 152
  City Council 110–11, 122
  Commission of Public Works 110–11
  Hôtel du Ville 108
  Institute for the Blind 53
  large immigrant communities
    in 49, 50
  population of 49
  reaction to Festival Decree
    36, 39–44
  role of *sections* in FoSB 53,
    70–2, 158
Pascal, Blaise 16–17, 154
Pavillon de Flore 136
Payan, Claude 39, 150
Pentecost, feast of 26, 154
Phrygian bonnets 89–90, 120
Pierre, Constant 64
Pitt, William 136
Pleyel, Ignace 90
Pocholle, Pierre 130, 133, 140n5
Popincourt, *section* of 42

Postolle (Citizen, Mennecy) 95
press censorship 131
Prieur de la Côte d'Or, Claude-Antoine 105
Prieur de la Marne, Pierre-Louis 105, 145n54
Proyart, Abbé (aka Leblond de Neuvéglise) 12

Quimper 139
Quinet, Edgar 3, 69, 128

Reason, Cult of 2, 4, 33, 35, 37, 155
Reason, Temples of 13, 36, 89, 139, 152
Regnier, Auguste-Jacques 58
religious toleration 14
Républicain Français, Le 131
Republican Clubs 7
Réunion, Place de la (ex Place du Carrousel) 67, 76n41
Réveillière-Lépeaux, Louis-Marie de la 151
Révolution, Maison de la 68
Révolution, Place de la 51, 57, 61, 67–8, 76n41, 129, 154
Révolution, Pont de la (ex Pont Louis XVI) 67–8
Revolutionary Tribunal 136, 144n46, 148
Richter (musical director, Lyons) 119
Robespierre, Augustin 24, 29n39
Robespierre, Charlotte 149
Robespierre, Maximilien
　assassination attempts on 37, 41, 70, 135
　disappearing from public life 148–51
　personal attacks on 69, 71, 127, 149, 156
Rousseau (city engineer, Amiens) 115
Rousseau, Jean-Jacques 12–13, 19, 22
　Rousseauvian philosophy 151
　Social Contract 19
Roux, P.-C. 5, 148, 158
　see also Buchez, P.-J.-B.

Rovère, Joseph-Stanislas de la 70
Rowan, Archibald Hamilton 138–9, 145n54
Ruamps, Pierre-Charles 69, 130, 140n5, 141n8
Ruault, Nicolas 70, 73, 128, 134–5, 155

St André, Jeanbon 105
Saint-Just, Louis-Antoine 2, 88, 105
Sarrette, Bernard 64–5
Sceaux 94–5
Schneider, Euloge 88
Sempronius Gracchus *see* Vilate
Social Contract (of Rousseau) 19
Sociétés Populaires 4, 14, 32, 34, 38–9, 43, 83, 91, 96, 114, 130, 133, 156
stage payments, system of 112
Strasbourg 36, 38, 80–4, 88–91, 100n34, 119–20, 124, 133–4, 152, 155, 158
　annexed 89
　language problems in 88–9, 133
Supreme Being
　concept of 22–3, 38
　Cult of 4, 7, 10, 15, 26, 35, 38, 44, 128, 151, 154
　homage to 69, 80, 82, 85, 139, 146, 150, 155, 158
　Temples of 82, 87–93, 117, 152

Tarpan (Agent National, Lyons) 85
Tench, Major Watkin 139, 145n56
Terror, the 5, 13, 16, 106, 138, 140, 147
　hopes for end to 35, 39, 96, 129–30, 137–9, 146, 154
　use of to support virtue 17
Théâtre Nationale 111
Theophilanthropy 151
Théot, Catherine 136, 148
Theys (Goncelin) 96
Thirion, Didier 70, 130, 140n5, 141n7
Thuriot, Jacques-Alexis 71
Toulon, taking of 25
Tours 80, 82, 91–2
Trottebas (Metz) 43

Tuileries *see* Jardin National
Tussaud, Madame Marie 106

l'Unité, *section* de 53

Vadier, Marc-Guillaume-Alexis 19, 139, 149
Vaud (Secretary to the Convention) 1, 130, 147
Verneuil (Cher) 36
Versailles, Commune of 42
Vilate, Joachim 2, 62, 71, 73, 128, 134, 136–8, 144n46, 155
   execution of 137, 144n46
   using *nom de plume* Sempronius Gracchus 136
Villars, Noël-Gabriel, Bishop of Mayenne 43

Virtue
   men of 10, 16
   Republic of 7, 11–12, 21, 129, 140, 146–7, 154, 157–8
   supported by terror 17
   use of word by Robespierre 10
   virtuous nation, visions of 3
Voltaire 15
Vovelle, Michel 3, 5, 6, 79, 158

Weltbote, Der 89, 133–4
Whitworth, John 41–2
Wisdom, statue of 65–6, 80–1, 87, 92

Young, Mary 148

Zimmermann, F. 64
Zwinglian Protestants 89

EU authorised representative for GPSR:
Easy Access System Europe, Mustamäe tee 50,
10621 Tallinn, Estonia
gpsr.requests@easproject.com

www.ingramcontent.com/pod-product-compliance
Lightning Source LLC
Chambersburg PA
CBHW070239240426
43673CB00044B/1848